Light on the Devils

Light on the Devils

COMING OF AGE ON THE KLAMATH

Louise Wagenknecht

Oregon State University Press • **Corvallis**

The paper in this book meets the guidelines for permanence and durability of the Committee on Production Guidelines for Book Longevity of the Council on Library Resources and the minimum requirements of the American National Standard for Permanence of Paper for Printed Library Materials Z39.48-1984.

Library of Congress Cataloging-in-Publication Data
Wagenknecht, Louise, 1949-
  Light on the devils : coming of age on the Klamath / Louise Wagenknecht.
    p. cm.
  Includes bibliographical references.
  ISBN 978-0-87071-611-9 (alk. paper) -- ISBN 978-0-87071-650-8 (ebook)
  1. Wagenknecht, Louise, 1949---Childhood and youth. 2. Klamath River Valley (Or. and Calif.)--Biography. 3. Klamath National Forest (Calif. and Or.)--History. 4. Klamath National Forest (Agency : U.S.)--History. I. Title.
  F868.K55W35 2011
  979.4'21--dc23
                                    2011020349

First published in 2011 by Oregon State University Press
Printed in the United States of America

Oregon State University Press
121 The Valley Library
Corvallis OR 97331-4501
541-737-3166 • fax 541-737-3170
http://oregonstate.edu/dept/press

Contents

Acknowledgements

Thanks to Susan Marsh, good and patient friend, for taking time away from her own extraordinary writing to ponder and criticize my efforts. You took me seriously before I did.

Many thanks once again to Gil Davies and to the memory of Florice Frank, whose books remain indispensable for anyone investigating the history of Siskiyou County and the Klamath National Forest.

To my mother, Barbara, for cookies and criticism, for stories and patience and unstinting support, more thanks are due than I can ever give. Blessings on my husband, Bob, for his perspicacious reading of many drafts. Thanks to my brother, Tom, and sister-in-law, Mary, who read mounds of manuscript, gave me invaluable feedback, and helped me to deconstruct House Brannon.

Many thanks to Mary Braun, Micki Reaman, and Jo Alexander of OSU Press for their kind and careful work on the manuscript.

Last but certainly not least, this book is dedicated to the memory of Jim Rock, good friend and retired archaeologist for the Klamath National Forest, who never stopped trying to teach others about the riches of the past. We all miss you, Jim.

An earlier version of "The River," entitled "And the Salmon Sing," appeared in *The River Reader*, edited by John Murray (New York: The Lyons Press, 1998).

Where It Ended

IN A TOWN CALLED HAPPY CAMP, beside a river that he had known all his life, a man drove into the deserted parking lot of an abandoned lumber mill, sat for a while in the cab of his pickup truck, and then blew his brains out. I had known him for thirty years, and he had worked in that mill from 1965 until the mill closed. And when I heard the news, far away in Idaho, when I learned how he died and the circumstances of family and community that had led him down to the riverside that evening, I knew that the world in which we had both grown up, the world of logging and lumber that my family had also followed as long as they could, was really, really over.

The mill had closed in September of 1994; it had operated in that far northwestern corner of California for over forty years. For much of that time, it was just one of four or five mills within a twenty-mile radius. But by that year, the timber harvest on the Klamath National Forest had dropped to half of its peak in the 1980s, when 196 million board feet of timber had been dragged from the woods every year. The spotted owl, a drab and reclusive bird scarcely heard of two decades before, had at last been listed as a threatened species, and a new set of timber harvest guidelines now superseded all the old forest plans, wherever the owl lived. For many people in Happy Camp—and all over the Pacific Northwest—this sudden new reality was like hitting a wall at sixty miles an hour.

1

Over the next decade, even the lowered timber harvest target was seldom met. The last great surge of logging on the Klamath National Forest had, in fact, come years before, in the wake of the lightning-caused conflagrations of 1987. Those salvage timber sales would be the last big ones. After that, even though the early twenty-first century would bring huge and almost uncontrollable fires, the old days of logging and road-building were gone. The rules had changed. Having lost its greatest source of revenue, having lost its usefulness as a tool of the forest products industry, the U.S. Forest Service—the agency that manages the National Forests—was unable to compete for congressional appropriations. As the years passed and the foresters who knew how to "get out the cut" retired or moved, they were not replaced. The mill and the Forest Service had been two halves of the same whole, and with one gone, the other would never be the same.

The last eighty workers at the Happy Camp mill lost their jobs on the same day that workers at Oregon mills in Springfield and Albany, also owned by Stone Forest Industries, lost theirs. And despite the rather desperate optimism displayed in the local newspapers by economic development councils and other public servants, most of the region realized the game was over. Stone Forest Industries was headquartered in Chicago, Illinois, and people in Happy Camp, isolated on their stretch of the wild Klamath River, wondered if the men in the skyscrapers even knew about them. They knew, of course. They may even have cared. But this was, after all, just business.

I watched the drama unfold from another National Forest, central Idaho's Salmon-Challis, where in 1993 the federal listing of various species of Pacific salmon as endangered and threatened had done to its timber cut what the spotted owl listing had done to the Klamath's. The spotted owl was threatened by the loss of its old growth forest habitat. The salmon of the Snake and Salmon river basins had been nearly extirpated by erosion from roads, clear-cuts, and livestock grazing; by irrigation diversions; and by dams on the Snake and Columbia rivers. But like the mill in Happy Camp, the lumber mill in Salmon required millions of board feet of timber a year, and once the allowable cut in the surrounding area dropped to single digits, it also was doomed. What had happened to Happy Camp was happening all over the West.

After the Happy Camp mill closed, the men and women who had worked there moved on. Some left. Some went back to school at the nearest community college, three hours away. Some, whose wives had jobs in town, commuted weekly to Oregon lumber mills. The frenetic prosperity of the late 1990s, which enabled a few timber communities to start over, never came to isolated places like Happy Camp. I began to hear stories of loss and infidelity and desperation. And Gerald's story haunts me still.

He had married Carrie right after she graduated from high school, in my class of '67. All through our junior and senior years, whenever I

2

saw Gerald's tall form materialize in the hall to catch Carrie between classes—he must have zipped down the hill from the mill at every coffee break—I wondered what it would be like to want to be married and settled, to want to be a housewife or a millworker, forever. I didn't want what they wanted, but I envied them both their certainty about life.

When I came back home after college to take a job with the Forest Service, Carrie had a part-time job and two sons. Gerald was still thin and homely, his hairline square above an old scar. Carrie was slender as ever, her skin translucent under her flaming hair, and Gerald looked at her as though she were something rare and precious. The boys were the kind of quiet, well-behaved kids who made me think, now and then, "If I knew they'd all turn out like that …"

Early in 1987, I transferred to another Forest halfway across the country and lost track of my classmate. Three years later, she phoned me out of the blue to tell me about her experiences with the forest fires that had begun on the first day of September in '87 and very nearly engulfed Happy Camp itself. I had gone back for those fires, too, but we were based in camps fifty miles apart during that months-long battle, and I never saw her.

Like many other locals, Carrie became a driver; she spent virtually every waking moment transporting an Idaho Forest Service crew involved in the then-new technology of fire-retardant foams. In the excitement of learning new skills, of meeting new people, of watching blowups light the night sky, Carrie looked at her life and felt that something was missing. And then she fell in love with her crew boss.

Gerald scarcely saw his wife until the rains of November ended her job. He never knew that Carrie had fallen in love with a firefighter, even though Carrie managed to keep in sporadic touch with Ken for a year. But they had never actually met again, and from what I knew of fire-camp romances, I suspected that the attachment born in the smoke of that fall was probably not reciprocated.

But Carrie could not forget, and now she hoped that in the small world of the Forest Service, I might have met Ken, might know something about him. I hadn't, but I looked him up for her in the Forest Service directory, gave her his address and phone number. After twenty years in the outfit, I knew the type. Fire guys like Ken moved around a lot, I told her, were seldom home, didn't have a lot of attachments. And a

3

woman of forty-one with two kids was definitely an attachment. Forget him, I told her. But in her voice, along with denial, I heard the sound of someone who, her marriage ending, was looking for a way out. We agreed to keep in touch, but listening to her brought back memories of my own unrequited love affairs, still painful to the touch. I had no idea what to say to a broken heart, and in the end I didn't call Carrie back.

Four years later, with the mill closed forever, Gerald commuted to a sawmill job in Oregon. One weekend in Happy Camp, he drove up to visit the district ranger, and as they sat on the porch and sipped iced tea, he blurted out the reason for his unaccustomed visit. "I need you to talk to one of your engineers," he said, "and tell him to stay away from my wife."

They had been meeting, the engineer and Carrie, on a logging road above town, where Carrie rode her horse up the hill from her house. The road was blocked by a locked gate, but the engineer had a key, and in that secluded place they met as lovers. The district ranger was a tolerant man, but to use a Forest Service vehicle and a Forest Service key for what was assuredly not government business was unacceptable. He promised Gerald that he would speak to the engineer.

The warning was given privately, but the small-town grapevine was already ten strides ahead, and when the engineer's wife heard about the key and the gate and the woman on horseback, she threw Bill out. I had listened to the story with open-mouthed amazement, for I could not imagine how Bill had even met Carrie. He was a middle-aged man with the charisma of mayonnaise who went straight home after work and was always described by his wife as a fishing addict. Now he moved into the Forest Service barracks and put in for a transfer. Carrie told Gerald that she was leaving him.

On an evening when the big-leaf maples had turned incandescent yellow, Gerald drove his pickup truck on his last journey. He parked between the building where he had learned to pull greenchain and the rusted tepee burner, now cold and dark, that would never again throw sparks into the night and cover the town with the rich, sooty smell of money.

The sun had dropped into the Elk Creek drainage, and Gerald looked out through his windshield at the remains of his working life. Did he think, even then, about the tools of his trade, ready to go under the gavel at auction? The debarker and the bandmill, the resaw, the greenchain, the log carriage, the edger, the chipper. The hog, the cutoff saw, the planer. The sticker stacker, and the steam-fired kilns that sucked the moisture from boards of pine and fir. The boilers and the blowers. The saw sharpeners. The band saws, log kickers, belts, drives, rollcases, drill presses. Hydraulic operated timber toters. Truck scales that once groaned under 130,000 pounds. Fuel tanks, wiring, conduit, cylinders, chain, pipe fittings, nuts, bolts, motors, reducers, hose, welding rod. The yard lights that turned the winter fog above the river into a cloud of molten gold.

Behind the sawmill buildings, where the ghosts of log decks rose three stories above the mill pond, stood the rows of log loaders, Cats, Hyster forklifts, straddle buggies, loader backhoes, dump trucks, and water trucks, lined up like toys in a sandbox. Did Gerald wonder if Ernie Spinks's collection of pinup calendars still gathered dust on the walls of the scaling shack? Did he think about the nine-foot-long redwood conference table, around which the fate of men like himself had been decided?

With the auction, all the machinery that he had known would disappear. As would his life, once he had raised the revolver to his head, and splattered the road outside his open window with a shower of blood and brains, a last thin layer atop four decades of bark and chips, mud and spit and oil.

The town blamed Bill and Carrie in about equal measure, and although the Forest Service arranged for Bill's hasty transfer, Carrie was left to deal alone with the pain and the guilt. How she told her teenage sons that their father was dead, how the boys dealt with the rift in their world, I never learned. A story reached me that as he prepared to leave Happy Camp, Bill rested his head in his hands and moaned, "What can I do? I don't really love her."

But whether from affection or obligation, Bill did send for Carrie, who joined him, and they were married. And for all I know, the story was wrong, and they were in love, and are to this day.

IN SOME UNILLUSIONED CORNER OF MY MIND, I had known for some time that the old world of loggers and endless realms of timber were

5

gone. The news of Gerald's suicide simply crystallized that truth for me. I had seen piles of aerial photographs depicting the spaghetti-like maze of roads and endless cookie-cutter holes left in almost every drainage by forty-five years of mechanized logging. For all the talk of tree thinning preventing forest fires, for all the (correct) analysis of how ninety years of fire control had spawned overcrowded stands of young trees, I knew that the Forest Service had never been much interested in remedial vegetation management. It had cut its post-war teeth on the "harvest" of what it had never sown: old growth conifers, chopped down in neat blocks. When that ended, the agency simply did not know what else to do, and men like Gerald had become so accustomed to their work that they thought of it as a birthright, and forgot the shallowness of its roots.

I had spent my childhood and youth in communities that lived on logging and sawmilling. So had Carrie. And when that way of life ended, the Forest Service, in different ways, got us both out. But Gerald had been trapped in that world, and until it was too late, he hadn't even realized that he was its prisoner.

Downriver

IN 1962, MY STEPFATHER QUIT HIS JOB as a forester for the Fruit Growers Supply Company and joined the U.S. Forest Service. Fruit Growers—a subsidiary of Sunkist, the giant fruit cooperative—owned Hilt, where we lived in a safe and orderly community of four hundred people, governed by the company, ruled by the mill whistles that rang out across the railroad tracks. But Dad knew, because he had crunched the numbers, that Hilt was living on borrowed time. Ten more years would see the end of the company's old growth timber, and when that was gone, he didn't think that the company would be able to compete for National Forest timber sales, the only other source of raw material. So he looked for a place to jump, and found it in the nearby Klamath National Forest, where foresters were much in demand.

Happy Camp, the site of Dad's new job, was only seventy miles away from Hilt, but my sister and brother and I had never been to the old gold rush town. Still, even at the respective ages of eleven and thirteen, Liz and I had heard stories about it. As the dates of our packing and moving meshed with the tensions of the Cuban Missile Crisis, the thought of getting beaten up by tough Indian kids in a strange school was far more frightening to us than a nuclear holocaust.

We weren't the only ones who had heard stories about Happy Camp. When my mother announced her husband's plans at an Eastern Star meeting in Yreka, the Worthy Matron sitting next to her placed her hand on Mother's arm, her eyes full of concern. "Oh, my dear," she said, "you don't want to move down there. The Indian women all have scars on their arms from the knife fights."

Mother knew that most of the people who spread those stories about Happy Camp had never been there, but she had, years before. She remembered a long, winding road that descended into a land of tall firs on steep hillsides, and a narrow sky of intense blue. She remembered the Indians, but no knife fights.

Still, Mother did worry. She knew Hilt. Hilt was settled and cozy and substantial, a place where everybody knew everybody else and where most families had some claim to respectability. The company enforced minimum standards of conduct, and crime—except for the pettiest of larcenies—was almost unknown. But Happy Camp was notorious: a rollicking place with a bad, bad reputation that the *Siskiyou Daily News* was eager to augment, running the latest brawl or shooting above the fold.

The California Highway Patrol had installed a resident officer there only a few years before. On his first Saturday night in Happy Camp, Everett Collord watched as fistfights overflowed the downtown bars into the middle of the single main street. He waded into the mob, dragged out drunken loggers and millworkers, and tossed them one by one into the black-and-white. When the caged back seat was full, the deputy sheriff on duty with Everett drove two blocks up the street to the jail, unloaded, and rushed back. After a while the jail was full and the street was empty.

But Mother and Dad had no intention of hanging out in bars. So one day when my sister Elizabeth and I were at school, Mother loaded our three-year-old brother Tommy into the Ford sedan and drove down the Klamath River Highway to Happy Camp. Tommy threw up about thirty miles downriver, right after they passed the Horse Creek Store, where Highway 96 narrowed and began to follow the twisting Klamath River canyon in earnest. She stopped at the Steelhead Resort at the mouth of the Scott River, cleaned him up under their outside faucet, changed his T-shirt, then went inside and bought a bottle of 7 Up, which she made him drink as they set out again, her knuckles white on the steering wheel, her diminutive rump balanced atop the two pillows that allowed her to reach the pedals.

She thought the last twenty miles would never end, as the curves between Thompson Creek and Cade Mountain looped in and out of cool fern-clad draws wet with splashing creeks. On the downriver side of Cade Mountain, the road widened and straightened, and then she saw the lumber mills, Carolina Pacific and Siskiyou Mills, with their two tepee burners pouring smoke over the river flats just east of town. She turned off the highway and drove down the main street. The old Cuddihy Hotel still stood on the corner. She drove across the steel

At Uncle Charlie Taber's gold-mining claim near Happy Camp, mid-1930s. Left to right: Aunt Mae, her husband, Charlie, and Mother's parents.

bridge over Indian Creek and pulled up in front of Alice Dunaway's boarding house.

Alice Dunaway had been a friend of Mother's Aunt Mae. Back in the 1930s, Mae had been married to a man who ran a store and gas station next to the boarding house. Mae's husband had dabbled in gold mining, and we still had a tiny bottle with some black sand and gold flakes on the bottom that Mother had panned out during a trip to his claim on the upper reaches of Indian Creek.

Alice's two-story white Victorian sat behind flower beds and a square of lawn. Alice and her mother had once run the boarding house together, but now Alice just rented rooms. "I'm too old to do all that cooking," she told Mother as she welcomed her into her living room, where time had stopped in the Hoover administration.

Born in the last century, Alice had been married, once. She still used Mr. Dunaway's name, but she regretted his absence not at all. "Good riddance," she said to me many years later. "He thought he could tell me what to do." It was obvious to Mother, as she sat under a tall floor lamp and contemplated the other woman's electric-blue dress, that no one had ever told Alice what to do. They drank coffee in the cool, high-ceilinged living room while Tommy had another soda. Alice, her brown eyes snapping, combed through her mental file of possible rentals. She reached for the heavy black telephone beside her easy chair.

9

Five minutes later, Mother was driving up Indian Creek Road to meet Ethel Fowler.

Like Alice, Ethel was a Karuk Indian, married for almost thirty years to Hank Fowler, a white man. They lived in a house surrounded by dahlias and fruit trees, tucked into a curve between the dark mountainside and a narrow chip-sealed county road. After another cup of coffee and a piece of zucchini bread, Mother and Ethel drove half a mile up the creek to a blue house set on a narrow flat strip of ground. Indian Creek roared in its chasm of rock across the road, and the dark forest rose straight up behind. Across the driveway from the blue house was a pink cabin. Ethel and Hank owned both buildings.

The houses sat up on piers, open underneath. Inside, the blue house was clean, with warm knotty pine paneling, a propane heating stove and kitchen range, and a separate laundry house in the backyard. The single bathroom had no bathtub, only a concrete shower stall. One of the two bedrooms opened directly onto the back porch, and in a corner of the backyard sat a substantial outhouse of unpainted boards.

"Sometimes the electricity goes out here," Ethel apologized, pointing at the well house, with its electric pump, between the two rentals. "It's a good idea to keep a couple buckets of water handy."

As Mother and Ethel stood and talked, logging trucks raced by on the narrow road. But the large grassy yard was tightly fenced with good woven wire and a sturdy gate, and included a white oak shade tree. Snapdragons bloomed around the front porch. The rent, Ethel told Mother, was eighty dollars a month. This was four times what my parents paid in Hilt, but Alice had warned her about high rents in Happy Camp. "We'll take it," Mother said, and Ethel beamed.

"I don't like to rent to just anyone, but Alice says she's known your family for years, and I've always found that Forest Service people are good tenants," she said, as Mother sat down on the front steps and wrote a check. Mother drove Ethel back to her house, and Hank came out and handed a loaf of zucchini bread and a quart jar of sun pickles in through the car window.

THAT NIGHT, MOTHER MADE PANCAKES for supper and told us about Happy Camp, which had, she said, changed a great deal since her last visit.

The town had erupted beyond its old limits into a quondam wilderness of second-growth timber and hydraulic mining tailings above the original gold rush settlement along Indian Creek. Now the community boasted three grocery stores, a clothing-and-dry-goods store, three gas stations, the two lumber mills down by the river, and two more several miles up Indian Creek. Downtown were two bars, three restaurants (if you counted the Frosty-Freez), a movie theater, a drugstore, a hardware store, and the post office. The grade school was across the street from the Forest Service office, but she hadn't seen the high school. We would have to ride the school bus four miles into town. And since the house had only two bedrooms, Liz and I would have to share with Tommy.

As Liz and I listened, taut with excitement, what came through louder than anything else were the words "movie theater."

DAD TELEPHONED HIS BROTHER in Corvallis and asked him to drive a U-Haul truck full of furniture from Hilt to Happy Camp. He brought wooden dynamite boxes home from work in the back of his International pickup truck and packed the tools and treasures from his workshop into them, closing them with slats of cedar and finishing nails. He crawled into the attic above the workshop and brought down all the trunks and suitcases, and the boxes of Christmas ornaments, and the deer antlers from all the deer he had ever shot.

Mother went through all our clothes and sorted out the ones we no longer wore, and on our next shopping trip to Medford, she dropped the bundles off at the Salvation Army. Dad looked at our toy collections with undisguised loathing and decreed that most of them would have to go. You never play with those dolls anyway, he said. You can each keep one. So we trundled almost all our dolls, and the doll carriage, and the cardboard bureau packed with the doll clothes that Grandmother had made, down the hill to the little Marin girls, who, astonished at this good fortune, looked at us with the eyes of dogs. Their mother's expression asked if we were nuts.

We walked back up the alley with tears in our throats, and later I looked at the two ballerina dolls, one blonde, one brunette, both *en pointe*, their feet jammed into pink rubber ballet slippers, who still stood atop our dressers. "But where are the rest of our clothes?" they

11

accused us. And I knew that it was not the other dolls themselves that I would miss, for in truth I seldom amused myself with them. The five small drawers full of miniature dresses and skirts and blouses and hats, however, had been sewn by Grandmother herself on her old Singer sewing machine, as she sat by the window in the back bedroom of the old house in Hilt. To lose the things she had made—the things I saw her make in the days when all was right with the world—was like losing her again. Not that she was dead, of course—she was very much alive. But she had moved far from Hilt with Grandfather, when he retired, and we hadn't seen her since. Letters—and in those days people wrote letters—didn't fill the gap. Their old house had been remodeled, had new tenants, and would never again be our refuge.

Months ago, as we walked home in the dark from a Christmas program rehearsal at the Hilt community center, Liz and I wondered aloud if the old universe still lingered somewhere, on another plane. If we ran fast enough, hard enough, into the night, couldn't we break through and find it again? "When Grandmother dies," Liz said, as we paused at the foot of the hill behind the company store, "she'll come back here." Our speculations did not extend to Grandfather—we did not particularly care where he ended up.

DAD DRAGGED A STEAMER TRUNK into our room and announced that we could bring with us whatever property would fit inside. So I was able, after all, to bring along three escapees from the Marin potlatch. One had straw-colored hair that Grandmother had braided into two coils; both were dressed in doll clothes she had made. Each could sit in the palm of my hand. The third doll had been made from a sock and boasted embroidered facial features and hair of yellow yarn. I tucked them all into the trunk under an old brown leather jacket that I had taken to wearing in the unfounded belief that it made me look cool.

Uncle Charlie rolled into our driveway late on a chilly Friday evening at the wheel of Aunt Dorothy's station wagon. He picked Liz and me up in his great paws and lifted us to the level of the basketball hoop beside the woodshed door. As he and Dad loaded chainsaws and hand tools into the bed of Dad's pickup, they talked about their parents and about people and places up in Oregon, where Charlie drove a logging truck. He was, of course, losing money by helping us, but for forty years, whenever Brannons moved, Uncle Charlie was there.

"What's that thing still up in the attic?" Charlie asked as he peered into the gloom from midway up the steps nailed to the woodshed wall.

"Just an old bedstead. Barbara's sister's supposed to come get it, but if she doesn't show up today it'll be too late," Dad said.

When our grandparents moved from Hilt, they left behind a double bed with curved metal head-and-foot boards, chiefly renowned for Liz getting her head stuck between the uprights of the foot board when she was five. Mother agreed to store it because her sister, our Aunt Jo, wanted it. Dad grumbled about the space it took up, and said he wasn't going to take it over to her; she'd have to come get it. Jo now lived about twenty-five miles away in the small farming town of Talent, in Oregon's Rogue Valley. She had mentioned the bed in a hastily penciled letter to Mom back in March, but Mother wasn't holding her breath. Jo's husband worked the night shift as a cook, and to get the bed they would have to borrow a pickup truck and drive over the Siskiyou Summit on one of his few days off. Jo, exhausted from dealing with a two-year-old, might not be able to get Carl motivated.

But on Saturday morning, after Dad and Uncle Charlie had gone to Yreka to get the U-Haul, Aunt Jo and Uncle Carl rolled up in Carl's father's red Chevy pickup. Mother plied them with coffee and the last of the cinnamon rolls from the emptied freezer. Behind a heavy layer of mascara and blue eye shadow, Jo's eyes looked bruised. The scarf wrapped turban-style around her brown hair disguised the fact that it hadn't been washed lately. Jo was thirteen years younger than Mother, but that day she looked older.

While Uncle Carl loaded the bed, Aunt Jo walked with Liz and me to the end of the dirt alley, pushing Sidney in his stroller. We looked down the hill beside the deserted company hotel, where the street curved toward the railroad tracks. The white poplar trees near the old store were almost bare of leaves. "Remember how we used to rake up leaves into piles and then jump into them?" Jo asked. She had been born here in Hilt, twenty-six years before, and had been only fifteen when Mother had left her husband in Idaho and come home to Hilt with two daughters to raise. Until she married Carl and left us, a year before Mother herself remarried, Jo was our friend and adored older sister.

13

Since then, Jo and Carl had divorced and then remarried. After the divorce, Jo had come back to Hilt to stay with Grandmother and Grandfather, a long tense visit that convinced Jo of the wisdom of a reconciliation with Carl. Carl had his faults, but at least he was not Grandfather, whom she actively hated. Now, with her parents retired to their new house in Oroville, her sister's family was Jo's last connection to Hilt, and in her face, on that autumn day, I saw the knowledge that the place was lost to her. But as she and Carl drove away with a piece of her old home in the back of a borrowed pickup truck, it did not occur to me to wonder where the pain of that knowledge might someday lead her.

THE KLAMATH RIVER ROAD, State Highway 96, begins as a turn-off from Old Highway 99 about six miles north of Yreka, California. We knew the first twelve miles or so of this highway quite well, for we often traveled it on family fishing trips down the Klamath River to a wide sweeping bar called Humbug Point.

Beyond that, we knew the Klamath River only as far as Horse Creek, where we had gone to play volleyball and softball on school trips. So as our caravan rolled past the Horse Creek Store, we sat up straighter. I passed Tommy a cracker and hoped he would keep it down. The narrowed canyon squeezed river and road closer together, and the trees above us exploded in height and girth. I looked out on a new world.

The green river ran translucent on that sunny fall day, and every mile brought us into a wetter land. New trees appeared—madrones, with slick orange bark and large shiny green leaves; California live oaks with mossy trunks that grew out of vertical rock faces. The ground squirrels that played chicken with cars on the long straight stretch of road east of Horse Creek (and happily ate the carcasses of their slower relatives) were replaced by gray squirrels as big as cats, tree dwellers that danced on the center line, then panicked and hurled themselves under our wheels. I rolled the window down and leaned out into the warm afternoon to breathe in the smells of wet ferns, moss, shade, and the river. A great blue heron lifted away from the glassy surface of an eddy. Mergansers, some with red crests stretched out behind their heads, dove into swirls of foam. Trout jumped.

*Liz, Bob, Mother, Tommy, and Dad in front
of our first house on Indian Creek, summer of
1964.*

We crossed over the mouth of the Scott River, a smaller, clearer stream. Beyond the confluence, the highway ran on the shady side of the canyon. Riprap crowded the river, and the roar of the water drowned out the car engine. Near the moribund gold-mining town of Hamburg, an osprey—the first I had ever seen—lifted off from a snag overlooking the river and flapped away, its black and white wings bent in the sun.

Below Hamburg, we looked across the river toward a wasteland of red soil where old roads climbed through oaks toward an abandoned chrome mine. Five miles more, and we sailed across a steel bridge with a breathtaking view of the Seiad Valley dump, where avalanches of tin cans and washing machines reached the river's edge.

Across the bridge, the highway cut through an old hydraulic mine where manzanita and blackberries clawed at banks of red soil. Another curve, and Seiad Valley itself appeared, startling in its green openness, surrounded by forested peaks. Another mile and a half, and we dove back into the canyon. I felt the full force of it now: the confinement against which the river raged, the walls of trees and rock that rose higher and higher as the road dropped in elevation and the ridge tops cut off the sun; the dark old growth that loomed above moss-covered boulders. As we climbed toward the summit of Cade Mountain, the sun returned,

15

and we dove at last down a series of sunny west-facing slopes that fell into Happy Camp.

"Almost there, girls," Mom said, as Tommy slept on, his sweaty blond head resting on Liz's lap. Bob, the Australian shepherd puppy, lay panting and discouraged on the floor, trying to drink out of the fish bowl where Tommy's pet perch swam. We rolled past the lumber mills on the wide river bar. Mother turned right at the Shell station and began the climb up Indian Creek Road. We drove past a big meadow with a huge pile of decaying sawdust at its edge, then up into forest again. Within a mile, the road turned downhill once more, and we passed an unpainted cabin where a pack of hounds lolled in the shade. Indian Creek appeared off to our left, as big as the Scott River, churned to white as it fell over rocks just downstream from a concrete bridge.

We had fallen behind Dad and Uncle Charlie when we stopped at a campground near Hamburg to walk the puppy and let Tommy sip more 7 Up, but as Mom pulled into the loop road running in front of the new house, we saw them, already carrying furniture inside.

Liz took Tommy by the hand and began to explore the yard. I unsnapped the leash on Bob's collar and turned him loose. He ran up and down the side fence for a few minutes and evacuated his bowels on top of some irises. From the back of the house I heard Dad's exasperated "*will* you kids get out of the way?"

I walked across the road and looked down at Indian Creek, a white noise in the gray-green rock walls of the canyon. I looked back across the metal roof of the house at the green mountains beyond. Just behind the yard, the stumps began, cloaked with honeysuckle vines, overtopped by deerbrush. Stumps and shrubs climbed up to a line of uncut trees at the boundary between private land and the National Forest. As I walked back to the front gate, I looked down the loop road and saw a mélange of houses and trailers, backed up against the timber. We had neighbors, then, lots of them.

I watched Uncle Charlie carry our bicycles out of the U-Haul just as a loaded logging truck roared down the county road, the exhaust pipes above the cab bellowing as it accelerated down the short straight stretch before the big curve near Mrs. Fowler's place: not a friendly road for bicycles.

16

By the time the trucks were emptied, the sun had dropped behind the ridge across the creek. Charlie climbed back into the U-Haul's cab and waved to us around his cigar. "No, no time to eat, Barbie," he said to Mom. "Gotta drive tomorrow." And then he was off, headed for Yreka and the station wagon. We waved at him as he disappeared down the road.

"Let's go get a hamburger," Dad said, to Mother's evident relief, and we piled into the Ford again. We drove back down Indian Creek Road, turned right, and coasted down a long curved hill, which led past an actual high school with a real football field. Two blocks more, and we were downtown.

Dad swung the car into one of the parking spaces in front of Pence's Café. "Well, girls," he said, "you are now *in* Happy Camp."

Putewans

ON MONDAY MORNING MY SISTER AND I stood out beside the county road as Indian Creek roared in its chasm thirty feet below. Several other kids stood with us, and we exchanged nervous glances. A yellow school bus had stopped a few minutes earlier, and Elizabeth and I attempted to follow a short round girl with long black hair up the steps. A boy with acne and a large knife on his belt put out an arm to stop us.

"That's the high school bus," he said. We slunk to the rear of the little knot of kids. A few minutes later, another bus stopped in front of us and the doors flew open with a crash. We found a seat together near the front.

"What grade are you girls in?" asked the bus driver, a blocky man with straight black hair combed back over his ears.

"Sixth and eighth," we told him, and we exchanged names. His was Dave Titus.

The bus roared past the restaurant where we had eaten hamburgers the night before, crossed the bridge over Indian Creek, and pulled up in front of the grade school on the flat between Indian Creek and the river highway. Dave pointed us toward the principal's office, where Mrs. Lee, the thin smiling secretary, took our names, filled out some forms, and led us to our new classrooms.

At Happy Camp Elementary, sixth through eighth graders had a homeroom, from which they rotated out for classes. Mathematics, for instance, was taught in the sixth grade's homeroom. The sixty eighth graders had two homerooms, one of which hosted reading, the other geography and history. Mrs. Lee dropped my sister off at Mr. Casperson's sixth-grade homeroom, then led me two doors down to 8B, where Mrs. Aubrey ruled. A tall dark-skinned woman in her late fifties, she looked as if she tolerated no nonsense. She pointed me toward an empty desk, introduced me to the class, which was getting ready to leave, and handed me several textbooks.

For the rest of the morning, I followed my new classmates around to geography, arithmetic, and reading classes. At recess, I explored the basketball court and watched the primary grades climb over slides and monkey bars. I played tetherball with a girl named Sandy and watched Liz talking with several other girls in her class. They seemed much taken with her long blonde hair, which hung past her waist and was held back from her high polished forehead by a black headband. Her big incisor teeth flashed with laughter; her thin white arms waved in the air as she made a point.

I met her for lunch, as we carried our brown paper bag lunches into the gymnasium, where long tables folded out from the wall and the linoleum was marked with the lines of a basketball court. Steam floated from the kitchen. Trays banged and kids yelled. Mr. Casperson tried to keep order and was utterly ignored.

"What's he like?" I asked Liz as I bit into my tuna-fish-and-sweet-pickle sandwich.

"Nobody minds him, and the room's a mess and smells terrible," she said. I nodded, having noticed the smell when the eighth graders rotated into Liz's new homeroom for math class. Mr. Casperson wore a crewcut and a short-sleeved white shirt, the tails of which dangled outside his brown corduroy slacks. The end of his belt waved to and fro. His tie had worked loose around his sweating neck. Little flecks of white spittle clung to the corners of his lips.

"Ick," I said.

"Yeah, that's what we all think," Liz said, as one with the rest of the sixth grade.

We ate our sandwiches and escaped onto the playground again, to wander the lawn west of the gym. Near the tall cyclone fence that marked the west boundary of the campus, a few kids crouched in the grass and picked up round black objects, only to smash them with rocks and excavate something edible.

"Walnuts," one of Liz's new friends called out, and we joined them and munched the sweet soft flesh of the green nuts.

As I waited my turn at the best nut-cracking rock, I glanced across the street toward the Happy Camp ranger station. One of many Forest Service compounds built by the Civilian Conservation Corps in the

19

1930s, it sat dark and cool in a grove of oaks. A green pickup truck pulled into the gate and stopped at a set of gas pumps under a shingled shelter. I froze until I saw that the truck didn't carry my stepfather. Not that I was doing anything wrong, but six years of living with the man had taught me to keep a low profile.

After lunch, Mrs. Aubrey led us over to the school library. I had never before seen an entire room in a school devoted to books. At the Hilt school, each classroom had only a single row of library books set atop the built-in bookcases under the tall windows. Every few months, a librarian from the county library in Yreka brought new ones—never enough, as far as I was concerned. But now Mrs. Aubrey turned us loose among the high bookshelves that circled the walls. I noticed some of my favorites in different bindings, and many more new to me. I finally chose something called *The Sword of Saladin* and lined up at the desk to check it out.

At three-thirty I made my way to the gate beside the gym, clutching my books and a handful of mimeographed notices for my parents. When the bus pulled up I climbed aboard and sank down behind Dave Titus. Liz followed me, deep in conversation with another blonde girl. The bus didn't retrace the morning route, but climbed up the hill to the highway and went the long way around to Indian Creek Road.

Alone in my seat, I looked at the thick stands of fir trees that slid past the window as we retraced Indian Creek Road in low gear. Once over the summit and headed down toward Indian Creek, we stopped in front of the cabin I had noticed the day before. Two girls stood up and walked by me to step off the bus, the older walking proudly in scuffed black flats and a tight skirt. I hadn't remembered them boarding the bus that morning. The younger girl had a harelip—the first I had ever seen— but what made my mouth fall open was her costume: a red-and-green plaid dress with a collar of two-toned green lace. Mother had sewn the lace onto that very dress last year, before I grew out of it and we took it to the Salvation Army store in Medford.

Their skin was the color of creamed coffee, and although their faces were clean, their bare legs were mottled with dirt. They must live in that cabin, I thought, appalled, and it doesn't even have electricity. A dozen hounds emerged from under the porch, yawning and wagging their tails. An outhouse perched on the hillside above the cabin. An old man with short gray hair, clad in filthy trousers and a ragged red shirt, split kindling at a chopping block. As we pulled away, I turned around in my seat toward the girl behind me, who shared my homeroom.

"Who were those girls?" I asked.

"Oh, those are the Southards," she replied with a curl of her red upper lip.

"Do they live there?"

"Oh, yeah. Their mother's dead, or gone, or something, and their old man hunts cougars."

"What for?" I asked.

She looked at me as though I were retarded. "For the bounties—it's fifty dollars apiece."

"Does he get a lot of them?"

"Well, no. There's hardly any around anymore."

"But how does he make a living the rest of the time?"

"I don't know," she said, as if the matter had never crossed her mind. "They have an uncle who lives below town and sells car parts," she added, as though that explained everything.

The bus stopped at the bottom of the hill, and my informant stood up and switched down the steps and walked across Doolittle Bridge as we pulled away again.

THAT FIRST WEEK GAVE US A SKETCHY EDUCATION in the local ethnography. Many of our classmates were Karuks, the tribe that for thousands of years had lived on this middle stretch of the Klamath River. The Tituses, Atteberys, Davises, McCulleys, Waddells, and Aubreys all considered themselves Indians, but their surnames came from a few white miners who, after the gold stampede of 1850 receded, had remained on the river and sired families with Karuk women. The children grew up and married the half-Karuk children of other white miners, so that now you couldn't always tell, just by looking, who was Indian and who was not.

Mrs. Aubrey, and her fellow teachers Mrs. Fitzer and Mrs. Fowler, were Karuks, as was Dave Titus, and Mrs. Attebery the postmaster, Ethel Fowler our landlady, and of course Alice Dunaway. Ernie Spinks, the Forest Service's top log scaler, was the offspring of a Welsh father and a Karuk mother. These people were the backbone of the community. They owned property and held down good jobs. Some of them—Alice Dunaway, at least—looked with varying degrees of pity or contempt at what she called Bad Indians. Bad Indians got drunk and drove their cars into the river, or got into fights and knifed each other at dances. Listening to her expound on this to Mother one day, I thought of Norma, a huge and aggressive seventh grader with the shoulders of a fullback, who would shove you out of the lunch line as soon as look at you. Even eighth-grade boys gave her a wide berth—a wise decision, since she outweighed most of them. But except for Norma the juggernaut, our new Indian classmates refused to live up to their off-river reputation: none of them beat us up.

Once Mother mentioned Lafayette Dick, a local character, to Alice. Dad had come home one day praising his work on a forest fire crew. But Alice clicked her tongue and shook her head. "He could have got on permanent with the Forest Service years ago," she said, "but he was a drunk. They say he's stopped drinking, but now half the time he's in jail for not paying child support to his ex-wife."

"Can't he afford it?" Mother asked.

Alice shrugged. "He claims none of them are his kids."

This was the sort of conversation you just couldn't find in our old circle in Hilt.

Our new school embraced its ethnicity; the football and basketball teams were called the Putewans, an Anglicization of the Karuk word *apurevan*—meaning sorcerer. Such characters were almost always men, and always malevolent. (Karuk shamans or healers, by contrast, were almost always women.) Our classmates translated the word as "Indian devil."

IN 1962, HAPPY CAMP NEVER REALLY SLEPT. Four lumber mills ran day and night. The bars had barely closed when the coffee shops opened. Roads were alive with the screaming brakes of logging trucks; their huge grills leapt into view in rearview mirrors, accompanied by a rumble of downshifting. At one of the first Forest Service parties Mother ever attended, another forester's wife described how a trip to Yreka had turned into two hours of horror as a logging truck camped on her rear bumper. She had driven as fast as she dared on the narrow river highway, but was unable to shake him.

"Why didn't you just pull over at a turnout?" Mother asked, imagining the frustration of the truck driver, who couldn't pass her around the curves. The woman shook her head, and the ice cubes in her highball glass rattled.

"I was just too terrified," she said.

On Saturday nights in Happy Camp, loggers and millworkers staggered from bar to bar, while in the rooms above Pence's Café a few whores were said to ply their ancient trade. A hundred and twelve years after the first white men burst into the country looking for gold, Happy Camp still looked raw and unfinished.

The town stood on the site of the Karuk village called *Asisufvunupma—* Village at Hazel-Withe Creek. In the fall of 1851, a group of white Americans working their way up the Klamath River from the coast found abundant gold, built some log shacks, stayed the winter, and called the place Happy Camp. Five years later, only a few well-financed mining companies remained to work groups of claims that later still were sold to Chinese mining companies.

The easy gold was gone by 1860, but then miners dug ditches to carry water from far up Indian Creek and Elk Creek. The water was funneled into pipelines and used to blast terraces into mountainsides and wash the hidden gold from prehistoric river gravels. (One of these terraces, perched above the ranger station, later became the town's airport.) Small sawmills mushroomed near each mine. Some white men came for the gold but stayed to become storekeepers and homesteaders, and raised hay, fruits, and vegetables on the flats near the river. 23

In a world turned upside down, those Karuks who survived violence and measles epidemics salvaged bits of their shattered culture. Karuk men who had fled to the high country in the face of guns and overwhelming numbers returned a few years later to find many of their relatives dead and their wives and sisters appropriated by white men. But they managed to carve out a niche in the new order. They adopted the implements of the whites that seemed useful to them. They learned to ride horses and to pack supplies on mules for white miners. Karuk women learned to use flour and brew coffee and make pies in cast-iron cookstoves. Everyone lived in frame houses and wore the white man's clothes, and many of them drank whiskey, but their inner life remained Karuk.

In 1908, Mabel Reed and Mary Ellicott Arnold, field matrons for the Bureau of Indian Affairs, came to live on the Klamath River below Happy Camp. "In the sixty miles between Happy Camp and Orleans," they wrote many years later, "the social life of the Indian—what he believed and the way he felt about things—was very little affected by white influence ... in regard to birth, marriage, death, the status of women, feuds ... the satisfaction of injury or murder by a fixed money payment, and other customs, the Indians on the Rivers ... thought and acted as their fathers had done before them."

But by 1962, the automobile and its roads had undone the world that those educated eastern ladies saw. In the Happy Camp that I first knew, a few older Karuks still spoke the language, but one of my classmates confided to me that her grandmother wouldn't speak Karuk in front of her. "She says it won't do me any good."

Still, Ernie Spinks often called out the Karuk "hello"—*ayuki!*—as he came in the ranger station door. A few old women still gathered bear grass and hazel shoots and the black stems of maidenhair fern, and cut yellow pine roots exposed by winter floods, all to make their intricate, watertight baskets. Families gathered in the fall to harvest tanoak acorns in traditional groves, but now they ground the acorns in blenders and fed the mush to their children with milk and sugar. In August, families piled into pickup trucks and drove downriver to Ishi Pishi Falls to dipnet the salmon coming up the river, even though the old people grumbled that without the world renewal ceremonies—*pikiawish*— to honor the coming of the salmon, without the white deerskin dance, without the medicine man saying the proper formulas at the proper places and times, then the world was no longer made right, no longer made at all, and must be coming to an end.

But the Karuks had achieved something miraculous in their steep and remote canyon. They had survived, long after most native Californians had vanished under the tidal wave of the American invasion. Their home had been unattractive to most settlers, so the Karuks, with their downriver neighbors the Yuroks, and the Hupas on the adjoining Trinity River, remained. The Hupas had a reservation on the lower Trinity near

24

its confluence with the Klamath; because it had no gold, white men had not even bothered to steal their land from them.

In Happy Camp, Indian and white children had always gone to school together, but for a long time what was acceptable in Happy Camp was just not done out in Yreka, in the white man's country. Happy Camp had no high school until the 1930s, so Indian children whose parents wanted more education for them often sent them away to the government-run Indian schools.

When Alice Dunaway was about twelve years old, an Indian agent came to visit her mother at their homestead near Clear Creek, nine miles downriver from Happy Camp. "My mother had a little fishing platform down on the river below our place," Alice said. "The agent came down the path and watched her netting salmon for a while. He asked her why she was doing that, because usually men did the dip-netting. My mother looked at him like he was crazy and said, 'Well, I have to feed my family, don't I?' Then he offered to take me up to the Indian school near Salem, in Oregon." Alice's mother jumped at the chance to have one less mouth to feed.

"That must have been hard on you," I said, thinking of the horror stories I had heard about Indian boarding schools where children were beaten for speaking their native languages.

"Oh, no," Alice said, "I was happy to go. There were lots of other kids to play with, and they bought us new clothes, and in the summer we all went out to pick beans and strawberries and made a lot of money." Her eyes sparkled at the memory, after the poverty on the river. Coming home from Chemawa at eighteen, Alice brought with her the knowledge that museums and collectors now prized the hand-woven baskets of her childhood. With money saved from school and earned at her mother's boarding house, Alice began to buy baskets from the Karuk women who still made them—"I never had the patience to learn," she told me—and in her sixties, she put the entire collection on the market. She sold it to a museum in the Bay Area, invested the proceeds, and retired in comfort.

But by 1962, such thrift and foresight seemed less important in Happy Camp. As loggers and millworkers followed the postwar lumber boom into the Klamath National Forest, the town's population doubled. Anyone willing to work in the woods or in a sawmill could earn more

25

money than people of Alice's generation had ever seen. And if the new money was often spent on foolish things, no one doubted that for each dollar squandered, another and yet another would come to take its place, in an endless series of second chances.

Year after year, new logging roads advanced into the Klamath Mountains. Year after year, more and more logs were dragged from the forest, and no one could see the end of it, for young men with long legs and a vision strode the ridges, and repeated a mantra: Multiple Use, Sustained Yield.

Piss–Firs

LIZ AND I RARELY TALKED ABOUT our mother's first husband, a man we could remember seeing only twice. Our mother hated him and had always been afraid that he would try to take us away from her. Many years later, we figured out that since this was the last thing in the world our father's second wife wanted, it would never have happened. Both women, for different reasons, greeted our adoption by John Brannon with relief. And since divorce was a stigma in Hilt, Liz and I were more than willing to forget our former status, even though those first few years with our stepfather had been painful. We struggled to conform to strange new rules, and were punished with blows from stout sticks when we failed.

Still, when I saw my revised birth certificate, I experienced a sense of disorientation. It proclaimed, as it always had, that I had been born in Boise, Idaho, and Mother remained my mother, but the man whose genes I carried had been wiped from the page. In his place was someone who had been nowhere near Idaho at the time.

Not that it mattered in Happy Camp, where no one knew our history. As we slapped the falsified documents down on the counter in the principal's office, we were—although we didn't realize it—participating in the old western tradition of reinvention. Liz proceeded to make the most of it. Within a week, she had acquired a new nickname—Beaver— for the front teeth too big for her face. We hadn't, in those days, heard of the word's coarser meaning.

In our new home, birth and marriage meant little. Ruth, a pale thin girl whose father Ralph worked in the Forest Service's fire warehouse, told me quite casually that her father had been married "eight or nine times, I'm not sure." Her own mother had simply left one day, and over the years her place had been taken by a succession of stepmothers. None stayed long. In Happy Camp, divorce was unremarkable, as were common-law marriages and illegitimacy. Liz and I could have claimed to be the love children of Johnny Horton, and except for the sad celebrity of the thing—the famous singer having smacked his car into an immovable object the year before—no one would have cared. The one social disadvantage we faced was not that Dad was not our real father, but that he worked, according to our schoolmates, "for the Piss-Firs."

"Piss-fir" is logger slang for the white fir, *Abies concolor.* Today, when anything that will make a board is valuable, white fir gets more respect, but in those days it often ended up in cull decks to be burned as trash. When freshly cut, its pale, brittle, sappy wood smells exactly like hot urine. The thin gray bark is easily scraped, leaving the wood open to infection by fungi, fit only for chips—and in 1962 there was no market for wood chips.

No one seems to know when or where the name was first applied to Forest Service employees. The full moniker was "Piss-Fir Willie," sometimes shortened to "Willie," as in, "So, you're working for the Willies now, huh?" *Real* men, we were given to understand, were loggers, or at least worked in a sawmill.

But in Happy Camp, the lumber business was not, as it had been in Hilt, a secure job. Loggers made excellent wages when they worked, but winter snows or low lumber prices could keep them home for months at a time. Every January, bulletin boards around town sprouted desperate notices: "Ford ½-ton Pickup: Take Over Payments." But the next spring, loggers and millworkers would buy new vehicles "on time" and take their chances. Our parents had paid cash for both car and pickup truck, and looked upon debt with horror.

28

But Forest Service employees—at least the permanent ones, like Dad—had an extra measure of security: civil service retirement, health insurance, and disability payments if severe sickness or injury struck. The price of all this was less money per hour. Also, living conditions for many Forest Service families in boomtowns like Happy Camp were cramped. We had been lucky to find the blue rental: new hires were far down the waiting list for the few government houses available on the ranger station compound. We realized just how lucky the day we went to visit the Mostovoys.

We had known the Mostovoys when we lived in Hilt; Hank worked in fire control for the Forest Service, and his family had lived in a new house—much bigger and finer than ours in Hilt—in the pine groves just south of Yreka. Hank and Johanna's three obstreperous sons soon became our friends. The boys had virtually no table manners, which may have been part of the attraction: our pre-Dad table manners had been dreadful, too.

The Mostovoys preceded us to Happy Camp, but weren't as fortunate in their choice of rentals. They lived in a duplex at "the projects," a collection of pre-fab houses originally built for highway construction workers in the early 1950s, whose owner was now making a second killing from the lumber boom. We stepped into the tiny living room and were nearly impaled on the antlers of Hank's stuffed mule deer head. In Yreka, the buck had been a rustic addition to a spacious den; here, it was as though a cow had camped in the kitchen.

While the adults chatted and Johanna fetched us glasses of iced tea, Liz and I gazed at walls painted an unhealthy green. The small rear windows gave us a fine view of a neighbor's quadriplegic truck raised on wood blocks. Hank was cheerful and talked to Dad about deer hunting. Johanna looked grim and said that they hoped to rent a bigger house soon. Or Else, her look told Mother, I Will Leave Him and Get the Hell Out of Here. This was the downside of working for the Forest Service: when they sent you somewhere, you had to go, and your family had to put up with it. Mother and Dad had been lucky so far, that was all.

But no matter how constricted their living quarters, the lives of Forest Service wives in outposts like Happy Camp were far from solitary. Marooned in the dark woods, far from family and friends, they formed new attachments with remarkable speed. Numerous Forest Service parties—held at the least excuse—ensured that everyone met everyone else, and Mother was surprised and delighted to find that some of them shared her interests. She began dropping by Mrs. Younkin's house on her way back from the post office, and Carolyn, a native of Virginia who said "hoose" for "house," began to teach Mother and Liz and me to knit. Once a week after school we walked to her house, across the street from the high school, to meet Mother and struggle with the mysteries of knit and purl. Young and energetic, she kept her house and her toddlers in good order, baked homemade pizza, and belonged

29

to book clubs. In her comfortable living room, she fed us cookies, introduced us to Constant Comment tea, and told us about exotic places like Washington, D.C.

As Liz and I manipulated our size fifteen needles, we listened to our mother laugh and chat with this woman from three thousand miles away, their talk ranging from gossip about goings-on downriver in the even more isolated Ukonom District—where the inmates were rumored to resort to wife-swapping to kill winter boredom—to discussions about possible Republican nominees in '64. Whatever the move to Happy Camp had meant to Liz and me, as it took us away from the juniper-scented hills of home, for Mother the journey downriver opened up a new world in which the uncomfortable past rarely intruded. Strangers themselves, the Forest Service wives—Mrs. Younkin from Virginia, Mrs. Mollish from Georgia, Mrs. Williams the district ranger's wife, ditsy Mrs. Johnson—needed each other. So Mother, who in Hilt kept to herself and rarely visited the neighbors, was deluged with invitations to baby showers and Tupperware parties and luncheons. She danced until past midnight at Forest Service parties and met the men her husband worked with. Sometimes the summer parties were cut short when a fire was reported, and the men, hammered or not, shot out the door, leaving their wives to drive home alone and wait.

Older than some, Mother comforted the spouses of young foresters when they telephoned in the small hours, frantic because Joe or Frank wasn't home yet. She told them that John was still gone, too, and that she didn't expect him back until the next day at the earliest. Go to bed, she said, and don't worry. Then she poured herself another cup of coffee and sat down again to read in Dad's chair.

A FEW WEEKS AFTER OUR FIRST DAY in Happy Camp, as the morning bus ride took us by Chez Southard, our jaws dropped to see the carcass of a mountain lion hanging from a madrone tree near the cabin. We knew it was a mountain lion, even though it was skinned, by the size and long tail. The pack of exhausted hounds lay beneath it, bellies distended. Over the next couple of months, as the carcass turned gray and rotted in the winter rains, the dogs leapt and chewed at it until the flesh on the tail, hind legs, hips, and rib cage disappeared. The head and neck hung on, out of the dogs' reach, but pecked at by blue jays and ravens. The rope holding the carcass to the tree limb rotted through a year later and dropped its burden, but shreds of the rope clung on for another three years before a winter storm tossed them away.

WHEN THE STEELHEAD RUN BEGAN on the Klamath in late October, we loaded fishing tackle into Dad's pickup truck and drove downriver: Dad and Mom and Tommy in front, Liz and I in the back, where we leaned on the rack that Dad had built of two-by-sixes and carriage bolts. The river highway ran through the flats west of town where Doc Chambers had his ranch, then dove once more into the dark river canyon. We passed a cove in a draw, where a brook tumbled down over the rocks. Tucked far back under some live oaks, a gray house trailer sat surrounded on three sides by hundreds of dead automobiles, eviscerated engines, and piles of tires. As we unloaded the gear at Clear Creek and prepared to walk over the bar to the river, I asked Dad about the junkyard.

"That's one of the Southard brothers," he said. "They're an Indian family. He and his brother Johnny were famous long-distance runners when they were young."

"Does he own that place?" I asked.

"No, he's just squatting there. It's a mining claim, but the only thing he's mining is parts from those old cars. They'll let him stay there until he dies, though. He's got nowhere else to go."

"Like his brother?" I asked.

"Yep. That's a mining claim, too. No one in the Forest Service wants to go to the trouble of throwing him off, especially since he has those girls to raise. But if he ever leaves, they'll burn the place down."

Like us, our stepfather was getting a crash course in How Things Were Done On The River. He told stories at the supper table about who was related to whom, who was honest and who was not, and we compared his stories with the gossip we inhaled like air at school. Slowly the jigsaw puzzle of Happy Camp fell into place.

We learned that Ralph really had been married nine times, and that although never drunk at work, he knocked himself out with vodka every night. We learned about the perennial poker game in the back of the Log Cabin Bar, where fistfights broke out. We learned that Rhonda's mother drank and frequently banged up her car on her way home from the bars. Maybe, I thought, that was why her daughter bit her nails down to the quick. We learned that some families had good branches and bad branches, and that it was better to avoid the latter, whose perpetually mean expressions were more than just bluff. We learned that the women who turned tricks above Pence's Café did business under the protection of the county sheriff, who had run for office years before on a promise to close down Siskiyou County's whorehouses—a promise he kept, except for those in which he had a financial interest.

One Saturday at the drugstore, while Mother shopped, Liz and I looked up at the many labeled photographs that Doc Kevershan, the druggist, had blown up and hung on the walls. Mr. Kevershan's toupee glided behind the counter like a dead mink on a stick as he filled prescriptions, while his wife pointed out some of the people in the pictures. Old Johnny Grant was the grandfather of the Meinert girls we knew from school. Two strong young men clad in racing shorts and undershirts, arms crossed over their chests, were labeled "Mad Bull" and "Flying Cloud." The nicknames had been adopted for a footrace of several hundred miles up the California coast back in the 1920s, part of a Chamber of Commerce effort to promote tourism on the new Redwood Highway. So this was Johnny Southard and his brother. I tried to reconcile the black-and-white photos of these fierce-looking muscular athletes with the thin old man, surrounded by hounds, splitting wood for a cabin with no lights or running water.

The big sawmills and large-scale logging that brought prosperity to Happy Camp arrived only in the early 1950s. Before that, the few hundred people who lived in and around the town survived by subsistence ranching and mining. Only a few people—teachers, postmasters, Forest Service men, state and county road department employees, storekeepers—had full-time employment. In the sleepy town and the homesteads roundabout, life went on much as it had for decades. Hay was cut, cows were milked, trees were felled and made into lumber for local use, deer were hunted for meat, fires were set so local men could hire on as firefighters with the Forest Service. Some of that still went on. Dad came home one night chuckling over a man who had walked into the Ranger Station declaring that he wanted to go fight the fire up Phillips Gulch, when no such fire had been reported—yet.

In that old world, rents and taxes were low, and consumerism was limited to what Evans Mercantile stocked and the mail-order catalogs shipped. The law's writ barely ran past the Scott River. People solved their own problems, or not.

After the Second World War, the Forest Service hired foresters and began selling timber in earnest. Lumber mills followed, by invitation. Roads were improved and extended into the Forest, and one day the town woke up to full employment, at least in the summer. Hordes of newcomers created an insatiable market for rentals. The old residents still hunted and fished, still grew gardens and picked blackberries, but by the early 1960s they could also buy frozen foods in Ealy's Market, and drive to Medford to find a better selection of clothes and a new pickup to drive on the improved roads. The old ranches were bought up by southern Californians for fishing retreats, as the descendants of homesteaders dumped their inheritances in favor of the wage economy. Locally grown hay all but vanished as bales arrived on trucks from Scott Valley, eighty miles away. Behind the disintegrating barns, dump rakes and mowers rusted beneath the engulfing blackberry vines—themselves invaders, but valued for their heavy dark fruit.

33

Tommy in the spring of 1964 at our first house on Indian Creek. On the porch behind him are the sleds on which, during the following winter, Liz and I would be hauling wood through deep snow.

The new prosperity in the Happy Camp of the 1960s boiled down to good wages and cheap gasoline. New house trailers perched on quarter-acre patches of dirt, carved out of 40 percent slopes by D-8 Cats. Then came wooden porches, and woodsheds out back, a new pickup truck to haul the firewood to fill up the woodshed, and toy trucks and bulldozers for the children who played on the dirt bank behind the trailer.

And those children were not the children of Hilt: compared to my former companions, they were loud, profane, and tough. Their snobbery was limited to disdain for flatlanders and the Forest Service, positions firmly grounded in short-term economics. Good loggers—especially the most skilled fallers—made three or four times the wages of the Forest Service men who told them what trees to cut. Boys knew that when they got out of high school—with or without a diploma—they had a job. Their parents were more prosperous than their grandparents. As they drove on the new logging roads, they looked out on ridge after ridge of unbroken timber. The Forest Service, for its part, assured everyone that the Happy Camp Ranger District's annual cut of 55 million board feet per year was sustainable. And the parents of the children who played in the dirt behind the trailers believed this, and the children believed their parents. Only a few old Karuks, like the Southards, seemed indifferent to the new paradigm and refused to abandon the old ways.

Entrepreneurs followed the lumber mills into Happy Camp. They bought up flat pieces of land and chopped them into lots that sprouted frame houses or trailers. By 1962, Happy Camp was what the Forest Service called a "full-service community." Gwen cut women's hair and gave permanent waves, Dr. Edmunds filled teeth, Dr. Chambers patched up injured loggers, Doc Hall the chiropractor cracked strained backs and sold groceries from his store. Wes Curtis filled propane tanks. Art Tisdale dug up and repaired septic tanks—if you were lucky enough to have one. Many people in Happy Camp remembered a time before lumber was king, but few people now could imagine the future without lumber mills and logging. Certainly the Forest Service couldn't. At full speed, they had developed a grand plan, in which our stepfather was now a very willing, able, and skilled cog. The cutting of trees and the building of roads to reach those trees was his profession, and for this job, and this place, he had in fact been training his whole life.

34

Origins

IN IRELAND, IN COUNTY LAOIS, old leases record that wood was once so plentiful that peasants were required to use it as fuel so that coal could be saved for industry. But by the eighteenth century, the forests were gone, and the poor had to be content with turf. In 1760, John Brannon, son of Patrick, ran off to America, where there was lots of wood.

In 1766 he married Rebecca Baldwin and settled in what is now West Virginia, where Mr. Brannon was considered exotic enough to be known as "Irish John." They raised a large family and their descendants blanketed the Appalachians, adopting the culture of the Scots-Irish backwoodsmen around them. By 1920, my stepfather's branch of the family was divided between Oregon and California; he and his brother were born in San Diego just as the Great Depression began.

Irish John's brother Thomas also came to America. He settled in Maine, where his youngest son grew up to spell his name Brannan and to become famous in the wild San Francisco of the 1850s—Sam Brannan. A one-time Mormon, a vigilante, a newspaperman, a speculator in real estate, he made and lost a great fortune and died poor in San Diego in the 1880s. By my stepfather's time, the exact relationship was forgotten, except for the fact that Sam had been "some sort of cousin." Indeed, the kinship was now an embarrassment—less because he had been a rascal than because of his association with Brigham Young. Antagonism toward all forms of authoritarian religion ran deep in the family.

My stepfather and his brother knew only that their name was Irish, and that their grandfather Bushrod Brannon had brought his family from West Virginia to Nebraska before moving on to Oregon. County Laois and its denuded hillsides were forgotten, and now the forests of another continent beckoned; by the early 1950s, my stepfather and his father and brother were loggers in western Oregon. And in Oregon, thanks to chainsaws and Cats and logging trucks, the work would go much faster.

35

As a child and a teenager, I wondered why the brothers were so different, and decided that it boiled down to education. Dad had escaped the grinding labor of the logging woods for the less dangerous life of a forester by going to college. Charlie had gone straight into the woods after graduating from high school; then he had been drafted into the army during the Korean War. Always tall and strong, Charlie was an easy target for the heaviest tasks; his family assumed that those were what he wanted. He matured at six feet, four inches and 250 pounds; in the army, he found himself the smallest man in a barracks full of MP trainees.

Two years later, he returned from Asia bearing stories of infiltrators who slipped into camp at night, knifing one man in a tent while leaving the other. Before going to bed in his old room, he told his family that if they had to wake him up, they should shout at him from the doorway. "Just don't touch me," he said.

Charlie and John had grown up on a farm near Lakeside, east of San Diego, where their father Al raised beans and worked as a well digger on the side. The farm offered security in a cash-poor world, and security was needed, for John, older by a year, fell ill with leukemia at the age of three. Doctors told his parents that he would be dead within a year, but they started a series of blood transfusions that were thought to sometimes bring a short remission. The skinny blond child confounded everyone by slowly getting better, although he would forever remain shorter and thinner than his husky younger brother. In deference to his early weakness, little in the way of farmwork was required of him. His mother, Tudy, had already decided that if Johnny survived, he would go to college.

Tudy's parents were German, and she grew up speaking the language and absorbing her family's awe of educated people. She never questioned the custom of giving the lion's share of family resources to the oldest son. Younger children were supposed to help the family educate the oldest. So John was encouraged to study, and in his free time he hunted. He caught snakes and sold them to the San Diego Zoo. He ran a trapline in winter and caught coyotes and foxes and bobcats and sold the pelts. Charlie, who liked horses while Johnny was afraid of them, Charlie, who was big and strong and never sick, hitched up the cultivator and spent long hours in the southern California sun, tending row crops.

When World War II broke out, Al began commuting to San Diego to work in an aircraft plant. But his mother in Oregon wrote letters complaining of her advancing age and her husband's poor health, and begged them to move north. So Al and Tudy settled on a stump ranch near Wren, Oregon, a few miles from Corvallis, where Al's parents lived. Although Al was glad to live closer to his father, Pops did not look like dying just yet, and his mother Rosa, besides owning and running a busy trailer park in wartime Corvallis, had enough energy left to try to convert her grandsons to Christian Science. This was the beginning of Al's long disillusionment with his mother. But at the time he just shrugged and made allowance for her gray hairs. If life was lean now, he thought, eventually most of his parents' property would come to him, for his younger sister Peggy and her husband, a man named Olds, were prosperous in southern California and seemed likely to remain there.

On their 160 acres of hillside, Al—now called Pappy by his sons, after the patriarch in the comic strip *Li'l Abner*—began building a house and clearing land for pasture. The boys went to high school in Philomath. After school and on weekends and in the summers, Charlie did farmwork at home and for the neighbors and earned enough to build up a small herd of Jersey cows; the cream checks kept the family in groceries. And every couple of weeks, John sat down on the hillside above the apple orchard at dusk and waited for the black-tailed deer to rise from their beds in the dark forest and come out to feed.

With an old .22 single shot Remington balanced on his knees, he shot yearlings and does and spike bucks. The Remington made only a sharp crack like the snapping of kindling, and in that well-wooded country could scarcely be heard a quarter-mile away. Even if the neighbors heard something now and then, they paid little attention, for most of them did the same thing. Still, John was careful. He shot in poor light, and got rid of the hide and head and lower legs, so that if someone should see a carcass hanging in the shed, it could be explained as one of the milk goats they kept to feed bummer lambs.

The blacktails weighed only about eighty pounds, and John soon learned to drag them up to the shed, hang them from the rafters, and skin them out with swift clean strokes of his pocketknife before wrapping

37

them in an old sheet. The next morning, before he caught the school bus at the bottom of the hill, he covered the sheet with a couple of old blankets to keep the carcass cool through the day.

When the deer had hung for three days, Tudy went out to the shed with a kitchen knife and peeled the tenderloin away from either side of the deer's spine. She sliced the long roll of meat into steaks, rolled them in flour, and fried them up in lard. In summer, she canned some of the meat, but four hungry people made short work of a carcass: first the tenderloin, then round steaks carved from the hind legs, then meat stripped from the front legs and run through the hand meat grinder, then stew meat carved from the neck. Last of all, she chopped the ribs free of the backbone with a hatchet, boiled them, slathered them with catsup-based barbecue sauce, and broiled them.

John carried the skeleton away to the oak grove above the barn and gave it to the scavengers.

Trees grew so fast in this wet green land that a pasture left ungrazed for five years became a young forest again. Early settlers of the county stood in awe of this fecundity as they wrenched fields from the woods with hand tools and oxen and fire. Later came steam donkeys and railroads, spurred by developing markets for lumber in Portland and Seattle. The 1920s brought the first primitive chainsaws; the 1930s gave birth to logging trucks. In the 1940s, a few people sensed that once the war was over, logging would grow bigger than ever.

They were right, for the late 1940s saw the end of living off the cream check. Western Oregon was suddenly full of lumber mills and logging operations as men came back from overseas and went to work. Barns fell into disrepair and herds of dairy cows vanished as their owners abandoned farming for a logging or sawmilling paycheck. Some even stopped poaching. But the Brannons, always careful with money, did not. John, studying forestry at the state college in Corvallis, still had time to provide venison for his mother's table. He grew at last, too, shooting up until he stood only three inches shorter than his brother, and gained weight and muscle as he began working in the woods in the summers. His long-fingered hands acquired calluses.

In the summer of 1947, the year he graduated from high school, John worked away from home for the first time, commuting to a job as a fire suppression crewman on a state wildfire crew. Charlie, almost a senior in high school, looked up one evening from the milking to see his mother standing on the other side of the stanchion. Years later, as he told the story to my brother Tom over a campfire, Charlie's voice still held anger. "She wanted me to quit school and go to work full time to help John through college," he said. "I just told her no, I wasn't going to do it. My God! The woman's buying groceries with my cream check, and she has the nerve to ask me to quit school!"

"What was she thinking?" Tom asked.

Charlie added more whiskey to the coffee in his enameled cup and shrugged. "That was the way things worked in her family. The oldest son got the education, and the rest of the family helped. But I wasn't going to do that."

In the summer of 1948 John set chokers on a high-lead logging operation, or "side," for two months. Setting chokers was hard, dangerous work everywhere, but especially so in high-lead, or cable, logging. Choker-setters climbed down steep hillsides littered with slash and felled trees, carrying lengths of cable fitted with a bell attachment that looped around a log. The ends of the chokers were then hooked to a larger cable dangling from the biggest cable of all, the mainline that descended from the yarder far above on the landing. (Think of snapping a dog chain onto your clothesline.) The most dangerous part of the business was attaching the chokers to the logs—often six feet or more in diameter—by climbing over and under them while balancing on rain-slickened bark in "cork" boots armed with spikes on the soles. The logs had already been limbed and bucked—cut into lengths—and rested like pick-up sticks in a bed of limbs. Sometimes men slipped; sometimes logs shifted and broke a leg or crushed a chest or pelvis. When a group of chokers was connected to the mainline, the choker-setters scrambled out of the way, signals were exchanged between woods and landing, and as the mainline tightened, the logs stood on end and were dragged to the landing. Once in a great while a yarder fell off the landing and tumbled downhill, crushing any choker-setters who couldn't get out of the way. Sometimes an overhead cable snapped under the strain of its load, whipped sideways, and cut a man in two.

When the woods crew shut down that winter, John worked as a handyman around Moser Lumber Company's mill in between classes. The next summer, he worked for Simpson Lumber Company, cold

39

decking logs—running the loader that removed logs from around the yarder and piled them up in a deck, to be loaded later onto the waiting logging trucks. When there were too few logs to deck, he set chokers behind a D-7 Cat—a safer job, generally, for Cats worked on flatter ground. In June of 1950 he began contract logging for Moser Lumber Company. He surveyed property lines, built logging roads, felled timber, learned to use blasting powder, and helped build a sawmill. By the time he graduated from Oregon State in 1951 with a degree in logging engineering, he had done every job in the woods. For the next five years, he and his father and brother were Brannon Logging, with up to ten loggers working alongside them. They bought standing timber from landowners, logged it, and sold the logs to local mills. They never had a man killed, but the work remained hard and dangerous, with injuries and close calls all too common. For a man with a college education, it simply wasn't worth it, especially as the "gyppo"—independent— logging business grew more competitive. In 1956, the family company broke up. Pappy took a job as a millwright for a lumber mill. Charlie, now married to a redoubtable woman named Dorothy, became a contract log hauler, and struggled to make payments on his logging truck. And one day that spring, John walked into the office of Fruit Growers Supply Company in Hilt on the California-Oregon border. Within a year, he had married our mother and changed all our lives forever.

Sandbagged

AS A CHILD, I PREFERRED TO SPEND TIME during family gatherings with the men. They talked about interesting things, like politics, and their travels. The conversation of the women tended to veer toward horror stories about childbirth and operations. One day, well lubricated by Grandfather's martinis, one of my great uncles asked me what sort of husband I wanted. "A rancher?" he asked. "You like animals."

"I don't want to get married," I said. "When you're married, you have to do what your husband tells you."

This was the message that I had absorbed from Mother and Grandmother, whose lives seemed circumscribed, sometimes bitterly so, by the desires of their spouses. But the men in the room swiveled their heads and stared at me. Uncle Nick guffawed. "Where did you get that idea?" he boomed, and they all laughed.

The expressions on the faces of the men puzzled me at the time. Not until many years later was I able to decipher their silent messages. The older men were saying, "*My* wife never does a fucking thing I say," while the younger men looked up at the grizzled silverbacks of the troop and asked with their eyes, "You can do that? You can tell them what to do?"

"Don't even think about it, kid," came the unanimous replies.

BY THE TIME I WAS TWELVE, five years after the man from Oregon married my mother, I had achieved a sort of armed truce with him. I got good grades, did my homework and my share of the housework, followed his arcane rules (or hid the fact that I didn't), and was silent in front of company. Sometimes weeks went by, now, without punishments. But after I turned thirteen, I faced other changes. I would remember that, even if my old diaries didn't exist.

I had enjoyed being twelve. Twelve meant the dignity of a training bra instead of childish undershirts. Twelve meant growing tall enough to put a ball through a basketball hoop. Twelve meant going to the spring basketball tournament in Alturas and eating supper in the old Alturas Hotel, where superannuated ranchers gathered to talk and read newspapers on deep brown leather sofas.

Thirteen started out well. I learned to serve overhand in volleyball, and as I watched the gray ball crash down on the other team, I heard Mrs. Aubrey say from the sidelines, "That new girl's a good player."

But by the spring of 1963, as the winter rains stopped and the weather turned hot again and the sun rose higher above the green walls of our canyon, something happened to me and to many of the other eighth graders. Thirteen-going-on-fourteen—my birthday fell early in June—was an age at which we regularly wanted to jump out of our skins. As the world around us burst into new life—roses along the fences, hillsides bathed in pastel blooms of deerbrush, apple trees exploding in every lot and pasture—we didn't care about school anymore. We talked instead about summer, and how we would swim all day in the hundred-degree heat. We didn't care about our gloomy teachers and their useless assignments. We looked forward to the dignity of high school, where boys were said to hide bottles of whiskey in their lockers. Leave us alone, our glazed eyes begged as Mr. Maxon gave us an English assignment, which we forgot as soon as we tumbled out of the classroom into the May sunshine. We paid even less attention than usual to Mr. Casperson. Our grades fell. Boys shoved each other and growled "no heh" as they stood in line outside the lunchroom. What I had thought was some cryptic Karuk phrase turned out to be slang for a lack of pubic hair. And in the back of classrooms and in corners of the playground, the girls, martyred but superior, whispered the dark secrets of their periods.

Mine had begun early in the spring, while cold rains still fell, and I rode the bus meditating upon my cramps. Every month I grew short-tempered just before the deluge. I shouted at Tommy, made bitchy remarks to Liz, cursed with colorful new words learned at school. I was always, always hungry, so that my painfully acquired table manners sometimes slipped. I grew taller, but my breasts and hips kept pace, and even as I devoured a dozen oatmeal cookies before supper, I bewailed the fact that I weighed all of 115 pounds.

I grew lazy, and my temper flashed when Mother asked me to do something unreasonable like vacuum the living room. I never seemed to get enough sleep. I talked back to Mother, although never when Dad was in earshot. Two years before, Mother might simply have slapped me for my impudence. Now, she narrowed her eyes and announced that I was "Acting Just Like Someone Else I Used to Know," a reference to her long-divorced husband in Boise, whose very existence still had the power to enrage her. I had no answer to the shame of my paternity, except to flee to the stash of candy hidden beneath a pile of slips in my dresser. A Three Musketeers bar always made me feel better. I had discovered eating as revenge, a bad habit with staying power.

A few girls in my class already went steady with high school boys. Some claimed to be engaged. They talked about where they would live and how many children they would have, but I wanted neither children nor a husband. I had been saying this from the age of ten, but now, an unwilling witness to my own metamorphosis, I was more than ever convinced that the last thing I wanted was to watch another person go through this hell. Bad enough that I would still be sharing a room with Liz when *her* face started to break out. And with Tommy in the house, I was all too familiar with the demands of infants and could not imagine why anybody would want one.

In our first six months in Happy Camp, some of the old draconian rules from Hilt slid away, never to return. In Hilt, I had been forbidden to read outside of school, due to my galloping myopia and the unwillingness of my parents to pay for new glasses every six months. Since books were my drug of choice, I read in secret. Now Mother discovered the branch library in Happy Camp on her own account and took out children's books for Tommy, and novels and biographies for herself. As she sat and read in the evenings, while Dad perused newspapers and hunting magazines, somehow the message was passed that it was now all right for me to read, too. Besides, in Dad's eyes, what was on television was far more objectionable than Agatha Christie. I gave silent thanks and wallowed openly in the printed word again, when Tommy wasn't begging me to read to him from the collected works of Beatrice Potter.

43

But even as my breasts exploded out of my chest like alien parasites, Dad looked up at me one day and saw a whole new series of faults to correct.

I ate too fast now, he told me. As he watched me across the supper table, I knew that he saw the table manners he had so painfully hammered into me as an eight-year-old going down the drain with every forkful of

Mother's good plain cooking. He saw large grocery bills, coming out of his now-smaller paycheck. He invented new rules to slow me down: I could, for example, no longer be the first to finish a meal.

Before my eruption into puberty, neither parent had paid much attention to the finer points of my grooming; now, every day brought new criticisms—of my hair (not set), my eyebrows (not plucked), my clothes (you're not wearing *that*, are you?), my nails (why can't you grow them longer and put on some nail polish?), and my face (shouldn't you be wearing a little lipstick now?). I was "supposed" to be doing a lot of things that had never occurred to me and that—when brought to my attention—seemed a total waste of my time. Girls at school who worried about their hair and nails were fluff heads who couldn't hit a ball out of the infield. Why in the world would I want to be like them? But my parents seemed to think that not wanting to wear lipstick was some sort of character flaw. And whatever my parents' quarrels with Liz—she remained determined to slip through school without "working up to her abilities," for instance—a lack of fashion sense would never be one of them. Liz instinctively knew what I should be doing to my hair, my lips, my eyebrows, because it was exactly what she wanted to do with her own.

"I would kill to have your figure," she mourned. "Can I borrow your lipstick just to see how it looks?" As I tossed my tube of Coral Pink across the gap between our beds, I wished that I could want what she wanted, be what she wanted to be—what my parents wanted me to be. But I couldn't, and the conflicts emerged in my diary:

44

> *Burped at dinner table and got excused.*
> *We are going round and round about the table manners again.*
> *This morning Dad gave me Father-to-Daughter Talk Number*
>   *Uncountable about table manners. And not doing work and budgeting*
>   *my time.*
> *Dad got mad about my manners—sent me away from the table to eat my*
>   *cake in the bedroom without a fork.*
> *At dinner this afternoon, I began eating too fast and Dad took away my*
>   *silverware. So I polished off two spareribs and began eating with them.*
>   *Of course it was difficult, and at last Dad said, "Are you open to a*

> deal?" I said yes and he said, "Next time you finish first at dinner, the
> next meal you eat without silverware."
> Last night it happened. I finished my plate at breakfast first, and at
> dinner I had to eat without silverware. Chocolate pudding for dessert,
> too.
> No supper tonight—I forgot to set my hair. That ultimatum was issued
> last night, you will remember, and I forgot it today.
> And then yesterday when I didn't set my hair before dinner I went to bed
> without dinner ... One more job to do—I gotta set my damn hair
> before dinner, or no dinner.
> Dad says I walk too heavy and must learn to walk lighter.

When I started high school in September, Dad noticed that I preferred reading at home to going to the high school dances. He ordered me to go to dances and to talk to boys at school. For a few months, he interviewed me at the supper table about the boys I had spoken to that day. At first, I actually did talk to boys, and dutifully noted down their names in my diary (Les, Bill, Robert) and what we talked about (hunting, football, algebra). But the list of boys who didn't actually repel me was short, and most of them already had girlfriends who glared at me, mystified at this breach of bus protocol, when I turned to talk to their beaus over the back of the seat. To avoid this embarrassment, I fell back on lying, which was a great time saver. With a little imagination, I could turn an overheard bus conversation into my own, and get in half an hour of reading besides. Dad didn't seem to know the difference. The summer vacation put an end to the daily reports, and when school started again, Dad had either forgotten about them or become as bored with my life as I was.

I would never be as good an actress as Liz, but eventually I managed to convince Dad that I wanted to go to the school dances. I received my reward one day when Dad forbade me to go to the Valentine's Day Dance, as a punishment. I tried to look sulky as I played Monopoly that evening with Liz and Tom at the kitchen table.

Dad rarely spanked me now. To spank a child was one thing, but to haul the large hips and bouncing mammaries of an adolescent over his knees was quite another. Sometimes, though, matters escalated on their own, as in the aftermath of one basketball game.

45

Tonight at 4:00 we freshmen girls played the eighth-grade girls. We won, 30-7. Afterwards, in the dressing room, Jennie pretended she was hurt in the shower and we tried to throw Mrs. Schaefer [our gym teacher] in, but she wouldn't let us—had a wool dress on. I'm not your coach, Jamie is, she said, so we threw Jamie & Jackie & Sandy & me in. We tried to throw Vicky in, but she ran into the toilet booth and got mad. We had a blast, my hair and undies were all wet, Jamie's gym clothes were sopped, and we couldn't get our coats nor books because the panels were across the hall and Mrs. Schaefer wouldn't open the restroom door for us. So I didn't bring my homework nor my coat home. Anyhow, we got home (Dad was waiting for us) and first thing, 'mid all the excitement, Dad started bellering at me to stand up straight and stop chewing my gum like an old cow. I couldn't take it any longer—so I said, 'Oh, be quiet!' quite disrespectful, but I wasn't thinking, and next thing I know I was crouched behind the door getting a licking! I didn't cry out, nor bawl afterward.

I can still mentally rip the roof off that blue house, so long ago, and watch myself come through the door, my bra and panties soaked, my damp blouse clinging to my breasts, their nipples hard in the cold air. I see the wet shorts on my hips, the goose bumps on my thighs. I see myself laugh, my mouth opening and closing on a wad of chewing gum. Hair damp, face flushed, I erupt into Dad's orderly world, a hurricane of energy and raging hormones. I see Dad's horror as this apparition talks back to him and sends all his training and discipline galley-west. I must have scared the hell out of him.

As Liz and Tommy looked up from their game of Candyland with wide eyes, Dad seized the spanking stick—eighteen inches long, two inches wide, and sharp at the edges. I crouched behind the bedroom door, cornered, as he struck me again and again. But this time, alone out of so many physical punishments, the blows didn't have the desired effect. For the first time in my life, I endured a beating without a scream or a cry. Dad turned on his heel and left, and the door slammed shut behind him.

I sat on my bed and dabbed witch hazel on the welts on my thighs, between bites of a Snickers bar. I hummed to myself with a strange sense of triumph. Only then did it occur to me that I hadn't seen Mother. The door to my parents' bedroom was closed, and as I opened it to slip into the bathroom, I passed her, lying flat on the big bed with a wet washcloth over her forehead and a migraine behind her eyes. "Eat some cereal before you go to bed," she murmured.

I made my way to the dark kitchen to follow her instructions, and my eyes were drawn to Dad's hands as he sat in his easy chair near the front door, the newspaper before his face. His fingers trembled, ever so slightly.

DAD NEVER STRUCK ME AGAIN. Brannon men did not hit women, and Dad knew, now, that I was a woman. But how to regain control? Over the next few days, I could almost see the gears in his head turning when he looked at me. In the end, he came up with a method so foolproof that he must have kicked himself for not thinking of it before.

In those days my favorite books involved animals, especially horses. When careers were discussed, I said that I wanted to be a veterinarian. Dad frowned at that. Women, he told me, were almost never admitted to veterinary schools. Besides, I would marry and have children, and veterinarians couldn't afford to take time off to raise children. Teaching was a far better career for a woman. I should become a teacher.

To tell me I couldn't do something was to make me even more attached to my imprudent ambitions. I continued to read about animals and to talk about them at the supper table. But one night Dad ended all that with a single sentence.

I can't read any more books about animals, Dad says, or he will shoot the dog and cat.

47

Well, that was simple.

We had come to Happy Camp with Bob, a blue merle Australian shepherd puppy whose destiny was supposed to include hunting deer. When an eight-week-old gray tabby kitten showed up on the front porch one day while Liz and I were at school, Mother—who had resisted all entreaties to adopt kittens in Hilt—scrubbed the vagrant in the bathroom sink and fed him a bowl of milk and oatmeal. We came home to find Boots—half a pound of stripes and white feet—curled up on the couch with a smug look on his face.

Now, these dumb hostages to fortune offered Dad a method of control with none of the exertion of corporal punishment. Under that threat—renewed as needed—I set my hair, buffed my nails, plucked my eyebrows, and submitted to having my ears pierced. I wore lipstick, finished last at meals, stopped talking about a veterinary career, and assured any relatives who asked that the dearest desire of my heart was to become a science teacher. I still read books about animals, but I kept them in my school locker, a last stand of defiance.

The obvious way to call Dad's bluff would have been to ask him what he planned to do for an encore after the dog and cat were dead. But I already knew that Dad's family viewed pets as expendable. His own parents had recently taken their two cats and the border collies, Dinah and Dollie, to the local vet and had them gassed. They had sold their ranch in Oregon in preparation for a retirement of travel and rockhounding, a lifestyle that would have been inconvenient with four animals. So when Dad said, in effect, "straighten up or Bob and Boots will die," I believed him.

Only once did I get a clue that Mother didn't fully support the ultimatum. One day she dragged a dynamite box, full of her old books, from underneath her bed. She pried off the cedar slats and stacked the books on the end tables in the living room. I had almost forgotten some of them: Hawthorne's *Tanglewood Tales*, and a lavishly illustrated *Swiss Family Robinson*. But I felt my insides twist as I saw a familiar dark blue volume, *Further Adventures of Lad*. Once I had known Albert Payson Terhune's words about his favorite collies almost by heart. To camouflage my excitement, I picked up another volume and began leafing through the unintelligible regional dialect of Joel Chandler Harris.

"Can we read these?" I asked.

"You can read any of them you like," Mother answered, looking directly into my eyes. And I did, and Dad said nothing.

AS I STEPPED OVER THESE NEW EGGSHELLS in my path, our old ophthalmologist, Dr. Lemery, retired. He referred some of his patients to the new gun in town, Mary Jane Fowler. Dr. Fowler set up shop in a converted Victorian in Medford, Oregon, where her husband acted as her optician. He sat all day in what had been the front parlor and adjusted glasses behind a desk in the bay window.

Mary Jane was the first woman doctor I had ever met, and the fact that she worked as the senior partner with her husband impressed me no end. She seemed to explode Dad's theories about what women could do, but I didn't mention this to him. Dad went to see her first, and liked her. She practiced a holistic style of medicine: she prescribed reading glasses for Dad, but she also talked about vitamins and told him to wear a hat to protect his light blue eyes from the sun.

My own first visit to her began well enough. She checked my vision with an array of clicking lenses set before my face as my chin sat on a padded rest. The examining room was dark and quiet as she led me through the eye chart. Outside, in a neighborhood of old trees and screened-in porches, bees cruised the shrubbery and English sparrows chirped under the eaves. I heard a far-off hum of traffic.

Dr. Fowler had creamy skin and black hair that brushed her earlobes. I liked her air of calm competency. She looked about forty. Her voice was soft and—to my amazement—she began to converse with me. When Dr. Lemery spoke to children, his gruff voice sounded as though he was warning us not to chew the furniture. Dr. McNair, the orthodontist, made it very clear that my job was to open my mouth and be quiet. But here was a grown woman asking me questions as she worked. What grade was I in? Did I play sports? What kind of books did I like to read? I began to talk.

She put drops in my eyes and deposited me in a dim room to wait for my eyes to dilate. I was bored with no one to talk to. She had removed my glasses, and the drops rendered me almost blind. When she brought me back to the examining room, she peered into the backs of my eyeballs with a bright light, and I saw the veins inside them hover in the air out to one side, a creepy vision I tried to ignore as Mary Jane resumed our conversation. I chattered away now, out of politeness and to distract myself from the discomfort of the burning light in my naked eyes. I was happy to talk to her if she wanted to talk to me.

When the exam ended, Liz and I picked out new frames in the front corner of the office. We had both been told that our eyes had "progressed" a little, which had always seemed to me a curious choice of words. In school, progress was good. But not where our eyes were concerned.

Mr. Herbert (Dr. Fowler practiced under her maiden name) fitted the new frames to our skulls, while Mother and Dad were called in to consult with Dr. Fowler. When they came back to collect us and lead us out to the car, I knew something was wrong.

Dad didn't look at me or speak to me for the rest of the day. Mother glared at me over compressed lips but said nothing. My mind flew back over the day. What in the world had I done now? We ate at North's Chuck Wagon, my favorite place, but the fried chicken stuck in my throat.

The next day, a Sunday, Dad called me into the house just as I finished mowing the lawn. I had tackled that chore without being asked, in an effort to appear hardworking and virtuous and humble, and ward off whatever was coming. But it was no good. A kitchen chair sat in the middle of the living room floor: the dock. Mother and Dad sat across from it, Mother upright on her side of the couch. I knew the routine. I sat down, a roar in my ears, my head spinning.

Three years before, after a horrible day when I had accidentally burned my mother with scalding coffee, I had seen all my sins laid bare as I sat petrified in one of these same chairs. That day changed my life, and gave me such a sense of my own depravity that my very survival, it seemed to me, depended upon hiding my evil self from the world. My parents knew I was bad, and that could not be helped. I could only behave so circumspectly that the badness would not be uppermost in their minds. But right now, it obviously was. I sat, shoulders back, and tried to act as if I wanted nothing so much as to pay attention to them. But the passage of three years had changed me, and not just physically. I was frightened, but also angry.

"Do you know what we need to talk to you about?" Dad asked.

Long experience had taught me not to make assumptions about what my parents knew and did not know. Confession was not, in my case, good for the soul. This had something to do with Dr. Fowler, I guessed, but I didn't discount the possibility that something else was involved. So as I shook my head, my mind raced over various slips in behavior during the past week. On Thursday, I had once again forgotten to set my hair when I came home from school, and when I heard Dad's pickup pull up beside the house, I raced into the bathroom, flung on my curler cap, and shoved it full of bristle-covered rollers until—to the undiscerning male eye—it looked as though I had set my hair. Had Mother ratted on me?

But what could Dr. Fowler have told them? I replayed our conversation in my head.

OHMYGOD. I had told Mary Jane, when she asked me what kinds of books I liked to read, "Horse stories, dog stories, histories." Jesus. She must have let this slip to Dad, not knowing how dangerous it was. I thought of the books stashed in my locker at school. *Desert Stallion*, and *Arabian Cow Horse*. I might just have killed Bob and Boots. My heart started to race. How could I have been so stupid? Had I learned nothing?

"Dr. Fowler," Dad began again, seeing that I wasn't going to speak, "told us that she's very worried about you. She says you're extremely nervous, and she'd like us to take you to see a neurologist."

I let out an internal sigh. Thankyougod. Then I realized what he had just said.

In 1963, in the world of my parents, neurologist was a code word for psychiatrist, for shrink. "She's been seeing someone for her nerves," ladies whispered to each other at coffee klatches, when what they meant was that the poor woman had gone screaming 'round the bend and was about to be led away.

"They're coming to take me away, hey-hey, to the funny farm, where life is happy and always gay," sang Liz and her classmates at recess, and in those days, long before the state of California decided to save money by tossing the mentally ill out onto the streets, incarceration in an asylum was not an empty threat but an enduring shame. I remembered the wife of a neighbor in Hilt, who was always spoken of as dead, although in fact she was alive in the state mental hospital.

So my babble to Mary Jane had not condemned our pets, but another threat now leered at me from the past, for in the aftermath of the scalding incident, Dad had told me that I was crazy, and that crazy people were taken away and locked up. That day had never really left me. Now, with Dad's old diagnosis confirmed by an independent professional, my stomach churned beneath my pounding heart. The most powerful person in my life was telling me that I was a telephone call away from imprisonment at Napa. And a neurologist, should he take me to see one, might back him up, too, might tell my parents that yes, I should be taken away for my own good. Dad let his words sink in for a moment, then continued.

"Now, I think you can get control of this by yourself if you really try," he said. "You can train yourself not to be nervous. And if you can show us and show Dr. Fowler that you can do that, I don't think we'll have to take you to see that other doctor. But if you can't learn that, if you can't get control of yourself, then if Dr. Fowler tells us the same thing next time, we'll have to take you to see him, and he might decide that you need to be sent away."

On the wall behind Mother's silent face, the afternoon sun struck watercolor paintings of an old Western town, just as it had three years ago in another room, another house. Close up, the paintings didn't look like much, but from across the room, they came alive with the warm dustiness of another century. I wanted to dive into that lost world, climb onto the horse tied to that hitch rack, and ride far away. Outside, Tommy chased Liz around the house, their young voices rising and falling as they passed beneath the windows. Bob barked as he followed them. Across the room, splayed out on Dad's easy chair, Boots shot his front paws out in a stretch, then turned his head upside down and went back to sleep, a string of drool on his chin.

I had thought of Happy Camp as a new start. My classmates didn't care that my mother had been divorced. They overlooked Dad's job with the piss-firs, once I proved I could play volleyball and hit free throws. My grades were good. I'd ended up as the damn salutatorian at eighth-grade graduation, for cripes' sake! What did they *want* from me? Tears welled up in my eyes and slid out, borne on a flash of rage.

"I'm sure you can do this," Dad said. "And if you can, we'll say no more about this, and we won't take you to the neurologist. So go to your room and think about how you're going to do this."

I nodded and stood up. Good. Maybe they thought I was sorry, thought I was remorseful. I slipped into the front bedroom and closed the door, then bolted through Mother and Dad's bedroom to the bathroom. I opened the window and turned the taps on full force. I flushed the toilet, then sat down on the lid, and cried. After a while I stood up on Tommy's stepstool and looked out the open window at the tops of the oak trees beyond the yard. Liz stopped below me, her pale face lifted as she pulled Tommy in his Radio Flyer wagon. "Did he spank you?" she asked.

"No," I said. "He just yelled at me. Dr. Fowler told them I was too nervous."

"Jeez," Liz said. "Want to go for a walk?"

"No, I'm supposed to stay in the room for the rest of the day."

"You can read the comic books under my mattress," Liz offered, and disappeared around the corner of the house, Tommy squealing in her wake.

I thought about what Dr. Fowler had seen in me and not in Liz. Surely Liz had chattered, too. What was the difference? Had her interest in me been just a ploy to draw me out, to find something wrong? Well, next time, I wouldn't speak to her at all, unless she asked me a question. Next time, I wouldn't volunteer a goddamn thing. Bitch.

But how did people relax? I didn't know. Try to breathe slowly, perhaps, try to move slowly. Don't talk much. Don't chatter. The next week, I found a book in the school library called *Relax and Live*. The author recommended deep breathing, from the diaphragm. I practiced this in study hall, on the bus. I practiced moving quietly and deliberately around Dad. Sometimes I forgot, but then I remembered what would happen if I couldn't change.

BACK AT DR. FOWLER'S TO HAVE OUR NEW GLASSES FITTED, I sat in her waiting room in a meditation of my own invention. I breathed slowly. As she checked my eyes once more, I kept my body still and was silent until she asked me a question.

"How's school going?"

"Fine." Just answer the questions. Don't elaborate. I looked at her calm face, intent on her instruments, and hated her. But she said nothing more to my parents about neurology, and although I saw her once a year until my sophomore year of college, the subject of my jangled nerves and their possible treatment never came up again.

In the second semester of my senior year, as I engaged in a neck-and-neck grade-point struggle with Lee Attebery for valedictorian, I broke out in a rash on my neck and arms. I scratched the itchy red skin raw, until Mother sighed and took me to see a dermatologist. He smiled at me and asked what was going on in my life. I told him about the race for graduation honors. He nodded. "I had a patient last year with a similar rash," he said. "Turned out she was getting married in a month." He reached into a drawer and pulled out a tube of ointment. "I gave her a tube of this, and the rash cleared up in time for the wedding."

I stared at him. "I think this is just nerves," he said, and patted my shoulder. "Probably it'll clear up soon. If it doesn't, come see me again."

"Just nerves." So other people had them, too. The dermatologist did not seem to think that made them crazy.

DAD'S MARRIAGE TO MOTHER and the birth of their son were happy events marred by the presence of two boisterous stepdaughters. We were expensive, with our teeth and our glasses and our need for shoes. Dad couldn't afford our neuroses, too. That was the real reason why I never saw a neurologist. But in those days I didn't know that. In fear, I changed my outward behavior. I tried to breathe deeply and remember all the rules. And after a while, repetition became habit. I learned to curb my temper. I grew used to the monthly hormonal surges and—without a choice in the matter—reconciled to my new body.

Now and then I still wonder: what did Dr. Fowler really see? A kid who seemed too eager to talk? I never found out. Mary Jane didn't bring the subject up again, and I was afraid to peek beneath that particular rock. With hundreds of patients, perhaps she simply forgot what she had noticed on that first visit. And the last thing I needed, as I dealt with monthly bloating and cramps and headaches, as I walked with strange lusts and swift rages, was any reminder of my warped mind. I had learned a strange and unintentional lesson from Dr. Fowler: when people know what you're really like, their knowledge is a threat. So I battened myself down, took a shaky refuge in the rugged individualism that refuses to ask for help, drugged myself with books, and told myself that it was good.

Into the Woods

IN THE KLAMATH MOUNTAINS, winter storms began in the first week of November. For six months, with only minor breaks, wave after wave of storms crashed against the Pacific coast and rolled inland. At Eureka, on Humboldt Bay, annual precipitation was thirty-five inches; at Orleans, in the Klamath River canyon fifty miles inland, rainfall rose to eighty inches as the mountains raked moisture from the clouds. Forty miles farther upriver, at Happy Camp, precipitation dropped back to sixty inches. By the time the storms reached Yreka, sixty miles east of Happy Camp, only twenty inches of rain and snow fell in a year.

Four miles north of Happy Camp, the steady thrum of rain, day after dark day, pounded on our metal roof and almost drowned out the roar of Indian Creek across the road. Even when the rain paused, fog blocked out the pointed green peaks. At ground level, almost no wind blew, but at night a soft roar over our heads tracked the storms through the tops of the trees. My sister and I missed the occasional heavy snowfalls of our old home in Hilt; missed the sight of snow clouds flattening into a uniform gray and dropping lower and lower until they blotted out Mount Ashland as the flakes began to fall.

During our first winter on Indian Creek, no snow came, and only a few inches of fast-melting slush the second winter. Sometimes when the weather cleared, we saw the flat snow-covered top of Slater Butte from our school bus windows, and we heard the other kids say that the gravel road called Grayback that led to Oregon was snowed in. But in our rain belt below the clouds, we lived confined in a narrow, watery world.

Above us, the endless conifer forest loomed, home to uncut giants, their tops hidden in fog. On rare rainless days, as the sun rose at eleven o'clock behind Indian Ridge, beads of water in the flattened branches sparkled, hundreds of gallons caught in every tree, shielding the forest floor from the pounding raindrops.

Humidity crept in everywhere. A framed photo of our grandfather as an infant, which Mother kept in a cabinet in the parental bedroom, grew dark as mildew blackened his long white gown and baby face. Mother wiped the edges of windowpanes with dry rags to forestall the black sludge that seemed to grow overnight. Doors swelled and stuck; window frames warped and refused to open. People told her that propane heaters seemed to increase the moisture inside a house. She said she didn't see how it could possibly be any wetter unless raindrops fell from the ceiling.

One Monday at school, after a drenching weekend, we entered the girls' locker room to find the drains backed up and a confused salamander trying to escape from the shower stall. The creature was half the length of my hand, and shiny brown, his skin flecked with tiny white dots. The end of his tail had been smashed. I carried him to the science room, snipped off the end of his tail with scissors, and placed him in the terrarium. I spent my lunch hour watching him and leafing through natural history books, while the salamander burrowed under the damp moss and wood chunks in the glass enclosure. Sewers were not his natural habitat. He was a lung-less salamander, a creature of the forest, washed down some draw by the storm. Secretive and nocturnal, the salamander proved to be an uninteresting pet, and in the end I took him out past the school fence and placed him under a fallen oak log.

In the woods behind our house, strange mushrooms with shimmering caps grew on the ground and on old logs and stumps. I knelt down to peer at the miniature bird's-nest mushrooms, cups in which round white sporophores floated. The bark of older trees was weighted with shelf fungi banded in brown and white. A rich wet smell penetrated to the back of my sinuses. Ferns grew out of the moss on the trunks of oak trees, and Dad told us it was licorice root. I dug the ferns out of the moss with the tip of my pocketknife blade, peeled the roots, and chewed them.

On weekends, I pulled on a pair of cut-off rubber fishing boots that reached to just below my knees, tugged on my leather jacket, dug a walking stick out of the jumble of tools in the outhouse, and led the dog out of the yard.

Above our house, on the sharp ridge that ran down to Indian Creek, stood an ancient Douglas fir. I climbed toward it, as Bob crashed through the undergrowth, clawed for purchase on logs, scraped eagerly at the secrets of rotting stumps with paws and snout. I fought my way up the slope behind him, boot toes catching in the snowberry and honeysuckle vines that laced the ground, my arms raised to push aside the soaking, brittle branches of deerbrush. On my first hike, the target tree proved smaller than I had thought, only four feet in diameter—solitary, broken-topped, and scarred by fire. I sat beneath it for a while, listening to sounds from below: Mr. Kuehl's truck starting, the barks of Mr. Mendenhall's two malamutes, a logging truck on the county road. I was invisible. My parents didn't know exactly where I was. I hugged my knees, delighted.

The scarred tree stood just inside the line separating the National Forest from the private land below. No signs or fences marked the boundary, but below it grew deerbrush and poison oak and patches of young trees; above stood the uncut ranks of old growth timber. Our house sat on land homesteaded long ago. The flat places, the gentler slopes along the canyon bottoms—these had been logged off, built on, or cultivated. Above them was a world unlogged since time began.

But not unmanaged. Once, our landlady's Karuk ancestors had burned parts of the forest landscape to encourage the growth of hazel and bear grass for basket-making materials. In autumn, the people started fires on the ridges and the flames crept downhill, keeping oak groves and hunting trails clear of brush. Lightning fires that started in the hot summers burned where the fuels took them, thinning young stands of trees, keeping the forest open and park-like.

But as I sat on the ground beneath the snag, picking deerbrush twigs out of my hair, I saw the result of over sixty years of fire control. Deerbrush (*Ceanothus integerrimus*) is a fast-growing, nitrogen-fixing deciduous shrub that can reach over six feet in height. It springs to life in incredible numbers after a fire, with as many as forty thousand seedlings to the acre. Deer browse it for its high protein content, but after twenty years or so, forest succession shades it out. Then its hard seeds lie dormant under the duff, waiting. With the deerbrush comes poison oak, reaching for the same sun, the same sky.

Poison oak grew tall here and, especially in leafless winter, looked so different from the discrete, polite thickets in the hills around Hilt that at first we didn't recognize it for what it was. Once Liz followed me up to the ridge, her face slapped by the slick brown branches that snapped

57

closed behind me. Within forty-eight hours, her eyes were swollen nearly shut, her face a mass of weeping sores. Mother consulted the litany of native remedies—washcloths soaked in manzanita-leaf tea, poultices of mashed plantain leaves. Some recommended eating a tiny leaf of poison oak when it first budded out in the spring, but Mother rejected this advice as unhelpful and fell back on the druggist's recommendation of calamine lotion and time. Liz accused me of deliberately letting the branches hit her. This I hotly denied, but she seldom came with me after that, and I had a guilty suspicion that she was right. I liked being alone on the ridge, alone under the broken tree, alone on the mountainside beyond. And unlike so many other things that I wanted to do, no one ever told me not to go hiking.

Beyond the snag, I followed a faint ridge trail up to a gentle curve where deer trails led off into the depths of the forest, into a quiet world where only the hardest rainstorms penetrated the giant crowns of ancient Douglas firs. Trickles of water ran over stones in the draws. I climbed, walking on trails that followed the land's contours, taking intersecting trails that led me still higher up the slope in a series of switchbacks. The noise of Indian Creek faded. The draws grew shallower and then disappeared; above them live oaks clung to the slopes of scree and thin soil.

Gray squirrels chattered at Bob. Land snails dragged their banded shells over the moss, leaving trails of slime. I touched their outstretched antennae and watched them recoil into the pink bodies. I pocketed empty shells to bring home, where I lined them up on the living room windowsills. Once I brought back a live snail, kept it in a jar half full of earth, and fed its alarming appetite with lettuce leaves. A few days later, it thrust its body into the soil and deposited a clutch of translucent eggs, then walled off the mouth of its shell with a curtain of dried saliva. I took the jar outside, placed the snail beneath some moss, and dumped the soil out under a log.

In the woods, Steller's jays followed me, squawking. Their electric blue wings swooped over my head in warning or announcement. When they tired of the game and left me, the woods grew quiet again. The thick boles of the trees, coated with moss and lichens, stood wide apart, like ancient temple columns. During a rainstorm, only an occasional drop of water reached the ground beneath them, but for days after a storm, the water caught in those treetops showered down with every breeze.

Few seedlings grew between the giants, for little sun reached the ground. In the rare openings, redbud and dogwood spread their thin branches, and now and then a madrone commandeered a clearing and grew to tremendous size, its slick orange branches spreading out, the ground below its shaggy lower trunk littered with orange berries. Sometimes I startled flocks of mountain quail or thrushes from beneath these shelters, or a blue grouse flew clumsily into the branches, and chinked at me in the half-light.

Clear water, filtered by standing trees and thick beds of needles, ran in the draws, unmuddied even under the hardest rains. Sword ferns and black-stemmed maidenhair exploded out of rock shelves and dead logs near these rivulets. Everywhere, moss cushioned the rocks.

Across the side slopes, the deer trails crossed fallen trees, some so old they had crumbled to piles of red duff. Some of the trails looked too wide to have been made by the dainty hoofs of deer. Larger creatures had gouged out these terraces—Roosevelt elk, the heaviest elk on the continent, and gone now for fifty years.

I seldom saw deer here, although sometimes I heard one crash away as I hiked up through the brush below. Deer did not feed in the deep forest, except to search out acorns or nibble a mushroom. I saw only tracks and droppings, and sometimes a bed, tucked under a shelf of rock or a fallen log.

I walked until I was tired, sat until I was rested. Other than my own clumsiness, or the unlikely chance that a tree might fall on me, few dangers lurked. Cougars were rare and shy after decades of bounty hunting. Bears and rattlesnakes slept in their winter dens. Not long before, local newspapers had been full of strange incidents near Orleans. Something had tipped over logging equipment and left giant footprints in the mud. Bigfoot, some people said. Some logger playing a joke, Dad scoffed. And if Sasquatch did roam those mountains, I never saw her.

But creatures stranger than Bigfoot did live here. The high branches of the trees held flying squirrels, spotted owls, colonies of bats, perhaps even tree voles—animals that rarely touched the ground and were utterly dependent on these rooted giants. Thirty years later, when wildlife biologists finally began looking for them, diminutive seabirds called marbled murrelets were found to nest in the tops of trees only a few miles to the west. They made daily trips to the ocean to bring back food for their nestlings.

The little I saw of that high and hidden world was startling enough. Sometimes a pair of pileated woodpeckers glided by—black and white, big as crows, with red crests from which the Karuks had made ceremonial headbands. Woodpecker scalps were treasures, and no wonder. How to kill such a bird with a bow and arrow? Downy woodpeckers and nuthatches and chickadees would have made easier prey, but no one ever hunted them. Small and noisy, they landed within three feet of me, unafraid, the nuthatches upside down.

As winter slid into spring, marked by longer and longer breaks between rainstorms and a slow warming, wildflowers appeared—purple shooting stars, fawn lilies, white and purple trilliums, delicate calypso orchids, Johnny-jump-ups in rare patches of sunlight. Pipsissewa was common in the acidic soil, and I stuffed my pocket with leaves to take home to Mother, who dried them for her herbal teas.

Mother's wildflower book showed only eastern species, but many of those pictures looked almost identical to the flowers in this Pacific forest—wild ginger tucked under a damp bank; miniature purple irises spread over the flat behind the house. Most startling of all was the snow plant, a thick pink neon confection that thrust aside rotting needles in the darkest corners of the forest, like some alien mutation of a fir cone.

I overturned logs and watched to see what scurried out—centipedes, millipedes, dangerous-looking scorpions, sometimes a salamander, twin to that refugee in the shower stall. The dog tired and fell in behind me, flopping down whenever I stopped, following me with a martyred look when I continued to climb toward the ridge, through the live oaks.

When I reached it, I turned to look across the canyon of Indian Creek and up into the Doolittle Creek drainage, with its narrow logging road that switchbacked up to Baldy Mountain. Behind me, more ridges flanked other drainages that emptied into Indian Creek, all of them leading up to Thompson Ridge, highest of all, and the Forest Service lookout on Slater Butte. The topography was steeper than a staircase, so steep that in these short days of the rainy season, a hiker ran out of light long before she ran out of territory. As the day faded, I followed the ridge trail back down toward Indian Creek, back to the old snag, down through the deerbrush and poison oak, and let myself and Bob in at the front gate, just as the lights came on in houses and trailers all around us.

Pleistocene, Ho!

WHEN DAD LEFT THE OREGON RANCH in 1956, he stopped poaching deer. In an apartment in Yreka, under the scrutiny of close neighbors and a landlord, there was no opportunity. After he married Mother and became the sole support of a wife, two stepdaughters, and later a son, he had too much to lose. So he bagged his venison more or less legally, with a license and tags. The tags were not always his—in years to come, they might be Mother's, or mine, or Liz's—but still, they were tags.

The Haystack Burn of 1955 cleared thousands of acres near Hilt, and over the next few years those mountains, where loggers salvaged scorched timber, teemed with deer, grown fat on the brush that sprang to life from long-dormant seeds. The black-tailed deer of the Pacific slope are a subspecies of mule deer, and distinguished from them by their small size—150 pounds at most and usually only about 100 pounds—and by their all-black tails. The antlers of both blacktails and mule deer fork like tree branches, while those of the white-tailed deer have tines rising from a single main branch. Since we had never seen whitetails except in the pages of hunting magazines, we scorned the effete eastern custom of counting all the tines on both sides of a buck's rack. A "ten-point buck," to our ears, sounded ridiculous. We spoke of "forked horns" and "four points."

When Dad worked for Fruit Growers in Hilt, he hiked the Haystack Burn and flagged out routes for the logging roads to come. Beyond the burn, he cruised timber for ever more logging operations, but while he measured and wrote in his notebooks, he also scouted hunting sites. He learned where the deer fed, where they watered, the trails they followed. He talked with loggers and learned something almost as important: how the game laws were enforced in Siskiyou County. California law, for instance, mandated that a game officer come to your house and stamp all the packages of venison in your freezer. But game wardens had no time to do that, so the provision was recognized for what it was: a means of nabbing poachers when no other evidence would stick.

Shooting deer from a vehicle was illegal, too, but this was interpreted to mean "when somebody's looking." Rather than spook a buck by stepping out of the truck, Dad—and everybody else we knew—steadied the rifle on the open window frame and shot.

To place another person's tag on a buck that you had shot was illegal, too, but again, the operative philosophy was: don't be stupid about it, and don't get caught. The local game wardens concentrated on hunters from out of the area and those who shot deer out of season. Even then, a local who was able to convince a judge of his poverty often received only a small fine.

In Happy Camp, rules were bent still further. Many Indians hunted year-round. Game wardens knew who was worth prosecuting and who wasn't. One evening, we stopped by to visit Ralph the warehouseman and found him in his kitchen, drunk on vodka and orange juice and attempting to cut up the carcass of a doe on his kitchen table. Ralph wielded the butcher knife with such inaccuracy that Dad made him sit down and began slicing up the steaks himself. Mother located wrapping paper and scissors, and Liz and I helped wrap the meat and tape it up. Tenderloin changed hands on that occasion, too. Mindful of his Forest Service job, Ralph didn't poach himself, but he accepted meat from his Karuk son-in-law. Dad soon began to follow the local Forest Service custom of bringing his rifle to work with him during deer season. If a buck just happened to cross the road in front of the green pickup, why waste the opportunity?

DAD HUNTED ALONE, OR WITH ONE OR TWO FRIENDS. Often, he ranged far off the roads and hiked for hours along open ridges to the brush patches where wise old bucks hid. He disdained the huge knives sported by many hunters, preferring a pocketknife. "You don't need a big knife to gut a deer," he told us. When he hunted, he closed the doors of his pickup with a gentle click. When he killed a deer, he didn't stop on the way home to drink beer and show off. He got the buck home as quickly as possible, skinned it, wiped down the bloodied ribs with a damp cloth, then encased the carcass in a cotton bag. Deer were not trophies; they were meat.

As the bucks hung in the shed—antlered head still attached, nose pointed at the rafters, forelegs cut off at the knees so that they poked forward like the arms of a sleepwalker—I sometimes visited them. I slapped the stiffened muscles of the shoulders beneath the deer bag. All the ticks that had crawled out on the deer's nose in the bed of the pickup were gone now, picked off and burned. The tongue, dry and pale, poked out from the side of the jaw. Just before bedtime, Dad covered the carcass with two heavy blankets and tucked the ends up underneath the white chin, folded their sides together, and roped them around the body with a length of twine.

Dad taught my sister and me, and in time our little brother, to shoot. He cut down the stock of his old .22 single shot to fit our shorter arms, and we learned to aim and squeeze, not jerk, the trigger. Sometimes he took us with him on evening hunts, and we followed him down deer trails, then sat silent beside him as the light dimmed.

In the wilder, damper world of the Klamath River, virtually all the land away from the bottoms of the major drainages was part of the Klamath National Forest. From November to May, especially, the wider skies and dry hills of Hilt seemed very far away. But Dad was too practical to abandon those long-scouted hunting areas near Hilt, and autumn drew him back to the pine-scented draws that fed into Beaver Creek, or the slopes of Sterling Mountain.

Dad soon learned the Happy Camp country, too, and found good hunting grounds on Grider Ridge and Thompson Ridge and in Stone's Valley in the Marble Mountain Wilderness. In the meantime, everyone knew that recent clear-cuts were good places to hunt, with their thickets of dogwood and deerbrush and big-leaf maple, and all were easy to reach via the new roads that sliced ever deeper into the ancient forests, those roads that our stepfather flagged for the Forest Service, one step ahead of the logging contractors. And where the loggers went, the deer, creatures of disturbed habitat, followed. So even as Dad changed the landscape, he made his own hunting luck.

FORTY-SOME YEARS LATER, I WONDER at the energy I poured into the annual quest to put venison in the freezer. I wonder at the strength of my desire, despite all that had happened between us, to learn to do what Dad did, and for him to think that I did it well. In the end it came down to respect. Much as I had feared him, I had also learned to respect him, and that not grudgingly. Children, and especially adolescents, have a sharp eye for competence in adults. At school, we knew that Mrs. Aubrey had it and Mr. Casperson didn't. I had always recognized it in Dad. We trusted his driving, even in the worst snowy weather. We trusted that he could fix anything that went wrong in the house. Dad knew about things.

There was still so much that Dad and I would never agree about. I would never be what he thought of as a proper daughter. Proper daughters were like Mother: quiet and domestic and unselfish. Proper daughters were realistic about the place of women in the world and accepted the fact that they couldn't compete against men. Proper daughters looked forward to marriage and families of their own. But even proper daughters might still want to go hunting. Dad would never have insisted on it, but once he knew I wanted to, he was willing to take me. Besides, it meant two extra deer tags.

But except for those evening hunts, I sat out the seasons of 1962 and 1963. I needed hiking boots to follow Dad on long hunts, and I had none. Boots cost money, as did licenses and deer tags, and money was scarce, so scarce that Mother no longer parceled out the dollar-a-week allowances that had made Liz and me feel rich in Hilt. To buy hiking boots for a girl still growing out of her school shoes was out of the question.

So I made cookies for Dad while he hunted with Max Younkin and Hank Mostovoy, and I practiced aiming and dry firing the .250-3000 from the front porch, while Mother picked seventeen pounds of white grapes from the arbor in the backyard and made wine. Dad took us all fishing at the mouth of Elk Creek, where we caught steelhead, and he put two bucks into the freezer. We ate venison and fish all winter.

When my fifteen-year-old feet stopped growing, Mother took me down to Hooley's—as everyone called Evans' Mercantile—and bought me a pair of Red Wing hiking boots. One evening in August, Dad and Tommy and I bounced up East Fork Road to a brushy clear-cut, and when a three-point buck stood broadside to us, one hundred yards away, we looked at him through our rifle sights. "Could you hit him?" Dad asked.

65

"Sure," I said.

Dad set up a block of wood on the logged hillside about two hundred yards from the road and tacked a paper target to it. We stuffed our ears with cotton, braced the rifles on a folded coat on the hood of the truck, and took turns shooting. My first shots through the open sights of the .250-3000 kicked up dust just below the target, as the metal butt-plate slammed into my shoulder. Dad's shots hit the target near the top of the black. He adjusted first my sights, then the telescopic lens on his .257 Roberts. We shot another group, then walked up to the target. Now my shots were all in the black, as were Dad's. We walked back to the truck. A jay landed in a madrone tree above the target, blue flame against the smooth orange bark, and scolded us. As the sun dropped away on the other side of the canyon, Dad crouched over the hood once more, the barrel of the Roberts cradled in folds of red plaid. A shot, an explosion of feathers, and the bird was gone.

Dad worked the bolt of the rifle, pocketed the empty cartridge cases, slid the bolt closed again, and pressed the trigger. It clicked on nothing, and Dad slid the rifle into the pickup cab. "Good enough," he said.

That evening, Dad pulled money from his wallet, and the next day I bought a hunting license and two deer tags. The season began on September 19, a Saturday. On Friday evening we loaded rifles and sleeping bags into the truck and drove upriver to the Haystack Burn.

The burn spread purple in the twilight above Beaver Creek as we parked the truck on the overgrown prism of a logging road that vanished into a washout just ahead of us. We loaded up and walked westward, the deerbrush rustling on either side of us as night creatures scuttled away. I could barely make out Dad's tall form in front of me. After half a mile of this, Dad put his pack down, leaned our rifles against a log, and covered them both with his coat. We rolled out our sleeping bags on top of a length of canvas and pulled the folds over them. Just below the road, a rivulet gurgled. I dug a flashlight from my pack and went to get a drink. Dad opened his pack and brought out cans of pork and beans and peaches, a bag of oatmeal cookies, and apples. He opened the cans with the can opener on his key ring. We ate sitting cross-legged on top of the sleeping bags, our boots off.

The stars winked on, and the pine-scented breeze moved past us, now warm, now cool. We drank again from the streamlet, then slid into the sleeping bags, Bob on top of the canvas between us. I looked up at the close and friendly stars, caught in the river of the Milky Way. A satellite wandered by, and a shooting star dove for the tree line. The red light of an airplane blinked its way north. I tucked my glasses into one of my boots and covered my head with the welcome warmth of the green sleeping bag.

Something shook my ankle. "Time to be moving," Dad said. I poked my head out and felt frost on the canvas under my chin. I pulled on my stiff, cold boots. We rolled up the bags and stashed them and the packsacks behind a log above the road. My rifle was cold in my hands as we walked down the road, and I pulled the sleeves of my hooded sweatshirt down to warm my fingers. Dad walked before me without a flashlight, the pale blob of his hardhat breaking the darkness. By the time my toes had thawed out in my boots, a pale swatch of light appeared behind us, and the world, although still colorless, was no longer black. We turned toward a draw, and Dad paused on a rocky point.

"Wait here," he told me, "and watch. I'll go across the draw." I nodded, still shivering under the sweatshirt. Dad's red hard hat now matched his red flannel shirt. Bob followed at his heels.

I sat down on the rocks, dangled my chilly legs over the edge, and watched the draw. Dad disappeared off to my left, and I watched the brush move until he reappeared on the other side. He sat down on a stump and glassed the hillside. Below me, the world broke into view as the edges of objects sharpened. A breeze stirred, and I huddled my hands into the pocket of my sweatshirt. Voices broke out above me, and I turned to see three figures moving above us at the head of the draw. When I turned back to look in Dad's direction, I saw a deer watching me from fifty yards away. Buck or doe? It stood before a clump of deerbrush, and twigs rose behind its ears. One ear twitched. One front leg stamped. The head moved against the background. No antlers—a doe. I looked across the draw and saw Dad nodding at me. I inched my head around to look at the hunters above me, but they were gone. I remembered what Dad had said once, that does often led the way for bucks. As the light increased, I saw the deer trail the doe followed, and I knew that Dad had been here before.

Far below us, another logging road crossed the draw, and now I saw someone walking along it. Above us, a rifle boomed three times,

67

and then voices came again. "Did he go over the ridge?" a man's voice asked.

The first rays of sun hit the ridge where Dad sat. He stood up and waved an arm at me. I crossed the draw to him, and together we walked back to our camping spot, retrieved our gear, and hiked back out to the truck. Breakfast was the rest of the oatmeal cookies and another can of peaches apiece. I drank my fill at the rivulet. A one-gallon canteen rode in the back of the truck, but that was only for places with no other water.

We drove out of the burn and back to the Klamath River Highway, then upriver to the Ash Creek bridge. Once over the river, we found ourselves beneath steep slopes covered with oak trees and poison oak thickets. If deer were to be found here, we would have to drive them out.

Dad's method for this was a lesson in timing. We hiked uphill, then took turns crossing draws, one ahead of the other. "I'll cross over to that ridge," he told me, pointing. "You give me about twenty minutes, then come across yourself." He handed me his pocket watch, with its braided black leather fob. He didn't own a wristwatch—they got hung up in brush, and sweat ruined them.

Sometimes, I crossed too high or too low, or walked too fast. Go slow, Dad admonished me when I caught up with him again. The day grew hotter, and none of the draws hereabouts had water. Dad owned a couple of Army surplus steel quart canteens, but he never carried them. In this country, he said, a person was never too far from water. "You can stand not to drink for a few hours," he told me. Easy for him to say, I thought, as I fought my way through yet another draw. I was sorry I hadn't drunk more water after breakfast. I thought about cans of peaches and bottles of soda. Bob clung to my heels, tongue out and breath rasping, and ignored the squeaks of chipmunks. With every draw we crossed, we climbed higher up the face of the mountain, until the Klamath shrank to a narrow ribbon below us. The distant noise of water brought a whimper to my dry throat.

By the time the sun dropped into the canyon and vanished, we had kicked out only four does. "Better head back," Dad said, and we descended, crossing other draws, until at last we hit the dirt road and followed it back to the truck. We drank deep of the still-cool water in the canteen, then drove a few miles downriver to Humbug Point and camped beside an old dredger pond, where we children had once fished for perch and bullfrogs.

As we set up camp, a truckload of people from Happy Camp lurched by over the rocks on the bar and waved to us. Salmon jumped in the river, the noise like shots across the water. Dad cut me a willow pole, and I attached monofilament line and a dry fly from a stash in the glove box. Nothing bit, but the river water was cool on my blistered feet. As the sun set, Dad built a fire in a ring of smooth rocks and fried up a can of Spam in a blackened frying pan. I opened a can of applesauce and spread margarine on slices of white bread. We ate off paper plates, and by dark we were in our sleeping bags. I stared from the glowing coals to the stars and back. On the highway far above us, lumber trucks groaned through their gears as they rounded the hairpin turn and accelerated into the long straightaway, headed for Yreka and the railhead.

We drove back to Beaver Creek before dawn, and at first light sat perched on a point above yet another brush field. Once more we waited for what might jump out between us. My socks were damp with fluid from my ruptured blisters, and I wondered if I could make it through another hot afternoon. At least I had remembered to drink as much as I could hold this morning. But—to my relief—as we ate lunch back at the truck, Dad looked at his watch. "Might as well head home," he said.

He took the long way around through Cottonwood Creek, and then down into Hilt. My job as passenger was to look, look, look out the window—far view and near view—and hold the rifles steady against the seat. Dad had good eyesight and remarkable peripheral vision, and even as he drove, he often saw deer that I missed.

69

"Most people," he said after he had stopped short to check out a doe invisible to me, "they're looking to see a whole deer. But usually you don't see all of it. You see a head, or a tail, or just part of the body. You have to look for the parts." He told me how to tell the head of a buck from a doe even if you couldn't see the antlers: a buck's face was much lighter than a doe's, almost white in the older ones. As we pulled into our driveway on Indian Creek that night, I was tired to the bone and limping, but I had survived my first hunting trip without major disgrace, and my blisters had a week to heal up.

The next weekend we hunted closer to home, in the Elk Lick country far up the South Fork of Indian Creek. No elk remained in 1964—not for thirty years would they trickle back from their last refuges on the coast. But the land was still wild and roadless, and dotted with boulders the size of cars. At these higher elevations, Douglas fir gave way to true firs; deerbrush was replaced by fragrant slick-leaved snowbrush. "There's not a lot of deer up here," Dad said, "but the bucks are big."

We saw none of them that day, however. I slipped while scrambling over a boulder and scratched the stock of my rifle. Bob whined as he tried to follow us. We saw more bear sign than deer pellets—piles of scat the size of dinner plates, full of berry seeds.

SOMETIMES WHEN DAD HAD TO WORK LATE scaling logs at Siskiyou Mills, Mother drove us up the East Fork of Indian Creek in the car. She carried her .222 rifle and her deer tags, but she also carried a sketchbook and pencils tucked into the front of her red hunting shirt. While she went off in one direction to "sit on a stump," I led my brother and sister off for a walk along the edge of a clear-cut. I never really expected to see a buck on these trips—too many people drove to this accessible area—but one evening, Liz heaved a rock into the brush and a buck leapt from his bed not fifty feet from us. By the time I got the rifle to my shoulder and the safety off, he had disappeared. Bob bounced in his wake, his high breathless yips fading into the distance.

Once I proved that I could keep up with Dad even in rough country, he began to take me along when he hunted with other Forest Service men:

Today Dad & I and Mr. Miller and his boy Dewey went hunting up West Fork of Indian Creek. We went up a ridge but had to fight the worst brush you ever saw in your life to get through as we couldn't find the trail. We found a lot of good country, including a huge alder thicket, and although we saw many tracks, we saw no deer. Coming down after a waterless and thirsty lunch, Mr. Miller and I went down to the station wagon via the trail (which we found). Dad & Dewey went on down the ridge. Mr. Miller and I drove around in the wagon to meet them at the bottom of the ridge. On the way we stopped at West Branch for a drink. Mr. Miller saw a 6-8 inch fish. We drove around and waited for them at the bottom of a clear-cut... The dog worked real well today but there just weren't any deer around for him to spook out, although we saw many tracks.

A week later, I saw my first buck killed, on another trip to the Beaver Creek country. On Bullion Mountain, Dad and I hiked downhill from a road, sat on opposite sides of a draw, and waited for daylight. We worked our way across to a timbered point, where so many gray squirrels scolded us that Dad had to secure Bob with a length of twine to keep him from chasing them. Toward evening, as we worked across a brush-covered basin, I saw Dad pull his rifle to his shoulder. A stab of flame, a blast, and ahead of us the brush thrashed and something fell heavily into a draw. Dad ran ahead, shot three more times, then called me over. Bob bounded ahead of me, the smell of deer and blood in his nostrils, and we found the buck before Dad reached us: a forked horn, dead on an old skid trail. I could see the bullet hole through his lungs, and his head twisted beneath him. When I grasped his antlers and pulled his neck straight, I saw the wound at the base of his spine. His mouth hung open, and his tongue lolled out.

After Dad gutted him, I carried the two rifles over one arm, my other bearing the weight of a heart and liver swaddled in my sweatshirt. The binoculars bounced against my chest as Dad dragged the buck down to the road. There, he hooked a strap around the antlers, and pulled the buck along for several hundred yards until we reached the pickup. We hoisted the carcass into the back and drove home.

I liked the Beaver Creek hunts, because we often came home through Cottonwood Creek, and Hilt. In the initial excitement of moving to Happy Camp, I had not missed Hilt all that much. But now, I clung to everything that reminded me of the place. When I walked toward downtown Happy Camp at noon, I chose a route that took me past some houses with deep shady yards, black locust trees, and wooden fences much like those of Hilt. And when Dad and I drove through Hilt on these autumn days, I rolled my window down and drank in the scent of the pines across the road from the sawmill. Nothing in Happy Camp smelled like those dry ponderosas on the hill known as Little Italy. As we drove down that last grade and passed the box factory—now closed and

71

deserted—where my grandfather had worked for thirty years, I looked beyond it to the town, and drank it all in, this place like no other, now lost to me.

Dad knew the land behind Hilt far better than I did. He could see whether the roads he had laid out had been built as he had designed them, whether a stand of timber had been logged yet or not. He knew what lay beyond every ridge, up every creek, and told me exactly what I would find as he sent me off on a sweep that might drive out a buck. I knew that for him, the Forest Service was a far better place to work than Fruit Growers, so the thought that he, too, might miss the landscape around Hilt never crossed my mind.

DAD'S PARENTS WERE RETIRED NOW and sometimes came to Happy Camp so that Pappy could hunt with Dad. They brought their trailer with them and so were little trouble, but sometimes Mother still escaped to the washhouse to get away from Grandma's endless anecdotes, and then Liz and I crept out to join her. We stood around the washing machine—the new Maytag wringer model that had replaced the pink automatic—and nursed cups of coffee as the machine churned. In the warmth of the sunshine that poured in through the windows, I felt again the coziness of Grandmother's laundry room in Hilt, an age ago.

What impressed me about Pappy was how calm he was in the face of situations that brought Dad to white-lipped anger. One evening I set my rifle up against the living room wall, and it slid to the floor and broke off the front sight at the end of the barrel. Without this brass bead, the rifle was useless. I stood shaking, embarrassed and heartbroken, for Pappy and I had planned to go hunting the next day, since Dad and Mother had to go to Medford. When Dad stopped shouting at me, I handed him the few dollars I had saved from my birthday money, to help pay for repair of the sight at a Medford gunsmith shop.

I have a cough, I wrote that night, *and I feel miserable and Goldwater has lost the election and I have busted my sight. This is a terrible day. I am so miserable I could just die.*

The next day I borrowed Mother's rifle, and Pappy and I drove to Slater Butte, high above Indian Creek. As we navigated brush patches and discussed tactics, he never once mentioned the broken sight, or the fact that I was coming down with a cold. His forbearance made me feel so grown-up that, as we sat on the roadside and ate lunch, I ventured to offer condolences upon the death of his mother a few weeks before. And then his blue eyes did flash at me. "Well, thanks," he growled, and then stood up so suddenly that I feared I had offended him. Perhaps I never should have mentioned Grandma Rosa. But she had lived to a great age and her death had not been unexpected.

Pappy and Dad went hunting by themselves the next day. Mother took one look at my red nose and puffy eyes and said I'd better stay home. I helped her with the laundry instead, and as I poured Fels-Naptha into the Maytag while Mother stuffed towels into the steaming water, I asked her about Pappy's reaction of the day before.

Mother shook her head. "Not your fault," she said. "It's just that Pappy found out that his mother didn't leave him anything, out of all her money. It all went to his sister, and he swears he'll never speak to her again."

As I listened to the soothing swish of the agitator, I thought of how easily things could be broken, and how hard it was to mend them again.

Deep Waters

JOHANNA MOSTOVOY DIDN'T HAVE TO LEAVE HER HUSBAND, after all, to escape her creepy little apartment in Happy Camp. (That would come later.) What got her out was the uprooting of another family, when Trella Loquet's husband was transferred by the highway department to southern California. Trella, an Attebery who had never lived away from the river, cried as she watched her furniture stuffed into the moving van. But now, early in the summer of '64, Hank and Johanna would rent the spacious house on Deer Lick Creek, half a mile up Indian Creek from us.

While Mother and Dad helped them move in, Philip, Jimmy, and Ronnie played softball with Liz and Tommy and me in the big backyard of their new house. Deer Lick Creek ran past the woodshed and down into Indian Creek, and we waded up its gravelly bed. Philip was Liz's age, Jimmy a year younger, Ronnie an annoying six. We led them down the road and showed them our swimming hole.

Good swimming holes—deep, with a slow current—were rare on Indian Creek; in ours, the creek foamed around a bend and poured into a depression, twelve or fifteen feet deep at its upper end, two feet deep at its lower, where gravel kicked out from the depths formed a riffle. Framed by the smooth canyon rock, sculpted over millennia by the high water of winter, the pool grew clear as the summer turned hot.

The summer before, a new log stringer bridge was built across Indian Creek just downstream from our pool, balanced on the rim of the gorge. Across it, on an old homestead property, the Buchanan family built a new house. Mr. Buchanan was a retired Air Force non-com with a wife and six children. Mother rolled her eyes, as she always did at excess fecundity. Of course they could afford all those kids, she snorted, with the military paying for everything. Dewey, the oldest, was in Liz's class. The Buchanan kids all came down to swim. The little ones splashed about in the shallows and refused to drown, despite the fact that no one paid much attention to them.

With the thermometer stuck above a hundred degrees, the water was still shockingly cold, and we took that first daily plunge with gasps and shivers, then pulled ourselves out onto flat boulders to bake. Indian Creek was born below the great ridgeline that separated the Klamath River drainage from the Illinois River in Oregon. Dropping south from that land of hemlock and Brewer spruce, it picked up two major tributaries, the South and East Forks. The South Fork headed below Preston Peak, highest in the Siskiyous. From its summit, the ocean could be seen. The East Fork flowed west from Thompson Ridge.

Both drainages, in those years, were mostly unroaded, their dendritic channels shaded by groves of Douglas fir, Port Orford cedar, and Pacific yew. Below the East Fork, all the flat places along the main channel of Indian Creek had been settled for a hundred years. The stream itself was still healing from the effects of early mining. But along the ravaged streambed, dogwood and mock orange, serviceberry, alders, cottonwoods, and live oaks flourished. The last big flood, in December of 1955, was far enough in the past that the creek pools had scoured themselves clean of silt and gravel, and in their depths the cold of melted snows lasted all summer.

We borrowed face masks and eye goggles from the Mostovoy boys and wore them as we cruised along the surface or dove deep to peer at colored rocks and snatch at crawdads. Now and then we came face to face with steelhead that sheltered in the deeps and waited for the safety of darkness to resume their journey upstream. We hauled old inner tubes up through the riffles above the home pool, until we reached the foot of Puppy Falls, where the creek fell into a constricted rock formation carved out of the canyon, and where even the sluggish flows of August foamed and roared. As we paddled furiously to keep from being hurled back downstream, we turned our faces into the mist, senses overwhelmed.

Puppy Falls is now called Buchanan Falls, and it flows within rust-colored walls, the result of a flood of arsenic-laden water—long trapped in an abandoned copper mine upstream—that poisoned the creek for several years in the 1970s. But we first saw the falls slam against pale clean rock, and in winter the rapids burgeoned under heavy rainstorms. Our schoolmates said that the original name came from their ancestors, who threw litters of unwanted puppies into the maelstrom; if any lived, they would be good dogs.

75

The swimming hole never palled. We threw inner tubes off the high rocks and leapt in after them. We slathered ourselves with suntan lotion and dozed in the sun. I read a dog-eared paperback copy of *Hawaii*, and tried to surf the current on a water-chewed board. We skipped flat rocks over the smooth water. At an outcropping of crumbly red rock, we mashed the lumps into goo and daubed designs on our bodies. We braced ourselves into cliff crannies, as startled water snakes S-curved away over the water. We floated down the middle of the creek on the hot black surfaces of inner tubes, and tilted our heads far back, hair trailing in the water as we looked up between the canyon walls at the bluest sky in the world. After four o'clock, as shadows stretched over the water and the down-canyon winds riffled its surface into opacity, we trailed home, sated.

When Tommy woke from his after-lunch nap, Mother sometimes walked down with him and her sketching materials. She watched him wade while Bob barked at the swimmers and refused to come in past his belly. Liz and I were the only waterdogs in our family. Dad seldom swam, and sunburned when he did, in those days before decent sunblocks. Mother had learned to float and dogpaddle in the community pool in Yreka before we moved from Hilt, but she approached swimming the way other people did artificial respiration: a good thing to know, but no fun. Tommy was more interested in gathering mussel shells and colored rocks than in paddling, but he finally achieved a tan on his thin shoulders.

After supper, Liz and I often scuttled up the road to the Mostovoy house. Sometimes we stayed overnight, our sleeping bags spread out on the immense back lawn. Behind us, the forested slope rose at a steep angle. Johanna and Hank ran a loose ship, not caring what the boys did so long as they weren't fighting. We ate supper crouched in front of the TV, then hiked up Deer Lick Creek on a bulldozed trail leading to a concrete dam and a reservoir that irrigated the lawn. We played softball and badminton and explored the fields on either side of the house. The place had no visible neighbors aside from a green clapboard cabin, just downstream from the lower field, inhabited by an elderly bachelor.

We lounged in the cool living room on the dark hardwood floor, played records, and drank iced tea. The bright kitchen boasted a black-

and-nickel Monarch wood-burning range in addition to the electric stove. Outside, across Deer Lick Creek, an old horse barn stood empty, the walls hung with petrified harness and greasy truck parts, the loft weighed down with stacks of rough-sawn lumber. Behind the house, madrones and big-leaf maples shaded a woodshed, a tiny guest cabin, and a well house. An orchard of apple and plum trees grew between the house and the lower field; beside it, squash and tomatoes ran riot in an overgrown garden.

To Liz and me, the place was an estate, with its buffers of open land up and down the creek, its groves and brook. So when we learned, at the end of that summer, that Hank had snagged a promotion to the Gasquet Ranger District near the coast, we mourned not only for the company of our friends, but for this pleasure palace—until Mother told us that soon we would be moving into the house.

We packed up in October, just in time to pick the last zucchini from Johanna's garden, strip the apples from the trees, and harvest the plums. The days shortened and frosts came hard and fast. Mother canned applesauce and lined up the jars in the walk-in pantry. She bought boxes of canned goods on our trips to Medford to fill the rest of the shelves. I mowed the lawn one last time and raked leaves between the fall rainstorms. Dad cut pickup loads of firewood for the stove in our new living room, and Liz and I tossed the chunks into the woodshed; when we came home from school, we split kindling and chopped wood for the next day.

About a quarter mile up Deer Lick Creek, a mineral seep oozed from the hillside—the "deer lick" for which the stream was named. Wide game trails radiated from it, and in the autumn evenings I hiked up the hill and sat down across the creek to wait behind a fallen log. In my lap I cradled the .250-3000 as I sat and watched. Does and fawns, yearlings and spikes, came and went under my sights, but never a suitable buck. Still, I liked the feel of night coming on, the downhill breezes picking up as the day fell away, the smell of fall rising from the leaves as they melted into damp soil. On the hillsides around me, the leaves of big-leaf maples—turned incandescent yellow by the cold nights and short days—held the light, long after darkness had fallen in the deep timber.

NOTHING ABOUT THE START OF THE RAINY SEASON of 1964 seemed unusual. The first "real" winter storm arrived like clockwork on the first weekend of November. The wet orange bark of madrones gleamed in the dim light, and the last of the maple leaves fell and flattened into a brown paste. Indian Creek rose, snow appeared on Slater Butte. We wore our new wool skirts and sweaters to school.

On the last day before Christmas vacation, the first snow fell in our front yard. The school bus almost spun out as it climbed out of town that afternoon, and on his way home that night, Dad's pickup wheels locked up, and he slid into the rear bunker of a logging truck. The truck driver had been helping a motorist who had slid off into the ditch ahead of him. Dad helped shove the car out of the ditch and drove home with a broken headlight.

That night, the ground shook outside, and through the darkness came squeals and rolling snorts. In the morning, to our joy, four inches of heavy snow covered the front yard, and a band of horses stood in the orchard, pawing for grass and windfall apples. Liz and I dressed and ran outside. Six horses stood their ground as we approached, including a tall pinto gelding that we recognized from a pasture several miles up the creek. He raised his head to stare at us, his stout back wet with melted snow. Steam rose from his flanks, and bits of apple fell from his jaws.

A gray streak shot past our legs. Dad had unsnapped Bob's chain. The horses whirled and ran, across the driveway, over Deer Lick Creek, and into the upper field. Deadly hooves sang past Bob's head. Liz and I ran after them, whooping. They clattered over the fallen fence next to the road and disappeared around the bend as we screamed at Bob to come back.

After breakfast, Liz and I helped Tommy build a snowman in the backyard. The sun came out, and by noon we had discarded our coats as we chopped kindling in the woodshed. Dad looked at the thermometer on the front porch and shook his head. Sixty degrees. That night, rain fell, hard and warm. We awoke on the twenty-first of December to find Tommy's snowman reduced to a gray football-sized lump. The thermometer registered sixty-five degrees. Dad drove in to work.

Liz and I spent the morning mesmerized by Indian Creek. After breakfast, we ran down to look at the old swayback bridge that crossed the creek just upstream from our driveway. At mid-morning, the bridge

The swayback bridge over Indian Creek.

was almost submerged; the brown water foamed around its middle. Logs struck it with dull booms, and spray erupted into the pouring rain. Only the cables, hammered into the rocks on either side, kept it in place. I twisted a stick into the sand at the water's edge. We walked down the road to look at the swimming hole. The high rock from which we used to jump was now only about two feet above the creek. Puppy Falls had vanished, its curving rocks covered, the old alder trees around them battered down and gone.

We looked up to see Dewey Buchanan standing on his log bridge, sweatshirt hood pulled up, hands in pockets as he peered down at the water. We shouted at him over the roar, and he walked across. He had promised to feed the dog and cat while we were gone to visit the grandparents over Christmas, and now he followed us back up the road so that we could show him where the dog and cat food were stashed. We stood in the woodshed, the wet air bright with the scent of split fir, and watched as Boots the cat eviscerated a vole on top of the chopping block. Rain had flooded the rodents from their holes. We walked Dewey back to his bridge, waved good-bye, and ran up to the swayback bridge once more. In the space of an hour, my stick had vanished, and Dad's pickup had reappeared in the driveway.

We told him about our morning as he sat eating tomato soup and a toasted cheese sandwich in the kitchen. He nodded between bites, and told us the news. With the first winter storms, teams of Forest Service men drove the logging roads to clean out culverts. They pulled away debris, shoveled mud and rocks aside, then drank hot coffee from their thermoses and talked of seasons past. But this year, as Dick Priddy and John Koenig drove up Indian Creek, something was different. They saw our swayback bridge engulfed by dark waves. Six miles up the creek, water tossed behind the levee next to Sharp's sawmill. Seven miles up the creek, they turned off on the South Fork Road and ground up through the mud to Tennessee Gulch, where water poured down the ditches in torrents. Even when cleared of all debris, the culverts couldn't handle the flow; water washed over the roadbed. "I should have brought my high water boots," Dick joked.

Koenig, a lit cigarette between his lips, as one had been almost every minute since he came back in '45 from a Japanese prison camp, leaned on his shovel and squinted into the fog. "This is just like '55," he said. "The snow's going off all the way to Preston Peak. We'd better get back before we're stuck up here."

At the ranger station, Dad, just back from a similar trip up Elk Creek, heard them talking and decided to go home for lunch.

"Don't try to go to town," he said now as he rose from the table. "That slide below Doolittle Bridge looks like it wants to go out again. And you'd better call the folks, Barbara. I don't think we'll be able to make it to Oroville."

We all stared at him. This was serious. Dad hated all trips not involving hunting or fishing, and he disliked Grandfather Roush, but he tolerated these holiday jaunts because Oroville was the headquarters for RCBS—a company that specialized in reloading supplies and equipment. Dad always spent a day there, stocking up on ammunition components and engaging in long consultations with the staff about bullet weights and gunpowder. For him to give up on Oroville meant that he thought we simply wouldn't be able to get out at all. We heard Mother slamming the lunch dishes around as we walked down off the porch, leading Dad toward the swayback bridge.

"It's gone!" Tommy shouted, pointing to the place where it had stood only an hour before. We heard the muffled thump-thump-thump as boulders rolled beneath the waters. At the edge of the creek, we looked out at water the color of creamed coffee. A refrigerator passed us, riding high above our heads on the hump of water in the midst of the creek. We looked up at it, mesmerized. Half-submerged logs shot by, and as one of them struck a tree, the twelve-inch trunk groaned and fell over into the water. We couldn't even hear the splash. Tommy clutched Dad's hand. We walked back up the driveway, and Dad climbed into his pickup and started the engine. "I'll call your mother when I get to town," he said. "Keep an eye on the creek, and if you see the water level drop suddenly, get on up the hill as fast as you can."

"Why?" Liz asked.

"Because if Koenig is right, the log deck at Sharp's may wash away. That's six million board feet, and it may jam up at a bend, and dam up the creek. When it breaks, everybody better be out of the way."

That afternoon, in between glances at the creek, I made molasses cookies. Mother expected the power to go off anytime now, so she filled the bathtub and set kettles and buckets under the eaves. When we told her what Dad had said about Sharp's logs, she drove the car over the bridge that spanned Deer Lick Creek and parked it in the barn, which at least stood higher than the house. She gathered sleeping bags and stacked them by the front door, and shoved warm clothing and matches into packsacks. She phoned her parents.

As I put the first cookies into the oven, Liz and Tommy came running in to announce that a man in a county road department truck had put up a sign on the road just upstream from our driveway. *Caution*, it said. When all the cookies were out of the oven, I walked to the foot of the driveway and looked at it. Just below the sign, water lapped up onto the road. I looked up at the middle of the creek again. By the time I got back to the house, the power was out. Mother got the kerosene lamp down, wiped the chimney clean, trimmed the wick, and told us to fill up the wood box beside the Monarch.

Dad drove his pickup home that night, but by first light the next morning, water had covered the road in front of the house and was creeping up past the gateposts in our driveway, only forty yards from the house. The road department man, after spending all night in his truck farther up the road, came back to rescue his sign. Downstream, between the green cabin and the swimming hole, the road was also underwater.

Dad pulled his truck up behind the house, then started walking toward town. "I'll catch a ride farther down," he said.

Mother cooked oatmeal for us on the Monarch range, and Liz and I ate quickly, then ran through the orchard and climbed the ridge above the swimming hole. From there, we could see Buchanan's bridge, the deck awash with water and littered with stranded logs. Several of the neighbors had gathered to watch as Mr. Buchanan, clad in a yellow sou'wester hat and slicker, edged out onto the far side of the bridge to attach cables to the bridge stringers. The bridge bounced with every breaking wave. As we watched, a massive cottonwood tree washed up on the upstream side of the bridge, stood on end, and went over backward. We watched as its fifty-foot trunk was sucked beneath the bridge and spit out the other side. Mr. Buchanan ignored it and went on manipulating his cables.

The road beside our old blue house was still above water, so we climbed down from the ridge and walked another quarter of a mile downstream, to the log bridge that crossed the creek to the Attebery Ranch. But here, the canyon was deeper, and this bridge stood high above the flood. We turned and walked back home, pausing again to watch Mr. Buchanan's struggle to save his bridge.

All the rest of that day, Indian Creek rose, until our gateposts stood half underwater. Again and again we walked to the water's edge and stared up at the flood that towered over our heads, rushing by so fast that it had no time to spread out and engulf us. Bob barked from the porch at the rumbling boulders and at the people who walked through our sodden fields as they skirted the waters that poured over the road.

Dad phoned Mother and told her that Happy Camp would be flooded soon. Early in the afternoon, we saw him come walking back through the orchard. Rain sluiced over the brim of his hard hat. He wore his "tin" pants and coat—canvas rain gear treated with water repellent—and carried a Forest Service radio in a waterproof satchel. Once inside, he sipped hot cocoa and told us that the highway bridge at Seiad, twenty miles upriver, was underwater. The grade school in Happy Camp and the basement of Hooley's store were both flooded. The steel bridge over Indian Creek, hammered by logs and other debris, had drifted away from its abutments, only to crash against the new concrete highway bridge below. A good thing, Dad said, as it might shield the highway bridge from a similar fate.

Dad tried to raise the ranger station on the radio but found only static. The phone was dead. He put his rain gear back on and hiked up toward Sharp's sawmill to look for a log jam. As he disappeared into the rain, Liz and I ran down once more to check on Buchanan's bridge. The cables had worked after a fashion—the two main stringers survived, flung high up on the rocks. But the rest of the bridge was gone. Two hours later, Dad came back to tell us that the levee behind Sharp's mill was gone, along with the entire log deck, and the houses around the mill were flooded, but the logs had floated free and there was no jam.

We ate supper to the tympanic rhythm of rocks rolling in the creek. A power company man sat in his truck above the flooded section of road, his lights shining out onto the roily water. Dad walked up to give him some molasses cookies and an offer of shelter for the night. He declined the offer of the couch, but ate the cookies and handed out his thermos bottle for a refill. We spent the evening clustered around the kerosene lamp at the kitchen table, playing Monopoly while Mother knitted and Dad tried to decipher a two-day-old newspaper. Rain drummed on the metal roof.

In the morning, it was still raining, but the creek had dropped slightly. "It's taken all the snow off," Dad said. "That was the crest, last night."

Mud and rocks covered the road. The creek still flowed high in the middle, still ran the color of milky coffee. We cooked oatmeal and ate toast broiled on a fork. "Are you going to town?" Mother asked Dad.

"I ought to stop by the station, anyway," Dad said, and Mother produced a shopping list. "In case anybody's open," she said.

Dad looked at me. "You want to walk downtown?" I ran to find my coat and a waterproof hat as Dad shrugged into his rain gear. We worked our arms into the straps of two manure-colored Forest Service backpacks and started down the road. The water had dropped below what was left of the pavement. Half a mile down the road, Hank Fowler drove by and gave us a ride down to the slide area near the Doolittle Bridge.

But the bridge was gone. Nothing was left except the abutments. The people who lived on the other side waved at us as we passed, even

83

more isolated than we. Below the bridge, the county road had vanished into Indian Creek. Not even a footpath remained to bridge the gray gash sliced out of the mountain. Yet men had been busy here: two heavy planks, eight inches wide, had been hammered together to span a gulf about twenty feet across. The gap looked formidable to me, for there were no railings, no protection except balance from the angry waves that hammered the bank below.

"You've got to be kidding," I muttered. I didn't like heights. Dad looked back at me. "If it was lying on the ground, you could walk over it easy enough," he said.

"But it's not," I squeaked. "It's a long way down." Dad walked across, his heavy logging boots firm on the boards, which bounced a little. I froze as I watched him reach the other side and begin to talk to another man in a hard hat. Ike McCulley was a logger, right down to his stagged-off Frisco jeans, White's boots, Big Mac shirt, and the red suspenders that framed his round belly. I went to school with his sons, Kenny and Pat. If their father told them that a piss-fir girl was afraid to walk across a board, I'd never hear the end of it. I stepped out onto sixteen inches of Douglas fir, glad of my rubber-soled boots, my eyes focused on the far side. As I stepped at last onto solid ground, Dad glanced down at me as though he had never doubted that I would follow him.

We waved to Ike and hiked uphill through the corridor of dark trees, following the road as it climbed toward Southard's place. A truck stopped beside us, and we caught a ride into town. Downtown Happy Camp was a sea of mud. The concrete highway bridge had indeed made it through the night, thanks to the twisted girders of the steel bridge, which had absorbed the pounding of the hundreds of logs now massed behind it. We waded to Ealy's Market, where Swede Sutcliffe was cutting and wrapping meat as fast as he could and selling it for ten cents a pound. "Help yourself to the vegetables and frozen food," he called as he tossed Dad a package of steak. Feeling like a shoplifter, I snatched packages of frozen peas and squash from the freezer unit and stuffed them into my backpack. Dad found some carrots in the vegetable bins. We waded out again and splashed toward the highway bridge, and saw for the first time the real power of the Klamath River in flood.

Just as I had spent the past two days looking up at the center of Indian Creek, now my eyes rose to take in the middle of the Klamath.

84

Below the highway bridge, the waters of Indian Creek hurled themselves against the brown wall of the river, unable to merge into that fierce traffic. The creek swirled, confused, unhappy. Happy Camp was flooded because Indian Creek could not escape. Just upriver, the steel bridge built to access the virgin timber of Elk Creek had survived, although I could not see how. Somehow, the waters had moved around it.

I looked out at the grade school playground, now a lake. Water rose to the doorknobs of the classrooms. A steelhead jumped and jumped again as it tried to escape the choking mud. We followed the highway around the schoolyard, then turned off toward the ranger station. We were on higher ground now, and we walked into the compound through the mud.

Ralph Sorensen, bright-eyed, shoved mud out of the fire warehouse with a push broom. The basement of the station was still full of water, he said. In the dim offices upstairs, the floors were dry, and Dad found a set of truck keys. We rode in a green pickup to Siskiyou Mills, where the tepee burner stood half underwater. Dad shook his head. "It'll take them three months to rebuild, if they do at all."

We stopped at Hall's Mercantile, on the unflooded upper part of town, and bought flour, salt, more carrots, bacon, soap, and two packages of cupcakes for lunch. As we pulled away, we passed Ranger Jack Williams, headed upriver in another Forest Service truck. Dad made a U-turn and followed him for two miles. Just beyond a fisherman's motel, half the highway had fallen into the river.

Williams pulled over to wait for us. "Get in," he said. "I'm going up to Cade Mountain to see if I can radio out." I sat between the two men and tried to keep my legs clear of the stick shift. We followed the highway to the top of Cade Mountain, where Williams pulled over and picked up the radio mike. "Klamath Dispatch, this is Happy Camp," he said, and after a few seconds a crackly voice answered from sixty miles away. "Happy Camp, this is Klamath Dispatch."

Williams pulled out a notebook and began reading off some messages. Then, breaking in, we heard, "Happy Camp, this is Ukonom."

Ukonom had not been heard from since the previous afternoon, when the flood overwhelmed the ranger station at Ti Bar and swept the office and the trailers away. Now we learned that the trucks were

85

parked on the highway above, and the people safe in some cabins nearby.

A Pacific Power & Light company truck pulled up beside us. Williams handed me the microphone and told me to listen for the radio while he and Dad stepped out of the truck to pore over a Forest map with Mr. Orrel. I sat with the mike in my hand, while over the radio came the siren song of dispatch, talking to Goosenest and Oak Knoll, to Scott River and Seiad. Some of the voices were familiar, some of the names belonged to men I had met. The tribe was talking, and I was part of it. That was the moment, with the defroster blowing and the rain splatting on the windshield and a chill breeze blowing in through the open window, when I fell in love with what my stepfather did for a living, and with the Forest Service itself. On that slick mountain road, sitting between two men in green shirts in a green pickup, I felt *connected*. I knew, as much as anyone did, what was happening in my world. And I loved that feeling.

As we drove back toward town and neared the washout again, Williams started laughing.

"Damndest thing," he chortled. "That poker game that's always going on in the back of the Log Cabin Bar? They didn't stop playing even when the water came rolling under the doors. They just picked up the table and chairs and the Coleman lantern and took it across the street to the old pool hall. Probably still going on."

He stopped the truck. "I'll just park it on this side in case the rest of the road falls in," he said, and rode back to town with us.

We stopped at Siskiyou Mills again, and the men left me in the truck while they strode among the ruins and searched for the plant manager. The Forest Service radio was quiet, but I read the ten-code guide taped to the dashboard and tried to memorize it. I twirled one of the knobs on the radio set, jumped at the squelch, and hastily turned it back. I pushed the button on the side of the microphone and listened to the click from the speaker. This entertainment exhausted, I ate my cupcakes and looked out at the remains of the sawmill. Most of the logs had vanished downriver, but a few lay scattered like pick-up sticks on the muddy plain.

Dad dropped Williams off back at the station, drove the Forest Service truck up Indian Creek Road, and parked it with several other vehicles near the Southard cabin. We tucked the groceries into our backpacks and hiked downhill in the rain toward the makeshift bridge, now (I was relieved to see) improved with railings on both sides. Once across, we caught another ride and crept up the road. Someone had bladed the boulders from the road in front of our house. As we neared the driveway, we saw Liz, walking arm in arm with the Larson girls from up the creek, "on the very brink of the raging torrent," I wrote that night. "Dad gave Liz hell," I noted smugly, "and sent her to bed." But my self-satisfaction was tempered by the knowledge that Liz had been unafraid out there, while I had been afraid to walk across a board. I had done it, but I'd been scared, while Liz, in the midst of isolation and destruction, had found her friends, and rejoiced, and danced.

BY CHRISTMAS DAY, A WOODEN BRIDGE just wide enough for a car had been built over the slide area. A "go-devil" took the place of the vanished Doolittle Bridge, and residents pulled themselves back and forth in the box that hung from the cables. The floodwaters dropped, and Dad invited a Forest Service family named Nichols up to eat Christmas dinner with us. They had a turkey in their freezer, but no power and no way to cook the bird. We had a wood-burning range but no turkey. We stuffed ourselves on turkey and smoked salmon the Nichols had brought down from Alaska, and Mother got tight on Tom and Jerrys.

On December 30, the weather grew colder, and snow fell, enough to sled on. Liz and I cleared a run on the trail that led to the dam on Deer Lick Creek. Four Army helicopters landed in Happy Camp, one loaded with CBS photographers. Outgoing mail arrived from downriver on one of the helicopters, including a letter with a nickel taped to it. Dad peeled off the nickel, bought a first-class stamp, and mailed the letter.

Two National Guard trucks, loaded with food, came to town that day, too, right behind the bulldozers that cleared the river highway. The dozers made it as far as Clear Creek, nine miles downriver, before they turned back because the bridge at Clear Creek was gone. Dad brought home onions, potatoes, milk, and eggs from the National Guard trucks. The electricity came on, went off, came on again, went off for good. We took sponge baths and kept the bathtub filled by hauling water from buckets set under the eaves.

On New Year's Day, Dad went back to work. A Red Cross volunteer handed Dad a newspaper, which said that this flood was twelve feet higher than the 1955 flood, and that all but one of the bridges between Happy Camp and the coast were gone.

More snow fell that night, and it continued all the next day in fat heavy flakes, an inch an hour. As Liz and I brought in wood from the woodshed, we heard something creak, and looked up to see an oak tree falling in slow motion onto the rear of the barn where Mother had stored the car when the floodwaters rose. The old building folded in on itself with a muffled thump. We ran inside to tell Mother, who was building a fire in the Monarch. She slammed the firebox shut and began saying words we had never heard her use.

All that day, the forest fell around us. A madrone limb—hard as steel—impaled itself in the woodshed roof, slicing through the corrugated metal like a knife through cream cheese. A fir tree almost struck the well house. From the slopes above the house came long death-groans and ground-shaking concussions as trees hundreds of years old found no purchase in the saturated ground and were felled by the heavy snow load.

Dad came home early and waded out through the snow to look at the collapsed barn. He crawled under the smashed roof to gauge the damage. "The body's totaled," he reported, "but it looks like maybe the engine's okay." That evening, he got out the ladder and climbed up onto the woodshed roof, shoveled snow for an hour, then moved on to the cabin. We stood below and took turns shining the flashlight beam onto the roofs, as other lights flashed above us in the close, black sky behind the snowflakes.

88

"Lightning," Dad said, but we heard no thunder.

The next day, ten quail paraded through the yard near the woodshed, ate madrone berries, and scuttled back into the woods. Flickers, Steller's jays, thrushes, and chickadees joined them. The snow slid off the metal roof of the house, forming piles three feet deep that pushed on the patio doors. Liz and I shoveled the snow away, and came in with our gloves soaked and our fingers white with cold. More snow fell and packed down under its own wet weight, so that it stayed about two feet deep, no matter how much fell. Dad shoveled off the woodshed and cabin roofs again. "If I ever hear you girls say you want snow again," he said as he put the ladder away once more, "I'll take a club to both of you."

Liz, Louise, Bob, and Tommy, in front of the woodshed behind the house on Deer Lick Creek, during the post-flood snow, January 1965.

We cooked and ate and hauled water. We chopped wood and shoveled snow. Mother ran out of eggs and baked something called a prairie cake that didn't need any. We ate leftover turkey and smoked salmon, kept cool in the washing machine on the back porch. We buried cartons of milk and frozen vegetables in snowbanks. In the woodshed, Liz and I leafed through stacks of old newspapers, talked about movies, and chopped more wood. Dad convinced the man who drove the county snowplow to clear out our driveway.

When we ran low on dry wood, Dad sawed up an oak tree that had fallen near the well house. Liz and I hauled it into the woodshed and split the rounds. Dad sawed up the tree that had destroyed our car, and we hauled those rounds back to the woodshed on our sleds. He hiked up the trail to the dam, his biggest chainsaw on one shoulder and a coil of rope over the other. Liz and I followed him, dragging our sleds and carrying the splitting maul. He sawed up two Douglas firs that had fallen across the trail, and we watched as the four-foot-wide cylinders fell from the logs. Dad swung the maul and smashed them into wedges, then showed us how to stack the wedges onto our sleds.

89

"Watch how I do this," he said as he roped the wedges onto one of the Flexible Flyers. He watched us do the second sled-load ourselves, then nodded. "Take it on in," he said.

I pulled the sled from the front, as Liz held the end of the lashing rope and walked behind to prevent the sled from running away downhill. But in the soft snow, the sled sank under the weight of the wood, and began to tip. Liz's eighty pounds were no match for gravity. As the sled tilted, she pulled on the rope, then knelt in the snow to help me push the sled upright again. Behind us, hollow sounds echoed off the trees as Dad wielded the maul.

On our second trip, Liz fled into the house, wet and angry, as soon as we reached the bottom of the hill. Enraged at her desertion, I made two more trips by myself. On my third trip uphill, I met Dad coming down and stomping out a trail as he came. "Go on in after this load," he said, and I nodded, relieved. My mittens were soaked. When I reached the house, Mother sat me down by the stove with a cup of the hot tea laced with brandy that Liz was already sipping.

With the schools still closed, our days devolved into an endless round of wood-hauling. When we had a good pile in the woodshed, we lifted the fir wedges onto the chopping block and struck off the dry heartwood. Then we split up the sapwood, as water oozed up around the axe blade with each strike. Mother started fires with the heartwood, then fed in pieces of sapwood. Cooking on a wood-burning range— or even just heating water—took a lot of wood, and the wood box never seemed full enough. For the first time in our lives, we wanted, desperately, to go back to school. We were terminally bored. But worse things than boredom were happening all around us, as we realized the day Dad came home and told us that Dr. Edmunds, Happy Camp's popular dentist, had dropped dead of a heart attack after shoveling snow off his sidewalk. Once more, Dad scowled at us, as though our long-regretted wishes for snow had caused the good man's death.

When the schools reopened late in January, Liz found her homeroom clean of mud and water, but the contents of all the desks had been dumped out onto the floor of the library and grown into a mound of mildew. At least the high school hadn't flooded, although our history classroom was full of racks of clothing rescued from Hooley's store, and old Mrs. Head was doing a brisk business behind a cash register on the teacher's desk. Out on the football field, stray horses foraged for grass. Other horses, marooned on properties far up Indian Creek, were rumored to have wandered off and starved to death. Our teachers tried to bring us back to a semblance of routine, but I had discovered *Gone with the Wind* in the high school library, and scarcely heard a word they said.

The weather broke, the sun shone, and the snow began to melt. By the end of January, just after we learned that Winston Churchill was dead, so much snow had melted that Liz and I could use Tommy's red wagon to haul wood down from the muddy hill. Dad climbed up an oak tree behind the woodshed, slung a rope around a madrone limb caught in another tree, and pulled it down so it wouldn't fall and kill someone.

The power came back on. The phones worked again, and Dad circled ads in newspapers for new cars. And one day he looked up from this recreation, pencil in hand, and looked at me as I brought in another armload of wood for the living room stove. My hair had not been set in weeks, and my hands were stained orange from the leather gloves I wore to chop wood.

"Henceforth," I wrote in my diary that night, "Dad says I am to spend fifteen minutes a day fixing my hair, and fifteen minutes a day fixing my nails, before supper, or else no supper."

Things were zigzagging back to normal.

When It Changed

SUCH A SIMPLE THING, WATER, yet it scoured away roads, destroyed houses and bridges, changed the courses of creeks and rivers, smashed our car, and killed people—not just anonymous people in newspaper reports, but people we knew. Now, when I walked downtown from the high school during lunch hour to have my hair cut by Mr. Lee the barber, Dr. Edmunds' office next door was closed and dark.

As late as March, the Klamath still flowed high and muddy, still churned with rocks and snags and root wads. In that month, Happy Camp's deputy sheriff drowned, victim of his own hubris and the terrible indifferent power of the river. He tried—against all advice—to run the nine-mile stretch between Happy Camp and Clear Creek in his motorboat. His body was found twenty miles downriver near the Hays Ranch; the boat was never seen again.

Far down the coast, beyond the mouth of the Klamath, the logs from Sharp's mill washed up on beaches, were identified by the brands hammered onto their ends, and salvaged.

When spring at last brought sun and warmth to the weekends, we piled into Dad's pickup and explored our changed world. We crossed the river on the miraculously intact bridge at Happy Camp and drove upriver to the old homestead where Hank Fowler had spent his boyhood. Here, water battering against a curve in the river had eroded the pasture, leaving earthen banks eight feet high above the wide cobbled bar. At river's edge, the willows grew upward again in the sunshine. A dying apple orchard huddled around the collapsed remains of the old cabin, and we looked up and across the road at limestone cliffs pockmarked by caves. When his parents first homesteaded this place, Hank said, condors had nested there.

"They were so big," he said, "a lot bigger than turkey vultures. But they didn't stay long after we came." As a boy, Hank had explored the cave but never found its end. "It headed south, right into the Marble Mountains, and maybe it comes out there someplace."

We walked under the banks and looked for obsidian chips in the fresh soil that had fallen since the river receded. Long ago, a Karuk village stood here, and the sheer number of obsidian chips indicated a stop on a trade route, where blanks of volcanic glass, carried from sites far to the east, were worked into tools and projectile points, then traded still farther west. I picked up chips and dropped them again as I walked. I poked at clumps of river-washed rocks and bits of charcoal stuck in the bank: hearths, where Indians once sat to cook acorn mush and salmon in watertight baskets. As I reached the upstream end of the bar, I looked down and saw a projectile point at my feet. I picked it up and held it to the sun. Translucent gray bands sliced across it. It was still so sharp that I could have cut my finger on it.

I knew how the point had been made, for Dad was a flint knapper and used the traditional tools: the tine of a deer antler and a piece of leather held in the palm of the hand. In the work of my stepfather and the ancient artists I saw the same pride of workmanship, the same long practice that gave a similar result. Back at the truck, he admired the piece, held it up to the light, and handed it back to me with a murmur of approval.

SISKIYOU MILLS AND CAROLINA PACIFIC REBUILT, sooner than anyone expected, and as the roads dried out, logging resumed, and once more the logging trucks raced down Indian Creek Road toward the mills. Early in April, a logger was killed when a log above him slipped as he was bucking timber. His son was working nearby, but the father was dead by the time he reached his side. Dad, inspecting another timber sale, heard of the accident on his truck radio and arrived at the scene in time to help haul the body up to the road. The dead man's face, Dad told us, had turned a deep blue.

I started going to dances again in March, but it became increasingly hard to pretend I liked them. One night in April, as Mother and Dad drove me home from yet another dreary evening, Mother asked me in her sweet voice if I had enjoyed the dance. It was too much: I burst into tears. She turned in the front seat and asked me what was wrong. "No one," I sobbed out, would dance with me. *No one.*

93

What I really meant was that boys never asked me to dance. I might dance the twist with another dateless girl, but that didn't count as a *dance*, not really. When I broke down and asked boys to dance, most simply refused. Once, I asked Charlie, a silent boy who looked exactly like Ishi in Theodora Kroeber's book about the last free-living member of the Yahi tribe. He had a habit of melting into dark corners, and I wondered why he came to dances at all. It seemed unlikely that his parents made him go. Charlie shuffled around the floor with me once, and except for his bad breath, I found him acceptable. Years later, I wondered if his silent acquiescence meant that he liked me or simply recognized my invitation for what it was—an attempt to avoid total humiliation—and took pity on me.

As the hours from six-thirty to nine-thirty stretched into infinity, I killed time by standing beside the record player and reading all the words on the backs of all the record albums, learning far more about the Beatles than I really wanted to know. I drank a great deal of Hawaiian punch, ate cookies, and took numerous trips into the sanctuary of the girls' restroom, where I fluffed up my hair and reapplied the lipstick worn off by the punch and cookies. With any luck, I could kill a few more minutes by joining a circle of girls as they discussed the latest catfight. But eventually I had to return to the crepe paper decorations of the dim music room, and pretend.

Mr. Tristan, band director and music teacher, often chaperoned these affairs, and sometimes when he saw me sitting alone, he sat down to talk—not about school, but about current events or books. He recommended titles, advised me to read, for instance, *Judgment at Nuremberg*. I looked forward to these conversations, for in choir practice I vacillated between hero-worship and terror of him. Everyone liked Mr. Tristan as a chaperone, though, for he allowed us to wander in and out, so long as we didn't stay outside too long. But on this night, Mr. Oamek, the principal, was on duty, and although he had allowed the double doors to stand open to dissipate the heat of jiggling bodies, he swiftly herded any escapees back inside, lest they take advantage of the darkness to smoke and neck behind the school buses.

True confession over, I slunk into the house, shamed. But my parents said nothing and allowed me to crawl into bed in peace. On Monday morning, after Dad left for work, Mother ladled oatmeal into my bowl and told me that I didn't have to go to dances anymore if I didn't want to. As I walked down to the foot of the driveway to wait for the bus, I tilted my head back to look at the sunlight slanting through the trees and felt a rush of unreasoning joy.

AFTER THE FLOOD, DAD SEEMED TO LOOK at me with new eyes. True, he had little choice but to make use of me. Next to him, I was the largest person in the house. Four inches taller than Mother, I outweighed her by twenty pounds and Liz by thirty. After that winter, Dad took for granted my ability to handle a shovel, wield an axe, pull on a rope, handle quarter rounds of split fir.

I went with him up Elk Creek to cut load upon load of firewood. Tommy stood up on the seat between us. We stopped near a tangle of Douglas fir logs between the road and the creek. Dad crawled over one of the bigger ones and scored marks across the bark at intervals with a hatchet, then told me to pick the pebbles out of the bark along those lines with my pocketknife, so he wouldn't ruin the chain on the chainsaw.

Later, as he worked his way down the log, cutting slices away in a haze of blue smoke with the big McCullough, I rolled the rounds away and attacked them with wedges and the sledgehammer. When Dad finished sawing the log and came back to take over the chopping, I tossed the chunks into the bed of the pickup, then climbed up to stack them neatly behind the cab. When the truck was full, we drove slowly back down Elk Creek Road.

I pried off Tommy's wet sneakers and held them in my lap to pick at the wet knots in the laces. I was sweaty and tired, and the knees of my jeans were muddy from crawling beneath the logs. With sawdust in my hair and fir slivers driven into my forearms, I was happy. At home, I would not have stayed alone in a room with Dad on a Sunday afternoon for five minutes, but somehow cutting wood was different, and a comfortable silence enveloped these trips.

TRELLA LOQUET CALLED MOTHER ONE DAY, and in a tentative voice confessed that the promotion Paul had moved south to obtain had just

95

become available in Happy Camp. They were coming back. But don't worry, she said, we can stay with my folks until you find another place. Mother hung up, sighed, and began the hunt for a new rental.

The flood had created a housing shortage, and although Mother burned up the phone lines, nothing was available. Then Trella's father, Cody Attebery, died, and in a series of phone calls, Mother and Trella and Eleanor Attebery, Trella's sister-in-law, worked it all out. Eleanor and her husband Frank would move into Cody's house, across Indian Creek. We would move into Eleanor and Frank's house on the opposite bank, next door to the Fowlers. Trella and Paul would move back into their own house. And all of this would happen on the same weekend.

Mr. Younkin and Mr. Ragsdale came up to help us move the heavy furniture while Liz and I stuffed the new Chevy station wagon full of kitchenware and linens. The cat fled into the woods and was still missing by the end of the day. By noon, the men had dragged our beds into the new house, and Liz and I were in proud possession of an actual attic bedroom. We flung the French window open to the spring sunshine and leaned out. In an alcove at the far end of the attic, stacks of *National Geographics* beckoned, and we stretched out on our beds and flipped through their Technicolor pages as thumps came from downstairs.

Frank Attebery had built the house twenty years ago from scavenged parts. The French windows in the living room and attic had been salvaged from a house at the old Gray Eagle Mine. Some of the interior doors were a little shorter than their frames. The words "Barber Shop" could still be seen beneath the last coat of paint on the bathroom door. But the yard was stoutly fenced, and although the kitchen and living room were drafty and innocent of insulation, they were bright on sunny days. Besides, we had lots of firewood now, and hundreds of veneer strips, four to six feet long, littered the backyard. Frank worked at the Carolina Pacific veneer plant, and evidently believed in that biblical verse about not muzzling the ox that treads out the corn. "Good kindling," Dad said, and over the next few weeks Liz and I chopped and stacked it up in the woodshed. It was peeled from clear old growth pine, and nothing like it will be seen again.

The next day, Dad and his friends moved the last of the large appliances the half-mile down the road. With all the excitement, it took a couple of days for Liz and me to realize that the television was missing.

Many years later, as I leaned on the mahogany bar at the Elks Club in
Yreka during a Forest Service party, Paul Salfrank, one of the movers,
confided the details to me.

"We had everything else loaded, and I pointed to the TV and asked
your Dad if I should load it. He said, 'You can have it if you want it.' I
asked him why and he said you girls spent too much time watching TV
and not enough time doing your homework."

I took a sip of my highball and smiled. "Well, we saw it differently, of
course. Did you ever get the vertical and the sound fixed?"

"Only needed a couple of small parts," Paul said proudly. "It worked
great for another ten years."

The truth was that, in the joy of having our own room, of reclaiming
Boots the cat (Trella finally coaxed him into the house with raw
hamburger, then phoned us to come get him), of wallowing in the
warmest, sunniest spring in years, we scarcely missed the television.
Dad had seldom let us watch the good shows, anyway. So now we
read *Huckleberry Finn* aloud to Tommy in the evenings, and after school
we sprawled on the lawn and watched as Indian Creek roared around
the bend below us. We wondered what we were going to do for a
swimming hole that summer, for the pool beneath Buchanans' vanished
bridge was gone, too. Our deep, mysterious water park had filled with
sand and gravel.

From our new yard, we gazed up across the canyon as a fresh clear-
cut grew, day by day, in the midst of a green velvet forest. With Dad's
binoculars propped on our chests, we watched the yarder pull logs up
the slope. We heard the toot of the yarding signals and saw the loader
stack logs onto the waiting log trucks. Day by day, a swath of destruction
crept down the mountainside, until a square brown cutout sat cooking
in the ever-warming sunlight.

One Saturday, as we were indulging in this recreation, Liz suddenly
bumped my arm and pointed down the creek. A quarter of a mile away,
smoke and flames rose from a point next to the road. We yelled for Dad,
who came out to look, went back inside to call the ranger station, then
ran out again to snatch a Pulaski and shovel from the woodshed. He
tossed the shovel to me as I handed the binoculars to Liz.

"Come on," he said, and we trotted down the road. Even carrying
the shovel and with my much shorter legs, I managed to keep up with

him. We climbed the road bank and Dad attacked the edge of the flames that hissed up the flanks of the deerbrush and gobbled last year's dead grass. He chopped at turf and duff and bushes, carving a line of raw dirt around the fire.

"Throw dirt on it," he told me, and I scooped up shovels full of soil and tossed them at the flames. The down-canyon wind filled our nostrils and eyes with smoke as I followed him up the slope. Men and boys came running from the Indian Creek Trailer Court. A large boy from the senior class snatched my shovel away; left without a tool, I scraped up double handfuls of soil and flung them at the flames. A smoldering piece of wood rolled toward me, and I kicked it back inside the fire line. The soles of my sneakers grew hot. A Forest Service fire truck roared up, siren wailing, and three men leapt down and unrolled canvas hose.

Later, Mr. Pence, the tanker foreman, questioned children from the trailer park and learned that three eleven-year-old boys had started the fire by setting off a homemade bomb. With water to douse the flames, the excitement was soon over, and most of the civilians drifted away. I got my shovel back in time to help with the mopping up. Dad showed me how to roll a log over, hose it down, and scrape the live embers away with the shovel blade. The tanker foreman looked at my blackened face and grinned at me. "Haven't seen a girl fighting fire since the war," he said.

"Girls used to fight fire?" I asked.

"Oh, just for a couple of years, when most of the men were gone," he said. "Some of those old gals were pretty good."

"Why aren't there any now?" I persisted.

Mr. Pence and Dad exchanged glances. "Well, it's pretty hard work, really too hard for girls, and besides, the boys need the jobs," he said, tilting his hard hat back to scratch the wet hair plastered to his skull.

"Here, pay attention," Dad said, and I turned back to stir the ashes as he directed a stream of water onto them.

Walking back to the house, covered with soot, holes scorched into my blouse, the air deliciously cool on my face, I turned Mr. Pence's words over in my mind. I knew Dad thought I had done a good job today, or he would have told me I hadn't. So who knew the limit of what girls could do? But I was not so naïve as Dad and Mr. Pence thought. This fire season had started early. Dad had already spent a couple of nights downriver fighting a fire on the Ukonom District. He led a crew consisting of unemployed men recruited from the bars of Yreka. Just getting them to the fire lines required a strong hand. I had heard him describe them, with a shake of the head and a roll of the eyes, to Mother. No respectable family, in or out of the Forest Service, wanted their daughters associating with such men. So neither Mr. Pence nor Dad envisioned a day when women would fight fires, or plant trees, or become foresters.

It was another in a long series of contradictions. The Forest Service had become like an extended family to me. But women were barred from all but office jobs. No future there for a girl who liked the woods. Dad demanded that I wear lipstick, and he would have preferred that I still go to dances. But he also expected me to help him get wood, to be able to shoot, to know how to use an axe. He wouldn't have forced me to do these things if I'd been the sort of girl who whined when she broke a nail. But once he knew the material he had to work with, he took advantage of it, even as he informed me that there was no possible way I could become a veterinarian.

School made no more sense. Officially, girls were supposed to play only half-court basketball. We were told we lacked the stamina to play the boys' version. Yet we played full-court ball whenever we could, charging up and down the court for forty minutes at a time, even playing against the boys in informal noontime games. One day, our gym class competed to see who could do the most sit-ups. My classmate Jamie did two thousand, outlasting all of us, though she rode the bus sitting on one hip for a few days afterward.

We wanted to play sports against other schools, like the boys, but when we asked Mrs. Schaefer, our P.E. teacher, why girls were not allowed to compete in anything but tennis, she said that "the bloomer set" was still in charge at the state level, and they would have to die before things changed. Only occasional all-day tournaments called "play-days" were allowed, the very name telling us that our efforts were not to be taken seriously by anyone.

EARLY IN MAY, TOMMY AND MOTHER FELL ILL, one after another, with the flu—an upset that Dad casually blamed on Liz and me spreading our school germs about. This was unfair, I thought. Tommy was going to kindergarten now every morning. He was bringing home just as many germs as we were.

Mother woke up sick on a Saturday morning. As she crept from bedroom to bathroom, heaving and groaning, Liz and I fixed breakfast, took care of the housework, and brought her small glasses of 7 Up. I cooked supper, and by evening Mother was feeling well enough to sit up in bed and read *The Return of Tarzan* as she sipped tea and ate dry toast. Dad and some other Forest Service men had planned a day of fishing at Kelly Lake the next day, and that night he gathered his fishing tackle and placed it near the front door.

I woke after midnight with a terrible stomachache. I pulled a pillow and a blanket from my bed, felt my way downstairs in the dark, and lay on the couch, suffering, until the saliva pouring into my mouth warned me that I was about to vomit. I scuttled into the bathroom and threw up as quietly as I could. Back on the couch, I felt a little better, but around dawn I vomited again, then dozed until everybody else was up. Dad brought me a glass of 7 Up. I raised myself on one elbow and drank it, but ten minutes later lost that, too. I dragged my pillow and blanket back upstairs to avoid the nauseating smell of frying bacon. I slept for a while, and at noon Mother climbed the stairs to tempt me with frozen Jello. That stayed down. I slept again. By mid-afternoon I felt well enough to sit up on the floor and prop my chin on the open windowsill. Below me, I saw Dad and Tommy climb into the pickup truck. "Didn't Dad go fishing?" I asked Liz as she handed me orange soda and cracked ice.

"No, he called Joe Ragsdale this morning and told him he wouldn't be able to go because you were sick." She sat on her bed, chin on fist. "He was pretty impressed with how quiet you were about it," she added. "He's taking Tommy squirrel hunting now, though."

I pulled my sweat-sticky pajama top away from my chest as the afternoon sunlight poured onto my bare feet, and wondered just what the hell was going on. First Mother had—against all custom—rested and read while we waited on her and cooked and did the housework. That was strange enough. But now Dad had passed up a fishing trip merely because I was sick. If I didn't know better, I thought, I'd almost think they were beginning to regard Liz and me as human beings.

Light on the Devils

IN LATER YEARS I LOOKED BACK on our few months in the Attebery house with unalloyed pleasure: a sunny place, where flowers sprang up almost overnight, where Boots stalked birds and once nabbed a hummingbird in the snapdragons. I took it from him and held the black-eyed jewel on the palm of my hand until it zipped away. I remembered the soaring optimism of spring, a puzzling kindness from my parents, and anticipation: in June Dad got a promotion and a transfer to the Seiad Ranger District. Mother and Dad started looking for a house in Seiad Valley.

To me, Seiad Valley had been just a place where, for a couple of miles, the highway ran blessedly straight and the walls of the river's V-canyon pulled back. Seiad Creek ran down from the north, from Cook and Green Pass on the divide that separated the drainage of the Klamath from that of Oregon's Rogue River. From the south flowed Grider Creek, born deep in the Marble Mountain Wilderness, and the two streams poured into the Klamath almost opposite one another. Seiad Valley meant meadows, lush and green in spring, wavy and gold in summer, and hillsides of oak and madrone.

Rising from its west side were three stair-step peaks that strode up to the divide: the Three Devils. On their slopes of serpentine grew scattered stands of Jeffrey pine, scarred by old fires, and dense swaths of manzanita. Behind the highest devil stood Red Mountain and Kangaroo Mountain. In a few years, hikers innumerable would cross them on their way up the Pacific Crest Trail, but in those days, only a few hunters, and the Robinson family who grazed their cows beside Lily Pad Lake in summer, roamed that high country.

In 1940, three hundred acres along lower Seiad Creek had been excavated with a dredger in search of remnants of gold. Mounds of gravel marked the machine's passage. The same thing had happened upriver in the Horse Creek drainage, but there the owners of the meadows had required the mining company to stockpile the soil and replace it when the dredging ended. No such deal had been made in Seiad, and now the creek ran between conical mounds of round rocks for a mile upstream from its mouth. Except for stringers of alders, the stream banks were still bare.

In the middle of the valley, just above this destruction, a sawmill smoked and clanked behind its deck of logs. Some of the millworkers lived in a cluster of frame houses known as The Grove, across the road from the tepee burner. Other rentals were scarce. The three houses and the trailer on the grounds of the Seiad Ranger Station were always full, and the two brown Forest Service houses near The Grove were occupied, too.

But a few houses in and around the valley were for sale, among them one belonging to an elderly widow whose husband had drowned in the Klamath River the previous fall. Mr. Baird had fallen into the Klamath while fly-fishing near his house at the mouth of Walker Creek. The green waders clipped to his belt filled with water and pulled him under, and his eighty-year-old body was dragged downriver and washed up two miles away, where the river made a sweeping bend near the mouth of Caroline Creek.

One evening early in June, our parents took us with them to look at the Baird place. Mrs. Baird, a round object in a flowered dress, greeted us in her living room, flanked by her son and daughter. The daughter did most of the talking. She wanted her mother to come live with her in Sacramento. The son had lost an arm in a logging accident, but he maneuvered his steel claw deftly as he shuffled papers with Dad on the kitchen table.

The house stood a mile east of Seiad Valley, on a bench above the mouth of Walker Creek. The '64 flood had not touched it, but between the front yard and the highway, a sea of sand and gravel marked where the waters had swirled. The property was bordered by tall Douglas firs. Two county roads met at its northeastern corner, below a madrone tree. One road led straight up Walker Creek; the other ran over a hill for half a mile, then back down to the river, which it followed west to the mouth of Grider Creek. A family named Alexander lived across Walker Creek Road, while across Grider Creek Road, a green clapboard cabin sat on a point above the highway.

Our house on Walker Creek, just east of Seiad Valley, December 1967.

103

Built for a retired couple, the house was small; Tommy would have to sleep in a sort of hallway between the bathroom and the only bedroom. Liz and I would take over the sunny laundry room—originally a porch, but now walled in. We didn't mind: we would have our own back door, and windows to open on summer nights. We could brush our teeth in the concrete laundry tub, and the wringer washer would make a dandy nightstand.

As an architect, Mr. Baird's priorities had been rocks, not roominess: although you couldn't swing a cat in the kitchen, the living room boasted a stone fireplace with a raised hearth, tidily built of river-washed stones, and an outside chimney of the same material. River cobbles, selected for flatness, had been mortared into place to make the steps that led up to the front porch. Behind the separate garage, a lean-to woodshed had been dug into the slope. All around the house, patches of lawn and flowerbeds were divided by more rock walls.

From the front porch, the Klamath itself was barely visible behind a screen of summer foliage—just a glimpse beyond creek banks stripped by the flood. Across the river rose a cliff face of pale rocks draped with live oaks; an osprey hovered over the green river, its wings held crooked as it watched for fish below.

A birdhouse, nailed to the madrone tree closest to the front porch, housed a pair of noisy tree swallows. Liz and Tommy and I wandered through the unfenced yard and came upon the irrigation ditch behind the house. Nearby, a garden plot, fenced against deer, lay fallow and engulfed in weeds. The irrigation system was clever, and I studied it. *The garden,* I wrote that night, *is divided in half by a long* [wooden] *water trough* [actually a raised flume], *fed by the ditch: the trough is about two feet off the ground, and below it, the ditch continues to flow. There are pipes coming out of the trough, stoppered by wooden plugs, and cement blocks are available, which one uses to dam up a portion of the trough, so that when a hose is attached to one of the pipes, water will flow out of it and the hose can be used for watering.*

We were enchanted.

A week later, Grandmother and Grandfather Roush arrived to take Liz and Tommy and me back to Oroville with them. When we returned in July, surfeited with swimming pool chlorine and orgies of late movies on cable TV, the garden spot was still rank with weeds. Mother and Dad had been busy seeding another lawn, repairing the rock walls, and cutting firewood. But we saw a use for the fenced garden, for in Oroville Liz and I had acquired four ducklings and half a dozen yellow chicks one day at the shopping center while Grandfather's back was turned. Grandfather held me, as the oldest, responsible for this breach of protocol, and he raged and sulked for days.

Grandfather's monumental temper tantrums were scarcely new to us, but this was the first time one had ever been directed at me, personally. Until then I had been his protégée, his favorite, the one he bragged about. For several years now I had despised him, knowing that the face he turned toward the world was not the one he showed to Mother and Aunt Jo and Grandmother. Still, hypocrite or not, he was my grandfather, and I was flattered by his pride in me. Now I learned the stark limits of his toleration. In the end, I was dreadfully sorry, not because I really cared what Grandfather thought, but because I saw, as if for the first time, how Grandmother suffered whenever he was "in one of his moods." I spent a lot of time with her in the kitchen over the next few days, and tried to make amends by helping with the housework. And all the while, I wished I could erase the pain on her face, caused—I was still self-absorbed enough to believe—entirely by myself.

One day, as I polished silverware at the dining room table, Grandmother sat down with me. She picked up a damp cloth and slathered Wright's Silver Cream onto another fork. She began to talk about her childhood in a river town in Iowa, where her father trained and sold buggy horses when he wasn't laying bricks. She talked about how her mother had allowed her, as a toddler, to run naked in the spring sunshine, because even she, a Danish immigrant who spoke little English, had heard of something called "vitamins."

"I had a happy childhood," Grandmother said as she glanced out the glass patio doors at the olive trees baking in the heat. In the distance, Grandfather's power mower roared. "Later on, though," she added, "it wasn't so happy."

A few years later, and I would have asked her why her post-childhood years were unhappy, would have seen her words for the invitation they were. But at the time I was only astonished that this parent of my parent, this infallible woman who had once switched my bare legs with a cottonwood branch when I left the yard without permission, should now confide something personal to me, should now hint that her present sadness stemmed not from my actions but from memories of a distant past. I said nothing, only stared at her hands as she rubbed the gray cream between the fork tines. Behind her chair, the dark sideboard stretched beneath an expanse of white doilies, topped by the cut glass punch bowl and a black-and-white cow creamer.

Waves of sadness rose from us both. Neither of us had ever read Kierkegaard or seen an Ingmar Bergman film, but our instinctive Scandinavian angst united us. Grandmother took a breath and opened her mouth to say something else, but at that moment the back door

105

flew open and Grandfather's bald sweaty head popped in to demand lunch.

GRANDFATHER'S MOOD PASSED. He got out his toolbox and built a portable pen for the poultry in the backyard and was pleasant to everyone again. When we returned to Seiad in July and lifted the cheeping boxes from the trunk of the Oldsmobile, Dad shook his head, rolled his eyes, and laughed. He pointed us toward the garden, the only logical place for ducks and chickens, and suggested we drag Bob's old doghouse in there for a roost. I had braced myself for punishment after the grandparents left, but that laugh had gone all the way to his eyes, and I relaxed a little. Long days later, I tumbled to what had amused him: at no expense to himself, Dad's two stepdaughters had tricked Bill Roush— Bill with his pretensions to gentility, his arrogance, and his silly pride—into hauling chickens—*chickens!*—in the trunk of his precious Oldsmobile. Dad could not have come up with anything funnier if he had tried.

THE DUCKS SPLASHED IN THE DITCH for several weeks and nibbled watercress, then caught coccidiosis. With no one to tell us about the virtues of Walko tablets (potassium permanganate) as a cure, they died, one by one. The chickens—all cockerels—proved hardier and soon grew white feathers and orange combs. When our store of feed from Oroville ran out, Liz and I fed them bread crumbs, table scraps, and stolen oatmeal until Mother handed us money and told us to go down to the Seiad Store and buy some chicken scratch.

So Liz and I walked, for the first time, along the edge of the two-lane highway toward Seiad. We stepped onto the pedestrian walkway of the steel bridge and leaned over to watch the dark waters of the Klamath sliding beneath our feet. We shrieked in mock alarm as a logging truck roared over the bridge and rattled the girders with a blast from the horn. We looked up at the trash cascading toward the river's edge from the community dump. Once across the bridge, we found ourselves in the hot canyon of the road cut, where gnarled manzanitas clung to walls of red earth, the scent of their blossoms heavy in the afternoon air. Beyond the cut, we walked downhill into Seiad Valley, past the old Reeves barn and the electric sub-station, past houses and trailers and the new school, to the store and post office building across the highway from the broad lawns of the Seiad Ranger Station.

Inside the cool shaded store, Liz and I followed Blanche Priddy's pointing finger to the feed room in back. We inhaled the rich smells of grain mixed with molasses, and I suddenly felt myself back at the store in Hilt, in the room behind the meat cooler where we had played with litters of kittens born between the grain sacks. As if she had read my mind, a gray tabby rose from her perch on a pile of burlap sacks, stretched, and strode forward to be stroked. Liz and I found the stack of paper sacks, weighed out several pounds of cracked corn and wheat from an open sack, and carried it back to the front counter. On the way, we passed the frozen meat case. I looked at the prices stamped on the packages of chickens inside. Math wasn't my strongest subject, but right then I knew that refrigeration had destroyed the only logical reason for going to the trouble of raising chickens. When Dad warned us later that the chickens must die in the fall, I nodded, understanding the cold equations.

But in the meantime, they were fun to watch, those young roosters. They raced about the garden on long yellow legs, gobbled grasshoppers, scratched dirt, took dust baths. When we found banana slugs in the flower beds, we picked them up with a stick, flipped them into the garden, and watched as the chickens converged on the hapless mollusks and tore them apart, then stropped their beaks on the ground to remove the slime. At night, we shut the birds up in the old doghouse. In the morning when we released them, they exploded outside with hysterical squawks and a cloud of white feathers that floated down in the early sunlight.

One weekend in the fall, just before deer season, Dad told us to leave the chickens in the doghouse the next morning. He brought a chopping block into the garden and reached through the door to snag the chickens, one at a time. He decapitated them on top of the block with a hatchet, and we stood back and watched as the birds flopped and sprayed blood over the weed stalks. Mother boiled a kettle of water and carried it out to us. Dad sloshed one of the twitching headless bodies in the scalding water, stripped off the feathers, then made an incision from breastbone to vent with the small blade of his pocketknife. Our noses wrinkled at the smell. "That's why they call them *fowl*," he said,

107

his upper teeth protruding as he made the only pun I ever heard from him. Then, having shown us how to strip the guts out, he handed me the knife and with a murmured "have at it," left us alone with the pile of white corpses.

Several hours later, we had buried the guts and feathers in the garden, slid the yellow naked bodies into plastic bread bags, and tucked them into the freezer beside milk cartons full of perch and trout. The chickens' meat proved darker, more flavorful—and tougher—than that of store-bought chicken, but it melted in the mouth beside Mother's dumplings that winter.

The chickens had not disturbed the strawberry patch on the south side of the garden, and the next spring Dad showed us how to dig up the plants, separate them, and replant them in rows. For days I worked at this, digging up plants in the mornings and evenings, transplanting them, watering down the rows, ministering to the wilted.

The soil primed with guano, we planted the rest of the garden space, too, and it grew lush with green beans, corn, crookneck squash, zucchini, Swiss chard, and cucumbers. The tomato plants towered over their wooden frames, obscenely prolific. Dad showed us how to construct hills of earth in the corners of the garden for pumpkins and winter squash, and their vines crept through the wire mesh of the fence and across the lawn, so that I had to shift them when I mowed. A toad, puffed to the size of a grapefruit when disturbed, lived beneath the broad leaves, fat and golden-eyed. We made entire suppers of garden produce: summer squash, corn on the cob, sliced cucumbers, green beans.

108   We bought vegetable and flower seeds at the Seiad Store—radishes, beets, parsley, Swiss chard, nasturtiums, and zinnias. Daffodils bloomed early in the yard. The new lawns filled in with plantain and dandelions, and we mowed them down with the grass, happy to see the green softness. Pacific tree frogs croaked in the irrigation ditch.

Late in summer, Dad cut down the old corn stalks, and we planted lettuce and radishes among the stumps for a fall crop. We picked more buckets of produce—tomatoes, squash, cucumbers—and Mother canned tomatoes and carried boxes of vegetables around to the neighbors. We traded vegetables to Mr. and Mrs. Rice up Seiad Creek for honey from their hives. Mrs. Alexander brought us buckets of plums and we returned them full of zucchini.

We pulled up the exhausted bush beans and planted more squash. All around the garden fence, pole beans climbed high, and one evening in August, the cucumbers overwhelmed us as Liz and I staggered into the house with two five-gallon buckets full. Mother groaned and dragged out her recipe box, and the next day the whole house reeked of vinegar and spices as she made pickles.

By the end of our first July in that house, while the chickens still lived, the wide swath of Himalaya blackberry vines between our property and Walker Creek Road began to bear. Watered by the runoff from the garden flume, the canes drooped with berries the size of our thumbs. All summer I cut the canes back to prevent them from overwhelming the garden fence, but now Liz and I filled gallon ice cream buckets with the dark berries, which Mother froze or made into cobblers. We ate berries for breakfast with milk and sugar. Robins, drunk and disorderly on fermented fruit, staggered by and squirted purple droppings onto the hot pavement.

Far into September, we picked tomatoes, cucumbers, and yet more zucchini. We grew a banana squash thirty-one inches long. The butternut squash filled out and turned golden. In the flower beds next to the house, zinnias, rock roses, marigolds, celosia, and nasturtiums bloomed. Sunflowers, their stalks choked by morning glory vines, nodded outside the kitchen door. Only the poison oak, its leaves turning red beneath the Douglas firs in the wild upper end of the property, signaled an end to summer—that, and the eighteen-inch-long sugar pine cone that Tommy found and set out to dry on a windowsill. One by one, the fat nuts fell out, and he sat at the table to crack and eat them.

109

THREE MONTHS AFTER WE MOVED TO SEIAD, Tommy started first grade. To our astonished delight, his teacher was Mrs. Davenport, who had taught me in first grade at Hilt. When I saw her again, clad in a flowered dress that overflowed the chair behind her desk, the round mole on her cheek as big as ever, I felt I had come home.

Thanks to a mother and sisters who had taught him his letters, Tommy could already read. He had always been a lean child, but now he grew taller day by day. And in this new place, he began to wander. He took long walks into the woods behind our place. With the dog and a walking stick, he strode uphill into the forest, and stayed away for hours. I worried about him, but Dad only shrugged. "He's got to learn how to take care of himself sometime," he said. If he or Mother were worried that their only son might never come back, they said nothing.

The woods held rattlesnakes, and nests of yellow jackets, and cougars—although the latter were rare, and likely to be deterred by the dog. So we let him go, and between hikes he caught gopher snakes and gentled them. One day he draped a snake around his neck and went to visit the Alexanders' teenage son Eddie across the road, where his burden made Eddie's mother shudder. One in particular he kept as a pet for a couple of months. We had found it slithering up the old madrone tree, intent on the birdhouse, while the tree swallows swooped and shrieked at the danger to their nestlings. Liz snagged the snake from the trunk with a leaf rake, and Tommy pounced on it. Dad built a snake cage from an orange crate, and Tommy force-fed his prize on chunks of meat and carried it about until the creature was fat, tame, and probably very confused.

SUMMER BROUGHT SUMMER PEOPLE: old Mr. Schultz and his wife, who owned the green clapboard cabin, and the families of their married daughters. The Montgomerys had two teenage daughters; the Whallons, two boys aged eight and ten. Even before I met them, I had been irrigating the orchard around the cabin to keep their apple trees alive. When I saw, one August day in that first summer, that the cabin was occupied, I reported back to Mother, who sent Liz and me back with a pie. Mrs. Schultz gave us a vague smile, but Mrs. Montgomery looked around for a return gift and snatched two Reader's Digest Condensed Books from a shelf. I hugged them to my chest, murmured a thank you, and fairly ran back home for some undisturbed reading in the cushioned Adirondack chair on our front porch. Liz disappeared upstairs with the Montgomery girls to play records and learn the tribal customs of the San Fernando Valley.

The Whallon boys followed me home to meet Tommy. I worked my way through the books, while Liz and Tommy played with their new friends. We gave the newcomers blackberries; they pressed buckets of apples on us in return.

FROM THE START, SOMETHING ABOUT GRIDER CREEK ROAD—that thread of gray chip seal that led west from our yard—drew me on summer mornings. I told myself that I needed to build up my legs and my wind for hunting season, so I rose early to run along that road: first the long uphill pull through an avenue of oaks, which tore at my lungs and made my side clamp down on a stitch; then the descent toward the river where I could lengthen my stride and grab a second wind. My thighs burned with exertion and turned red in the cold air, but by the time I reached the long flat beside the fenced pasture, my legs had fallen into a rhythm of their own. A hundred yards down the fence line, the chip seal ended and pale orange decomposed granite crunched beneath my sneakers. From here the road began to climb again and became a shelf carved above the river, which dipped down to the mouth of Caroline Creek and into a belt of timber. Beside the tumbling stream, a Forest Service campground had once covered an alluvial fan, but the '64 flood had chopped it away. At about this point, old Frank Forsaka usually passed me, pork pie hat atop his head, and waved from his white pickup truck as he rattled on toward his job at the ranger station.

Beyond the creek, the road rose once more, now built onto an even more precipitous slope, where chunks of the mountainside broke away every winter. And from here I saw my goal: an ancient scarred live oak that leaned over the river just below the road, the only living thing left on that sugary road cut. I pushed up the grade, past the tree, and slowed to a stop at the summit, beyond which the road rolled down toward Grider Creek.

I leaned over, hands on knees, panting. When I stood up again, the awakening world hit me in the face: the roar of the river, thundering over the rocks below and echoing back at me from the blasted road cut; the painful chill of the air—tinged with smoke and pine sap and the bite of the river—as it rushed into my throat.

Sunlight brushed the tops of all the peaks to the north, from Red Mountain down to the Lower Devil. Smoke from the tepee burner mingled with the valley mists and spread downriver. Often, a couple of turkey vultures regarded me from the top of the live oak, their wings outspread as they waited for the sun to dry their feathers. And as I looked at them and blinked the wind-blown tears from my eyes, this

111

new world reached out and gripped my heart as firmly as ever the round hills above Hilt had done.

Bob always followed me on these runs, his rump a white flash as he dove into the brush after squirrels. Tommy often came along, too, red sneakers in motion beneath the cuff of his jeans, his blond hair stirred by the breeze off the river. As I waited for him at the turnaround point, I looked back at my brother and marveled: he wasn't a baby anymore. When he reached me, we stood together for a moment and watched a blue heron rise, croaking, from the river island that we thought was shaped like the hull of a Viking ship. We looked at the smoke and the mist and the spreading wonder of pink light on the high shining peaks of the Siskiyou Divide, and morning by morning, I grew to love a landscape, and a vision of life. And as I looked across the Klamath at the rose-splashed Devils, I knew, with a certainty that still transcends the long years, that I didn't want anything more than this, ever.

Then Tommy and I turned back and began to run again, and as we raced each other downhill, gravity seized the muscles of our legs and propelled us onward, faster and faster, into a rising sun.

The River

GRANDMOTHER GREW UP ON THE MISSISSIPPI RIVER, where her father, a Danish immigrant, worked through the Iowa winters in his shirtsleeves, cutting great blocks of ice from the heart of the river. But when I first knew her, she had lived for over twenty years in the valley of Cottonwood Creek, a tributary of the upper Klamath River.

I remember watching as she cast a dry fly across the river, and asking, "How wide is the Mississippi?" And she would answer, "About a mile across, at Clinton. Now be quiet, the fish can hear you."

I stared at the green water purling around her hip waders, at the fifty-yard expanse of the Klamath, and tried to picture a stream one mile across. Impossible.

I saw the Mississippi only once, when I was seven: a great sluggish mass of brown water, and a line of trees over on the Illinois shore. Grandmother looked across it, her hand shading her light blue eyes, and smiled as she told us about the catfish—as long as a man, able to swamp a rowboat—that fishermen used to catch when she was a girl. The Mississippi was *her* river, and would be, as long as its vast presence lingered in her mind.

THE KLAMATH BEGINS WHERE the Williamson and Sprague rivers rise in southeastern Oregon, in the volcanic country east of the Cascades. They pour into Upper Klamath Lake in the cold, dry Klamath Basin. At the lake's southern outlet, the waters narrow and then drop eighty-seven feet in less than two miles, a stretch of water known as the Link River, almost entirely confined within the city of Klamath Falls.

Below Klamath Falls, the Link widens into Lake Ewauna; the water that leaves the lake is the Klamath. The new river turns southwest, headed for California. After three hundred miles, it joins the Pacific near a tired Indian village called Requa. On the way, it cuts through the Klamath Mountains, that collage of rocks scraped off the ocean floor,

The Klamath River at Happy Camp, December 1969.

folded, lifted, and eroded into a dissected plateau, through which also flow sections of the Sacramento and Rogue rivers. The mountains were born before the river, and the river has only one thought: to carve a path through them.

Bearing steadily southwest, the river takes in the waters of its largest tributary, the Trinity, then swings sharply north and pours into a dark canyon only twenty miles from the coast. So formidable are the slopes here that when mountain man Jedediah Smith reached this confluence in 1828, he spent fifteen days clawing his way toward the ocean.

Although the region around Upper Klamath Lake was known to the Hudson's Bay Company as "the Klamath Country" for years before Peter Skene Ogden actually explored the area in 1826-27, what he called the "Clammitte" River was actually the Williamson. Subject to the creative spelling of the early nineteenth century, the name was variously written as Tlamet, Tlameth, Clamet, Clammitte, or Klamath, its actual meaning lost, for the native people who still live around Upper Klamath Lake, although known to whites as the Klamaths, called themselves Maklak, meaning—of course—"the people."

My provisions are fast decreasing. The hunters are discouraged, Ogden confided morosely to his journal in November, just before some thirty Maklaks visited his camp. They told him that the river he sought, the one that emptied into the ocean, was "yet far distant." By January, the price of dogs for stew had skyrocketed. His party worked their way downstream. They trapped few beaver until February, when a white mountain rose above the southern horizon, just as they reached the main Klamath River.

I have named this river Sastise River, Ogden bragged, feeling better now that forty beaver pelts were drying in camp. *There is a mountain equal in height to Mount Hood or Vancouver, I have named Mount Sastise. I have given these names from the tribes of Indians.*

Ogden sent advance parties further down the Klamath; they returned with hundreds of beaver pelts and tales of large villages of plank houses with friendly inhabitants who crossed the river in capacious redwood canoes. His name for the river stuck for at least another decade, evolving into "Chasta" and finally "Shasta." The placid stream known today as the Shasta rises near that great mountain and joins its larger cousin a few miles downstream from the ford where Ogden's scouting parties crossed the Klamath on their way back to Upper Klamath Lake. The ford itself still exists, below a rounded peak known as Black Mountain. From it a trail headed north toward the summit of the Siskiyou Mountains. The trail led up Cottonwood Creek and passed through a valley where in the twentieth century a sawmill town called Hilt would rise, prosper, and then fade away.

When my grandparents lived in Hilt, they fished between that old ford—ten miles south of Hilt—and the reservoir upstream where, barely three miles south of the state line, the river slackened and widened behind the Copco No. 1 dam. On Saturdays from spring until late fall, they rose early to pack a lunch, load fishing gear into the Oldsmobile, and head south, where the Klamath ran through a gentle country of alfalfa fields and pastures below hills dotted with oak and juniper. On the high slopes beyond were the remnants of a pine forest that once supported a sawmill town called Klamathon, its site now lost under grass on a flat where winter rains brought twisted nails and chunks of melted glass to the surface.

In the years when we lived with our grandparents, Liz and I followed Grandmother along the riverbanks, searching for agates or the opalescent shells of freshwater mussels, trying to catch the trout fry and tadpoles trapped in drying shoreline pools. We poked with sticks at decaying fish carcasses, captured frogs, and returned at last to the car with sticky hair and sneakers full of sand.

Grandmother tied a mean fly, and they fooled many a trout. The fish wriggled frantically as she removed the hook and measured the fish against her hand, which from fingertips to wrist was the exact legal size, six inches. She inspected their flanks for the ugly round wounds left by the sharp mouths of lampreys. She slid the keepers into her wicker creel, seized her walking stick, and waded farther into the river, casting, the line snaking out into the riffles, flinging shards of water sparkling into the sun.

Between May and October the limit was ten fish per day, almost all of them steelhead smolts. Unlike the young of the Chinook and silver salmon, which fled straight to the ocean in early spring, the steelhead children started for salt water in June, taking their time and growing fat on orange salmon flies. In drought years, they might take refuge in the cool waters of tributaries and wait for autumn to complete their journey.

Sometimes Grandmother put her fly rod aside and brought out a newfangled spinning outfit, with clacking reel and monofilament line, which Grandfather despised and mocked, until she began to catch more fish than he did. Then he got one of his own. In winter, Grandmother's wet flies, wrapped with orange thread and trailing a hackle of polar bear hair, were deadly when attached to a flashing silver spoon. In summer the spinning outfit's lures sometimes snagged suckers, which she tossed back even though they often weighed several pounds. Indians knew how to cook suckers, but to white people their soft flesh and small bones were disgusting. We watched them drift downstream, their strange downcast mouths working, their beady, worried eyes staring back at us as they sank away.

Grandmother gutted her catch on the shore, while we watched and thought about death. The summer I was seven, I found a pocketknife in the road and graduated to fish cleaning duty. I squatted beside Grandmother and scraped at silver scales until speckled fish skin lay smooth beneath my fingers, then sliced upward from vent to gills. I cut through the cartilage under the lower jaw, hooked a finger in the gap and pulled to tear the pectoral fins loose, then the innards. I ran my thumbnail up the inside of the backbone, scraping away kidneys and blood, and finally rinsed the carcass in the river before stripping away that last little piece of intestine caught in the vent. I sliced into a stomach or two, to see what the fish were eating, then hurled the waste into the current.

Mother preferred sketching to fishing. She sat on fallen cottonwood logs and filled pages with pencil drawings and watercolors, enjoying the freedom of slacks and sneakers after girdles and high heels in the office all week. She also kept a wary eye on the river, for the first and great commandment of the Klamath was Don't Trust Me. Below the Copco dams, the river was subject to sudden rises of as much as four or five feet: when demand for electricity rose, huge amounts of water surged through the dam turbines, and fly fishermen drowned in midstream.

117

Tommy, Louise with steelhead, and Bob, December 1967.

WE NEVER SWAM IN THE KLAMATH. Born in a land of erodible volcanic soils, then passed through a lake that brimmed with runoff from overgrazed pastures and pesticide-dosed potato fields, its waters stirred to froth by the dam turbines, the river was not the clear stream that Ogden saw. Once, when beaver dams held back the silt loads from its tributaries, before crops and cattle and road runoff, the Klamath ran clean, but even then, the Karuks and Yuroks of the middle and lower Klamath never drank river water. An enemy, they explained, might have thrown a dead dog in somewhere upstream.

In summer the Klamath flowed a dark translucent green, the rocks slippery with algae, the quiet stretches sharp with the smell of fermenting water plants. Cattle stood up to their bellies in the water and inhaled green slime. Summer trout from the Klamath tasted slightly muddy. Real fishing, everyone knew, began in October, when the steelhead came home.

I have seen salmon so thick ... that fishermen would bait their hooks for steelhead that followed the salmon and ... the bait would ride on the salmon backs for some time before it could get into deeper water, wrote an old-timer of the fishing on the upper Klamath, before the California-Oregon Power Company blocked the river.

Those magnificent runs of salmon and steelhead were gone before my time, after decades of decline punctuated by occasional good years when it seemed as though the worst might be over. In 1932, commercial salmon fishermen took thirty thousand pounds of salmon off the mouth of the Klamath. The 1920s and 1930s brought a spate of state laws to ban salmon spearing, to regulate the timing of hydraulic gold mining, and to forbid the construction of any dams on the Klamath River below the mouth of the Shasta River, but still the runs declined.

The steelhead were more adaptable and resilient. I saw a few salmon rolling like saturated logs, but because they stopped feeding after entering the river, they were seldom caught except by snagging. Steelhead were the preferred quarry; silver torpedoes leaping and twisting above the current, their reentry splashes like gunshots across the water.

A good chunk of the upper Klamath was drowned in 1961 when Iron Gate Dam set its teeth against the river, just above Bogus Creek. Built to eliminate the dangerous water fluctuations below the Copco dams, it completed the destruction of the upper river. Returning salmon and steelhead were taken out just below the dam, milked of their eggs and sperm, and their offspring raised in a hatchery.

Below the mouth of the Shasta River, the Klamath growls and rushes, a wild child forced into a narrow channel by encroaching rock walls, dropping fast in elevation. As it falls, the canyon rises, the junipers and oaks and sagebrush fade away, replaced by ponderosa pine and Douglas fir. As the river meets the pathway of the Pacific storms, rainfall rises steadily.

Too steep for farming except on isolated river terraces, much of the land away from the river never passed into private hands, and became part of the Klamath National Forest. The gold-bearing river was punctuated by piles of dredger tailings, ponds, and the naked walls of nineteenth-century hydraulic mines.

WHEN JOHN BRANNON MARRIED OUR MOTHER, the world of the middle Klamath opened up to us. Dad took us to Humbug Point, about six miles downriver from the mouth of the Shasta. A narrow dirt road bailed off the edge of the Klamath River Highway and crept downhill to a deserted homestead, where in winter a rancher fed his cattle on the river bar near the ruined barn.

We seldom saw other fishermen here, except at the height of the steelhead run. A dredger pond full of bullfrogs and perch afforded amusement when the river fish weren't biting. Deep in its canyon, the river was louder and wider, almost frightening. On the south side of the river, a great triangular patch of Douglas firs pointed down at the river, foreshadowing the heavier forests downstream. In the homesteader's abandoned fields, wet weather brought flakes of obsidian to the surface of the silty soil. An old ranch gelding, turned loose to doze away his final summers under the witchy apple trees, lipped crusts of bread from our hands.

I caught my first steelhead at Humbug Point on a Sunday morning late in May just before my eleventh birthday. The whole family watched as Dad coached me, urging me to keep the tip of the pole up and not to horse her in. I finally beached her by backing up on the sand, while Dad slipped a finger through her gills and tossed her up onto the shore.

119

Mother ran to get the camera, and there I stood, a chubby kid in dirty glasses, hair wild, coat askew, holding up a three-and-a-half pound fish in triumph.

At Humbug Point, mourning doves called, and quail whistled in the brush, skittering away through the dry leaves beneath the poison oak thickets, while red-tailed hawks glided overhead and rattlesnakes waited for the cool of evening to hunt near the river. Great blue herons rose, croaking, at our approach, their necks folded back over their shoulders. Killdeer ran ahead of us over the bar and scattered mud flies as they dragged a wing to lure us away from their young. Black-tailed deer came to drink at dusk, and as we drove home, jackrabbits the size of fawns fled up the road, their eyes red and insane.

TWENTY-TWO MILES DOWNRIVER FROM HUMBUG POINT, the Scott River enters from the south, and now the conjoined rivers grow truly introspective and fierce, while the snows of the Scott Bar Mountains resist summer. After a rainstorm, the Scott ran muddy. In the 1850s, gangs of miners turned the entire Scott River out of its bed for three miles above the mouth with a series of wing dams. Some of the largest nuggets ever found in California came from the Scott. Granville Stuart, who died a cattle king in Montana, passed through Scott Valley, twenty-three miles upstream from the mouth, in the autumn of 1854. In his journal he wrote:

Camped in Scott's Valley which is perfectly beautiful, with a clear stream flowing through. The valley is different from most we have seen … all the valley proper is covered with yellow bunch grass, knee high, and waving in the wind like fields of grain … in the night we were awakened by our mules snorting and trying to break loose from the picket line … we saw a grizzly bear shambling off and disappearing in the brush along the stream. … During the night we heard continual splashing in the water near where we were sleeping, and couldn't imagine what kind of animal was in the stream all night, as we had seen no sign of beavers in California … In the morning we … found that all that splashing in the river was caused by salmon fish, from three to four feet long, flopping and jumping in, forcing their way up the stream over the riffles where the water

*was not deep enough for them to swim … we were told that every fall
these large fish came up from the Pacific Ocean to the upper branches of
all the streams as far as they can possibly go and there lay their eggs, then
start back to the ocean, but most of them are so bruised and exhausted
that they die on the way.*

Once, beaver were thick in Scott Valley. *The richest place for beaver I ever
saw,* said Stephen Meek, who accompanied a Hudson's Bay Company
party to the valley in 1836. He described the valley as "all one swamp"
and "full of huts" (beaver lodges). The trappers took eighteen hundred
beaver from Scott Valley in one month, then moved on. Other trappers
followed them, so that when Stuart saw the valley, the beavers were
gone, their dams washed out, and the wetlands they had maintained for
ten thousand years had turned to dry meadows.

Thirty years after Stuart saw it, Scott Valley produced so much wheat
and barley that its towns boasted breweries and flour mills. The river
was diverted into irrigation ditches that stranded both adult salmon
and ocean-bound smolts. Siltation of spawning beds, logging of the
headwaters streams, and high water temperatures doomed still more
fish. And every year of the new century, more and more roads appeared.

BEFORE THE MINERS CAME, the Shasta tribe harvested salmon in Scott
Valley and left obsidian flakes at Humbug Point. Below the mouth of
the Scott, the territory of the Karuk began and extended from Seiad
Valley almost to the mouth of the Trinity. Beyond that was Yurok land, 121
while the Hupa lived on the Trinity River.

Thirty miles below the mouth of the Scott was Happy Camp, and
about thirty miles downriver from Happy Camp was Katimin, the
sacred village of the Karuks, near the mouth of the Salmon River.
Between Katimin and the Salmon River stands a conical peak known
as Sugarloaf to the whites and Auich to the Karuk.

Atop Auich lived Aikren, "he who dwells above," the immortal
peregrine falcon who every year flew away with his fledglings to follow
the ridge traveled by the souls of the dead. The Yurok also revered the
bird, and called him Kerernit. Kerernit had two wives, Black Bear and
Grizzly Bear.

At Katimin, great ceremonies once stabilized the physical world and prevented pestilence and famine. The August new year festival at the time of the salmon runs, called *isivsanen pikiavish* or "earth making," was the most important of these, but by the time we moved to the Klamath, it had not been held for decades.

And thanks to DDT, there came a year when Aikren did not return from the land of the dead. The Karuks still dipnetted salmon at Ishi Pishi Falls below Katimin; once we journeyed to watch them. We were living in Happy Camp then, and we saw our neighbors balance unafraid on the rocks, wet with mist as they scooped up thrashing salmon in nets. In the 1960s old people yet lived who knew, as we did not, that salmon were first made at a village just downstream from this place.

All the salmon in the world, and the river itself, were once confined in a box owned by two old women of that village. When they wanted salmon to eat, they took one out and cooked it. Widower-Across-the-Ocean saw them one day. He waited until they left their house, then found the box and tipped it over. Water and salmon spilled out, rushing downhill. The angry women pursued Widower, and he called on two tan oak trees to help him. As they grew around him, joining to hide him, he called out, "Let the river run downstream!" and blew downhill. And the Klamath roared toward the ocean, bearing the salmon.

THE KLAMATH RIVER HIGHWAY, down which we traveled to fish and to watch others fish, existed because the men who first managed the Klamath National Forest thought about how to best extract timber. The disciples of Gifford Pinchot believed in a future timber famine, and they wanted to be able to supply a crying market when that day came. The famine never quite arrived, but the roads did, and with them the ability to transport a resource.

As early as 1914, the Forest's managers, overwhelmed by just how much timber they had, tried to sell more than two billion board feet of timber growing north of the Klamath River between the mouth of the Shasta River and the mouth of Indian Creek at Happy Camp. If they could build a railroad downriver from the main Southern Pacific line, they decided, the timber could be sold in three massive units, with mills spaced out along its length. But no bids for this bounty were ever received. "Too rugged, too much low quality timber," scoffed the lumbermen, as they chewed their way through the vast groves of more accessible—and privately owned—spruce, redwood, and Douglas fir near the coast.

By 1919, the Forest Service realized that the key to attracting buyers for government timber in the Klamath watershed was a road system. From then on, they pulled every string and greased every wheel to encourage the federal government to build a road system that would make the uncounted millions of board feet of old growth timber available to the saw. Even as my grandmother cast her hand-tied flies into the waters of the upper Klamath in the 1950s, the basic infrastructure was already in place: the state highway that paralleled the Klamath down to its confluence with the Trinity and there linked up with yet another highway leading to the coast. A dozen other roads, built with federal money, snaked up the main tributaries of the Klamath. Aggressive politicking by several Klamath National Forest supervisors paid off when the post-war rises in lumber prices began.

Production foresters tend to regard old growth forests not as assets but as liabilities, not as ecosystems valuable in themselves but as sinks of diminishing returns. Any tree not actively putting on volume is wasting space, wasting time, and should be replaced with a younger, faster-growing tree as quickly as possible. But in the first decades of the Klamath National Forest, the problem was how to make cutting timber worthwhile for the lumbermen. From the day in 1919 when Forest Supervisor Huestis persuaded coastal Humboldt County to lobby the state for a highway connecting the Klamath River with the coast, to the day in 1947 when Forest Supervisor James pushed through a plan to reroute part of the Klamath River Highway to the north side of the river to access the untouched National Forest timber in the Beaver Creek drainage, the overarching goal of replacing all the old growth in the Forest with plantations never changed.

123

Russ Bower, a retired Forest supervisor whom I knew as a gentle white-haired sage much honored at Forest Service picnics, reminisced about the process:

The reason the Klamath National Forest was able to get such a large portion of federal highway funds was interesting. The allocation of such funds within the state of California was guided by a three-way agreement of the Forest Service ... the State Division of Highways and the U.S. Bureau of Public Roads. The State Highway engineers' guidelines for funding was based on traffic counts exclusively. The Klamath River Highway was near the bottom of their list ... and was also far down on [the Bureau of Public Roads] list. The Forest Service had it as their top priority due to the selling job done by former Klamath Supervisor George James, who was now on the Regional Forester's staff. We needed one more vote to get the funds directed to the Klamath Highway. In the winter of 1950-51, I sat down to review the program with State Senator Randolph Collier of Yreka who represented Siskiyou County in the Senate and was also chairman of the Joint Legislative Committee on Transportation. He agreed that the project would be of great economic benefit to Siskiyou County but he would need some leverage to get it through the Highway Commission over the objection of the engineers ... I was chairman of the local Chamber of Commerce Transportation Committee. I prepared an economic analysis of the probable benefits to the economy of Siskiyou County from increased logging, lumber, and mineral development, with a plea to the Highway Commission to vary their normal basis for priority of allocation of funds ... When [the request] came up for consideration by the State Highway Commission, Senator Collier was able to persuade them to accept the proposal ... Senator Collier and I informally and verbally agreed that if I would continue to push for Federal Funds for the portion of the highway from Pacific Highway 99 to Happy Camp, he would try to get a State Inmate road camp assigned to the portion of the highway from Happy Camp to Orleans ...

124

The road that the timber finally traveled was greased with other people's money and slave labor. That's not how Russ Bower saw it, but that's how it was. By the 1970s, when the spawning beds of many of the Klamath's tributaries were choked with sediment, the Forest Service blamed the county road department and the California Department of Transportation, which over the years had indeed shoved many a load of dirt into streams during construction and maintenance. But the private deals of thirty years before, when a forest supervisor sat down with a powerful state senator, were never mentioned.

The logging roads drained into creeks, which now ran brown in winter. Culverts washed out, slides tore out whole drainages, clear-cuts stripped creeks and draws bare. But the logs came out of the woods, hundreds of thousands of board feet a day, fifty-five million board feet a year from the Happy Camp District alone. In the 1960s, the Forest Service hired more foresters and more engineers to build bigger and better logging roads. Dad, who from his days as a gyppo logger in Oregon knew that wider roads were more expensive to build and maintain, complained over the supper table about engineers who had never had to meet a payroll.

The timber sales attracted logging companies and ever-larger lumber mills. Even before we moved to Happy Camp, all but one of the family-owned mills on the river were gone, replaced by Josephine Plywood and Siskiyou Mills and Carolina Pacific. In 1953 the Forest Service built the largest two-lane bridge in the Forest over the Klamath River at Happy Camp. Two billion board feet of timber lay on the other side, sealing the fate of Elk Creek. Hundreds of miles of logging roads later, Happy Camp's municipal waterworks frequently shuts down after a storm to avoid sucking mud into the system.

I NEVER LEARNED TO CAST A DRY FLY. When I was in high school, Grandmother gave me her fly-fishing tackle, but the gift came without lessons. The first time I took her fly rod down to the river, I succeeded only in snapping the hooks off several of her precious flies. So I went back to my spinning outfit for river fishing, and saved the fly rod for use in mountain creeks, where I could pull the line out by hand and let it drift through the narrow pools.

In winter, I fished a deep quiet stretch of river, green as kelp, with Grandmother's steelhead flies, hackled with polar bear hair. Beaver swam silently past me as I stood between the willows, then slapped their tails on the water and dove for their burrows in the riverbank. Tundra swans flew overhead, and sometimes an otter or muskrat slid by my line as it cut through the water. Every couple of days I caught a four- or five-pound steelhead, and on most days a half-pounder. I brought them home and baked them in the oven with butter and lemon and dried

125

parsley, or froze them in milk cartons filled with water. In my mind, actually catching a fish took second place to learning the river, its holes and eddies, snags and rocks.

The 1964 flood changed the face of the river and of its tributaries. Creeks too cold to swim in except on the very hottest days grew warmer after the flood ripped out overhanging trees and filled deep holes with sand. "It's warm!" we caroled as we plunged into Grider Creek on a hundred-degree day, unaware that the cause of our swimming pleasure had also wiped out an entire cohort of young salmon and steelhead.

IN THE MID-1960S, the term "roadless area" had not yet entered the vocabularies of the Forest Service men who pored over maps in offices all over the West. In the Klamath National Forest, hardly anyone remembered what had happened in the summer of 1943, when a group of Forest managers climbed into two redwood canoes and took a strange trip down the lower Klamath River. Skillfully handled by Yurok guides, the canoes navigated the river canyon below its confluence with the Trinity.

The Forest Service owned no river frontage here, although some lands within the canyon were under nominal federal management. The foresters in the canoes had met to decide what to do about a proposal by the state to extend the Klamath River Highway all the way down the river canyon to the mouth of the Klamath. After all their efforts to introduce roads into the Forest, these men had now decided that they wanted the lower Klamath River canyon left alone. But they had trained the highway department too well. So if they couldn't block construction entirely, they thought, they would try to constrain the new highway's location: high enough on the ridges to preserve the natural beauty of the canyon. Perhaps they could also acquire strategically located parcels of land on the lower river and enter into negotiations with the state. Later, the Forest did scrape together funds to buy three parcels, and the state took the hint and dropped the project from the planned road system. Thanks to seven men in a couple of boats, the lower Klamath remains highway-free to this day. What, if anything, the Yurok boatmen added to the conversation remains unknown.

That representatives of the Forest Service defended the lower Klamath still astonishes me, but I suspect a darker reality: they wanted to protect the last canyon because they had no intention of protecting any of the others. By the 1960s, the men of the Klamath National Forest planned to build logging roads on every thousand feet of contour, wherever timber grew, outside of actual wilderness areas. They thought the battle was over, and they thought that timber production had won. If they had foreseen in 1943 that they might someday be deprived of that goal, would they have tried to preserve the lower canyon? In the beginning, they didn't even know how much timber they had; in the end, they didn't know how little they had left, or how many other resources had already been lost.

So the Klamath flows unfettered those last few miles to the sea, spanned at the end of its journey by one lone bridge on the coast highway. Although torn in half by the great flood of December 1964, the gilded statues of California grizzlies at either end survived—Aikren's wives, still staring sightlessly where real grizzlies once fished.

On the Road in Middle Earth

LIZ AND I ROSE AT SIX O'CLOCK, on our first school day in Seiad, and ate breakfast sitting on the raised hearth of the stone fireplace in our new house east of the town. By seven o'clock, we waited down at the highway with Eddie Alexander—a blond sophomore barely taller than Liz—and Mitch, a senior who sucked on a cigarette and hunched his shoulders inside his jacket. Liz was just starting high school; I had achieved the insouciance of a junior.

At 7:15, Bus Number 28 squealed to a halt beside us. Bob Mills, the old bus driver, sat behind Wendell Bussert, the new bus driver, to show him the route. Wendell lived at Scott Bar, three miles up the Scott River. Scattered around the bus were Marie and Ross, siblings who lived on a ranch just below Horse Creek and had to drive to the mouth of the Scott River to meet the bus; Wendell's plump daughter Nadine; and Mike and Charlie from Hamburg, a wide spot in the road halfway between Scott Bar and Seiad. Charlie immediately homed in on Liz and Eddie, who with their slender paleness could have been brother and sister. "Mr. and Mrs. Mousie!" he hollered, thus ensuring that Eddie would never, ever, sit any closer to Liz than he had to.

At the Seiad Store, we stopped for another clutch of passengers before taking the three-mile detour up Seiad Creek. We wound through oak groves, looped in and out of side drainages, and finally made a U-turn in front of the Robinson place, where the three tall fair Robinson kids and their darker cousin Georgia climbed aboard. Except for chance encounters at the store or swimming hole, I hadn't seen my bus mates all summer.

Between stops, I looked out the window and watched the light of the rising sun strike the row of high peaks that climbed from the valley floor north toward Cook and Green Pass. I watched the mill smoke drift up Seiad Creek, and as the bus halted at a side stream called Canyon Creek, I saw Robert Cooley stride across the road in front of us, behind his older sister Linda. They lived with their grandmother, Blanche

Priddy. Schoolroom gossip said that their parents were divorced and lived "down below"—which to us meant anyplace south of Redding. Blanche worked at the Seiad Store and was renowned for her earthy directness, exemplified by the day that her panties fell down as she was waiting on a customer. Without missing a tap on the cash register keys, she stepped out of the scrap of nylon and kicked it under the counter.

Robert—now a junior like me—was a tall redhead with an expression of deadpan solemnity and a reputation for effortless excellence in math. He made competent Bs in everything else, played no sports, and his only apparent passion was hunting. Linda, a dishwater blonde with muscular calves, stepped onto the bus wearing a narrow skirt with matching blouse, new white flats, and a disdainful expression. She scanned the vacant seats and finally perched her narrow hips on the edge of mine. Her upturned chin and narrowed eyes rejected conversation. As the bus eased back into gear, I looked across the aisle toward Blanche's house, and saw the green stucco with new eyes. Robert resembled neither his snooty sister nor his odd grandmother. His shoulders were wider than they had been last June, his legs longer. I wondered where he had spent the summer. I had never seen him at the store, or in the deep emerald swimming hole on Seiad Creek, although we often saw his noisy Robinson cousins there. With that coloring, he probably sunburned easily.

After another quarter of a mile, the bus stopped to pick up Bink Sherman, who began talking to Robert about hunting and where they would go on opening day of deer season. I listened to them while my eyes swept over the ridgelines above us. The Robinsons had horses and cattle, and during hunting season they packed far into the high Siskiyous. Perhaps Robert went with them. I tried to picture him on a horse.

I heard Bob Mills remind Wendell that if he missed the eight o'clock roadblock on the construction area, we'd be late for school. As we turned back onto the highway, Wendell ran through the gears, and we roared past the Wildwood Club, where the valley ended and the narrow river canyon resumed. He almost missed the next stop, and as the screech of brakes died away, Danny and Mark climbed up the steps.

In later years, whenever I heard the term "jock," I saw Danny. Tall, with thick brown hair that fell over his forehead in just the right assumption of carelessness, his broad shoulders were accentuated by a letterman's jacket clustered with thick decorations, his neck muscles straining at his

129

collar. A toothpick jutted from the corner of his mouth, and he smiled in a benevolent, *noblesse oblige* sort of way. Never without a girlfriend, he and his current squeeze could be seen draped around each other beside lockers or in doorways before every class, as though they were about to be separated for a year instead of fifty minutes.

A year older than his brother, Mark was shorter, slender, and tense in a kind of James Dean way. On his face, the family smile appeared as a rueful lift of one side of his mouth, accompanied by a tilt of the head, so that his blue eyes looked up at you, not down like his brother's. As Danny flung an arm over his seat and shouted pleasantries at his football teammates Charlie and Mike, Mark swung that upward glance around, then opened a worn blue loose-leaf binder and began to draw on a fresh page with ink-stained fingers. Liz turned and peered over the back of her seat and watched the drawing take shape, upside down.

From my seat on the right side of the bus, the vistas of valley and peak ended, and the dull gray metamorphic rock of the road cut slid by the windows. We shot past the old hydraulic tailings at Portuguese Creek, stopped at the crowded flat of Fort Goff to let Odette and Sharon on, and hit the roadblock at the entrance to the construction area near Thompson Creek.

The great flood of '64 was already receding into legend in the wider world, but here it had just ended. The damage inflicted on this five-mile stretch of the Klamath River Highway boggled our minds. Never more than a narrow shelf scraped from the canyon walls, the highway here had once been shady, even on the hottest days, as it snaked its way in and out of draws and creeks, following the contours of the land rather than creating its own. Although long since paved, the curves were those of roads from the 1920s and forced drivers to slow down. I had loved this section of road in summer, loved the cool breezes that flowed over my face as I leaned out the car window to look at fern-clad draws where trickles of clear water fell over mossy boulders. But the flood had scraped much of the old highway away, as a cook scrapes down a bowl of cake batter with a spatula. The bulldozers that reopened the road dug deep into the canyon wall to carve out a roadbed again, but now the highway department had come in force, to make the road wider and straighter than before. Between Thompson Creek and Cade Mountain, giant earthmovers and belly-dumps toiled. Within a week, we would know many of the workers on sight. *There is a Cat operator we all call Tarzan,* I would write, *because of his big muscles, and a guy with a reddish Norse-type beard, who is cute, and a crew-cutted flagman, who is very cute.*

Now the very cute flagman walked out in front of the bus and held up a stop sign. Wendell set the brake and turned in his seat to talk to Bob. I looked at Wendell. About sixty, he was slightly built, with a face like a pale prune. His thinning gray hair stood on end, as though he had left his house without combing it. When he spoke, his arms waved, and his voice rose to a squeak as he craned his neck to stare up at the road cut. A D-8 Cat worked high above us, carving away at a precipitous slope once clad in live oaks and madrones. From the back of the bus, the boys sized Wendell up for signs of weakness. I hoped that he would not make the mistake of treating them like human beings. Dave Titus and Curt Morey, our Happy Camp bus drivers, could keep rowdy boys in line with one narrowed glance into the rearview mirror.

The pilot car appeared, the flagman stepped back and reversed his sign, and we led a line of vehicles through the dusty construction zone. Back on the pavement, the bus groaned up the east side of Cade Mountain and flew down the west side. Wendell took the endless hairpin turn near the bottom so fast that a couple of kids were flung into the aisle. We rolled toward Happy Camp under a blanket of morning mill smoke that floated up the river.

Four miles from town, we stopped to pick up our last passenger: Beverly Collord, daughter of the local highway patrolman. Bev was a senior this year, but as she had skipped a grade she was only my age. Self-assured, with a smile for everyone, she managed to get straight As without being a grind. She played the piano and lived in a house full of books that her parents bought simply because they wanted to read them, and not just as occasional birthday or Christmas presents. Bev had read books I had never heard of, and sometimes she loaned them to me. Now she took the seat in front of me, smiled her wide smile, and asked how my summer had been. Even Linda unbent a little and talked to her, although she looked away again when we began talking about books. Bev rummaged in her purse and pulled out a thick paperback, worn at the corners. "You ever read Tolkien?" she asked.

I held the book in my hands and looked at the title. *The Fellowship of the Ring,* by J. R. R. Tolkien, it said. Monstrous black figures flew across the creased cover. "What's it about?"

"It's about some little people called hobbits, who have to destroy a magic ring," Bev said. "He's a friend of C. S. Lewis," she added, pointing to the author's name.

Thanks to Bev, I had read C. S. Lewis's *Narnia* books, but I had never heard of Tolkien. I felt a tightness in my chest. So many books in the world, and so little access to them. This year—because the upriver bus left right after school let out—I wouldn't even have time to run over to Happy Camp's branch library. That left the high school library—every title on its five shelves had been burned into my retinas—an occasional paperback from J. K. Gill's in Medford when I had the cash, or the kindness of Bev. "Can I borrow it?" I begged.

Bev reached into her purse again and pulled out a folded piece of paper and a pen. "I'll put your name down on the list," she said, scribbling.

"There's a *list*?" I wailed. Five minutes ago I had never heard of Tolkien; now I was desperate to get my hands on those pages.

"It won't be long," Bev soothed me. "They're all fast readers."

SEVEN HOURS LATER, CLUTCHING AN ARMFUL of textbooks, I waited for the bus at the back gate of the high school. I tilted my chin and smiled at Robert. I had an excuse to talk to him now, at least a little bit, for he and I were the only students in Mrs. Applegate's second-year Spanish class. He smiled back and held up *El Camino Real, Book 2*. I rode through the cacophony of the return trip absorbed in *Celia Garth*, but as Robert stepped off the bus, I looked up and watched him walk down his grandmother's driveway, his thighs moving under his corduroys.

132

As long as the fall weather stayed fair, the daily hurry-up-and-wait of the construction roadblock was not onerous, at least for me. The long book drought of summer was over, and I gulped prose like water as I made the best of the school's meager collection. I read *Moby Dick* and plowed through endless descriptions of nautical minutiae. *Jane Eyre* left me speechless for days with the kind of excitement that comes only when we are young and unjaded by the conventions of romantic plots. I almost gave up on *Rebecca* before the heroine finally grew a spine in the face of the welcome news that Maxim had shot his bitch of a first wife. Hadn't we all met evil girls we wanted to shoot? I read *The Game of Kings*, the first of Dorothy Dunnett's marvelous historical novels, and saw, in the slender blond bad-boy hero's rivalry with his responsible brown-haired brother, a parallel with two of my fellow passengers. When Kathy Robinson, desperate for book report material, asked me to recommend a book, I told her about *Gone with the Wind* and for the next couple of weeks had the satisfaction of seeing her walk between classes with the volume before her face, unable to put it down.

THE FIRST HINT THAT THIS WOULD BE a long winter came early in October, when the flagman stepped onto the bus one afternoon and told us about the belly-dump. The machine had slid into the river and sunk out of sight with its engine running as the driver took a lunch break. "They think they'll have to get a diver to find it," Mr. Very Cute told us, to admiring stares. The next morning, we crowded over to the river side of the bus, ignoring Wendell's pleas to sit down, and saw a pair of scuba divers adjusting their tanks on the riverbank. By afternoon, the belly-dump had reappeared as a shadow under the murky water. The next day, the behemoth rested on shore like a basking crocodile, looking none the worse except for a few dents.

Sights like this made me more than ready for something that would blot out the world for an hour and a half every morning and afternoon, so when I finally got Bev's book in my hands and learned that it was only the first of three, I settled into it with a sigh, as though placed before an all-you-can-eat buffet.

Once the rains began, workers burned the trees and brush that had been pushed together by the bulldozers as they cleared the mountainside for the new road cut. Fires blazed high in the half-light of morning and raised clouds of steam from the wet banks and roadbed. Our bus slithered past them, and one morning, just as we drove by the last roaring fire, Wendell noticed that the front of the bus was steaming, too. He stopped and got out and disappeared under the raised hood. "That's not just steam, that's smoke," Mike observed as Wendell climbed back in and drove on through a stench of burning rubber. By the time we reached the Shell station at the edge of town, we could lean out and see smoke boiling over the front tires. We abandoned ship and walked the last quarter-mile downhill to the high school.

133

In December, we wallowed through deep ruts every day, and flows of mud caked the sides of the bus. We slammed down into holes of brown water, but by then I was far away in Middle Earth. One January day, Mr. Carter, the road project engineer, stepped onto the bus as we waited at the roadblock. "All you kids sitting on this side," he announced, waving a hand uphill, "watch out for falling rocks."

"Oh, *great*," groaned Bink.

"Hairy, man," exulted Sid, an Indian boy whose instinct was to turn everything into comedy. I looked out the window, stared up and up at the road cut looming hundreds of feet above us, and saw trickles of mud and pebbles slide down toward the ditch. As we began to move again, I put Frodo's journey aside for a moment and looked at the overhanging rock outcrops, balanced on nothing, destabilized by bulldozers and explosives, and ready at any moment to obey gravity and tumble into the river. I felt the first stirrings of claustrophobia as I realized that we were trapped in this line of cars and trucks, unable to duck or dodge. I looked ahead at the pilot car and willed it to move faster. Across the aisle, Liz had stopped chatting with her seatmate; her eyes were wide and dark as they met mine.

Ahead of us, a tractor-trailer pulling two oil tankers slid out of the ruts and into the deeper mud on the river side of the road and groaned to a halt. We waited in the rain for twenty-five minutes before a D-8 crept over to pull them out. We followed in their wake, as the steering wheel spun almost uncontrollably under Wendell's clenched fingers and the engine screamed in second gear.

The next afternoon, with snow falling as we stopped to let Bev out, her father pulled in behind us, red lights flashing on top of the black-and-white. "Your bus body's at an angle to the chassis," he told Wendell. "I think your springs are broken."

Wendell turned around, drove back to Happy Camp, and found another bus to take us home. But we had missed the four o'clock roadblock opening, so for half an hour we waited in line and stepped out to throw wet snowballs at each other. By the time we piled back in to drive on, the boys were flushed and full of bravado. They jeered at Wendell as he steered past a mudslide pouring over the road. "Never fear, Wonder Buzzard is here!" shouted Mike, and the new nickname ricocheted through the bus.

"Out of the blue of the western sky comes: Wonder Buzzard!" Bink and Robert gasped, breathless with their own cleverness.

The next morning, the bus struggled through the construction area as Wendell tried to catch up to the car ahead of us in the procession. Behind me, I heard Charlie mutter, "Shift, for God's sake, *shift!*" Mr. Carter's advice about rocks came back to me as a boulder the size of a Volkswagen flew off the road cut, landed in the middle of the mud between the bus and the car ahead of us, bounced once, and arced into the river. We fell silent, and twenty-five heads plastered themselves to the right side windows as Wendell crouched over the wheel and floored the accelerator.

One day in February, a grim Mr. Carter drove his pickup into our path and sloshed over to the bus. "There's a slide further down the road, and we're letting cars through," he said, "but it's too narrow for the bus. You'll have to go back."

Back home by nine o'clock, I was never so happy in my life to tackle the ironing. Later, I sat by the fireplace and followed the Rohirrim to Helm's Deep.

The next day, despite rocks pelting down the banks, the bus went through, past a battalion of flagmen and flaming oil pots, and around the slide. In the afternoon we waited again for a few acres of mud to be scooped off the road ahead. As rocks rolled down from the road cut, Wendell made dire predictions, and a new song rose from the back of the bus. Faint at first, then louder as the improvised lyrics came together, we listened to Bink's falsetto revise "Yellow Submarine."

"And we called him Wonder Buzzard," Robert chimed in. The other kids got the idea, and soon the vehicle rocked to the Beatles tune, the refrain finishing with "*a yellow school bus, yellow school bus right now!*"

The final insult to our fraying sense of security came when the roadblock began near a mammoth dump truck whose rear wheels had gone over the bank above the river. Its load of boulders would already have dragged it down, if not for the cables that fastened it securely to a belly-dumper wedged in the ditch. I looked up from *The Two Towers* and watched as men scrambled around the dump truck and finally managed to raise its bed and send its gray burden shooting into the river. Another dump truck rumbled up to help pull the first one back over the lip. We

135

wallowed through the quagmire left by the bogged machinery, and I returned to Treebeard's monologue.

Bev's books were the pirated Ace editions, the ones that galvanized Ballantine into bringing out an authorized paperback a few months later. Later that spring I would find those books at J. K. Gill's and buy them with my first babysitting money. Today, when multi-volume fantasies constitute an entire industry, Tolkien has many imitators. But in the 1960s, the old philologist stood alone.

He wrote about creatures and places that I immediately accepted as real, and the deeper I plunged into those stained and dog-eared pages, the more Middle Earth seemed a familiar place, a world I had known all my life. Hobbits and orcs, elves and dwarves were as real as the people on the bus; the Shire and the wild places beyond it morphed in my mind's eye into mountains and rivers already familiar. One afternoon the bus pulled into Seiad Valley and turned up Seiad Creek just as a rainstorm cleared and the pointed mountains shook themselves free of the fog.

In that moment, Tolkien's geography assumed the shape of the land around me. From then on, as I followed Frodo and Sam on their journey into Mordor, as Pippin and Gandalf rode to Minas Tirith, I saw them in the familiar landscape of the Devils and Lake Mountain and Slinkard Peak. When Boromir's body tumbled over Rauros Falls, I saw the Klamath, brown and angry, racing past the bus windows each morning. Little by little, piece by piece, the landscape of Middle Earth took the shape of the one I knew, and in the midst of it all, Seiad Valley became the Shire.

136   Perhaps my perception of Seiad as a safe and secluded place came about because the wide world outside the river canyon seemed to be going crazy. Images of wars and riots in newspapers and magazines frightened me in a way that runaway boulders didn't. I was glad to live in a hidden place that no one important had ever heard of.

SPRING CAME JUST AS FRODO TOOK SHIP for the Gray Havens, and I closed *The Return of the King* and looked up for the first time in a long time and saw swaths of deerbrush blooming pink and blue on Cade Mountain, healing the scars of logging with a riot of delicate blossoms, their odor filling the air on a warm afternoon. The whole world seemed to ooze fertility, as we discovered when Mr. Very Cute vanished from his job at the roadblock. "He got a girl in trouble," I heard the other kids smirk.

By May, I found it increasingly hard to concentrate when Mrs. Applegate tried to pound the subjunctive tense into my lunch-addled brain. I wanted to watch the ospreys ride the updrafts beside the limestone cliffs above the river. I wanted to run in the cool of the morning and smell the river while my little brother's sneakers slapped the road behind me. I wanted to work in the garden.

Through the open classroom windows, the giddy scent of roses poured in, and when I turned my head to inhale it, I saw Robert's burnished head across the room. He didn't look around. The fact that Robert and I were the only students in Spanish II had not, after all, resulted in much conversation between us. Not that I expected a great deal: short of a nod as he got on the bus, he rarely spoke to me. I told myself that for all but the most secure of jocks, to notice a girl was to be teased about her.

On one of the last days of school, with the sun warming my shoulders as we rolled up Seiad Creek, the joy of life and youth and the coming summer caught us all, and even Wendell looked back and smiled as the boys stood up and leaned out the windows. Their cracked tenors echoed off the canyon, as they yelled once more about our home on a yellow school bus. The Devils shimmered in the heat, and the far-off snowfields of Red Mountain glared beyond them. I looked at the velvet green cone of Slinkard Peak across the river, and I wanted it all, forever: this ride, and this view, and this raucous company, and I wanted it not to stop, even as the bus paused in the shade of the Canyon Creek gorge, and Robert stepped off. I watched his long legs stride away, as they had so many times before, but now he seemed different somehow—whole and luminous in the afternoon sunshine—and I looked at his jeans and caught the movement of muscle in thigh and buttocks. I wanted him to look back at me, so I could smile at him, but he didn't. He moved down the hill toward the green house, eager for what was left of the afternoon. Next week, he would walk down that driveway and out of my life until September.

The bus lurched into gear, and I turned in my seat and caught one glimpse of sun-flecked hair through a curtain of young oak leaves before

137

the bus rounded the next turn. A Tolkien passage that I had memorized ran through my head, the scene in which the hobbits first meet Strider:

> *His legs were stretched before him, showing high boots of supple leather that fitted him well, but had seen much wear and were now caked with mud. A travel-stained cloak of heavy dark-green cloth was drawn close about him, and in spite of the heat of the room he wore a hood that overshadowed his face, but the gleam of his eyes could be seen as he watched the hobbits.*

It's possible to invent romance anywhere, even while riding a school bus on a spring day in Middle Earth.

Liz and Mark

AT FOURTEEN, LIZ WAS SLIGHT AND SLENDER, her chest still flat, her hips narrow. Her blonde hair hung to her waist, held back from her high forehead with a headband that made her look even younger. She weighed about eighty-five pounds and was so pale that in some lights her face looked slightly green.

Liz often complained that middle children got no respect. I didn't see that then, for the long armistice between us, brought on as we stood together against our stepfather, was showing cracks. As I passed out of what Jane Austen called "the most trying age" and Liz entered it, she woke one day to find that her older sister had drunk the Kool-Aid of self-righteousness. I only knew that somehow the formerly burdensome rituals of school and home had become rewarding. I discovered in myself the happy ability to absorb material and regurgitate it back onto test papers. In class, I was quiet and diligent and most teachers looked on me with approval. At the same time, I was competent enough in sports to be readily picked when we chose up sides for volleyball or basketball or soccer, which saved me from total social oblivion.

On an emotional level, to be in love with Robert—or rather, to attach a vague idea of romance to the cute ass of a boy who might speak to me once a week, if that—was both titillating and safe. But even if Robert had actually lusted after me, being alone with him would have been a challenge: he didn't have a car. Few boys on the river did, in those days.

The parental pressure that had once rendered Saturday nights horrible to me, as I dressed for dances I didn't want to attend, vanished and showed no signs of returning. I spent my Friday and Saturday evenings *en famille*, playing records, throwing Monopoly dice across the kitchen table, reading aloud to Tommy. Mother knitted, Dad read the newspapers, and the rhythms of Herb Alpert and the Tijuana Brass blared from the record player. The house was suffused with warmth and the peace of gentle amusements. We lived twenty miles from the bright lights of Happy Camp, and even after I got my driver's license, the last thing our stepfather wanted was to have us navigate the river road on a rainy night. Besides, a forty-mile round trip in the new station wagon cost money, and he was not about to drive us himself without a very good reason.

The new routine contented me, but not Liz. She had loved the dances in the grade school gym, and just as she had graduated to the more sophisticated pleasures of high school, she had to miss them. While her friends slid across the music room floor where I had spent so many martyred hours, Liz argued with Tommy over the rent for Ventnor Avenue. On Monday morning her friends talked about who had done what to whom at dances and beer busts, and Liz laughed at the stories and pretended she didn't care. She missed Vern, her eighth-grade flame, missed dancing slow dances with him in the dimness under balloons and crepe paper. But since Vern didn't have a car—or a license, for that matter—she saw him only at school, and knew he often fell under the spell of other girls and held hands with them in the dark depths of the Del Rio Theater. Ever practical, however, Liz looked for other options.

To this day, when Liz walks into a room, males trip over themselves to reach her side. They did it when she was six, and thirty-six, and they will still be doing it when she's eighty-six. Men want to wait on her—to take her coat, fetch her drinks, pull out her chair. Their faces light up with goofy and willing servitude, even as she fixes them with a superior stare that promises nothing. It isn't just that she's a slender blonde with wide and mischievous eyes, although that helps. Something else—sheer charm—brings the willing prey to her feet.

One morning in October of that first year in Seiad, Mark sat down by Liz, opened his binder, and began to draw a motorcycle. Liz lit up and talked, rattling on "like a sewing machine," as I wrote that night. Donna Robinson leaned forward and tapped me on the shoulder. "She sure can talk, can't she?" she whispered. I nodded, and noticed that Mark talked back to her, his head tilted down to catch her words despite the roar of the engine and the shouts of the passengers. The two of them talked all the way to school, and walked off the bus and through the school doors together, Mark's head still bent toward Liz's. I watched him nodding down at her as they disappeared into the din of the hallway.

Mark was a year older than his brother Danny, although both were
seniors this year. "Flunked a grade," Mark told Liz as they sat together
one morning. Five years is an eon when it stretches between a freshman
and a senior, so wide a gulf that although Donna and her sister Kathy
teased Liz about her "boyfriend," they didn't for a minute take the new
relationship seriously. Nor did Mark treat Liz the way his brother Danny
treated his buxom girlfriends. He didn't seek her out between classes.
But I knew that Liz liked Mark with an intensity not lavished on her
other crushes, even Vern. She talked about him to me, for one thing.
Mark didn't really want to play football, she told me. It was just that his
parents expected it of him. "Everything Danny does, they think Mark
ought to do," she said.

As for Mark, he had stronger defenses against male-on-male teasing
than his brother's celebrated muscles. In my sophomore year, Mrs.
Gosselink, a rumpled woman with short iron-gray hair who tried
unsuccessfully to control her classes and teach them a little English
grammar, pounced on Mark's artistic talent. She had him illustrate the
rules of study hall behavior, and pinned the new posters above the
blackboard in the library. I often glanced up to take in his complicated
artwork, the devastating caricatures that spared no one, not even his
teacher. The artist's eye caught everything, down to the eyelet lace on
Mrs. Gosselink's slip as it drooped beneath the uneven hem of her skirt.
He reproduced to perfection the oily swirls of Mike's hair and the way
Kenny slouched at his desk, picking his pencils into slivers with broken
fingernails.

One Friday afternoon, as the bus pulled away from the high school,
Liz plastered her face to the window and looked out at the football field.
On game days, Danny drove his car to school so that he and Mark could
drive home together. As the field receded behind a curve, Liz flounced
back down into her seat beside me. "That Sharon," she hissed, cutting a
glance back to a gangly sophomore several rows behind us. "She's asked
Mark to the Sadie Hawkins dance."

"Who told you that?" I asked.

"Donna," she whispered.

"Oh, come on," I scoffed. "That can't be true. Even if she did ask him,
I can't see him going with her."

"Why not?"

141

"Well, look at her. She looks like Gollum, for heaven's sake." Liz turned and stared at Sharon, whose pipe cleaner legs, none too clean, stuck out into the aisle.

"You're probably right," she admitted.

"I'll bet Donna's just teasing you. Anyway, why don't *you* ask Mark?"

"It's too late. It's tomorrow night. Anyhow, we have to go to Medford tomorrow and probably won't get home till late."

Liz sat silent and stared out the window as we drove through the construction area. As Sharon stepped off the bus at Fort Goff, Liz turned to me. "Mark flunked two subjects and he's going to have to drop football," she said.

I murmured something sympathetic, but Liz only shook her head. "He hated it, anyway," she added. "He's a lot better at wrestling."

By November, Liz and Mark often sat together in the very back seat of the bus. When I sneaked a look back, I saw their heads bent together, in contemplation of one of Mark's drawings. I worried about my sister, as she flirted with a boy old enough to be drafted. I told myself that she was in over her head. I told myself that I just wanted to protect her from hurt. I told myself a lot of things, and at last I told Mother, knowing that she would tell Dad.

"You're flirting too much," Dad said to Liz the next evening. "You'll be in hot water if he ever starts flirting back. From now on, you don't sit by Mark, and you don't sit in the back of the bus."

The next day wasn't pleasant. I had broken our pact.

"You spinster," she hissed as she bounced down on the seat behind me, using the worst insult she could think of. She folded her arms and stared out the window. By the time Mark and Danny climbed aboard, the rest of Liz's seat was occupied. She smiled at him, to tell him it was all right, and with a puzzled look he walked to the back of the bus. When we pulled up to the school, Liz stood up and waited for Mark to walk by. I heard her explaining to him, "It's her, it's Louise."

But when I passed Mark in the hall later that morning, he smiled at me and said hello. No hard feelings there. "He likes her," I thought, "but he doesn't think of her as his girlfriend."

On the way home that afternoon, Liz sat down behind me and let me have it. "You won't let me do anything," she accused. "You're such a jerk."

"It wasn't me who said you couldn't sit in the back with Mark, it was Dad," I threw over the back of the seat.

"But you told on me," she retorted. Well, there it was. I knew she was right. I shouldn't have said anything. *Who do you think you are, anyway?* said a voice in my head. *But she doesn't know what she's doing,* the other side of my brain answered.

Liz's discontent led to a Big Discussion one evening with Mother and Dad. I listened from the living room as I sat on the couch and read to Tommy, and Liz astounded me by telling our parents exactly what she wanted.

"I don't want to wear these clumpy shoes," she said, pointing to her brown oxfords. "I want to get my hair cut. I want to sit where I want to on the bus."

"I'm trying to guide you," Dad said, "and I only have four more years to accomplish the job. Both you girls were hard nuts to crack, although I think we may have finally cracked Louise. You need to keep both feet on the ground. It's dangerous to just see one boy."

"But how am I ever going to see more than one boy?" Liz demanded. "I never get to go anywhere after school."

"There are other boys on the bus besides Mark," Dad pointed out.

"Ewww," Liz said.

In the end, Liz agreed not to sit with Mark on the bus, and Dad agreed that she could get her hair cut if she brought home a good report card.

When Mark sat down next to Liz the following day, she fixed me with a they-never-said-he-couldn't-sit-by-me look, and I just shrugged and turned away. By January, the two of them were once again giggling over drawings and tattered copies of *Mad* and *Cracked*. I gave up. What Mother and Dad didn't know wouldn't hurt them.

143

But by late January, Liz's algebra grade had slipped to a C and she had flunked a home economics midterm.

"You need to buckle down and work!" Dad shouted at her. "I know you're smart enough to do the work. Why won't you?"

To make matters worse, her scores from the state scholastic aptitude tests—the ones we all had to take as freshmen and juniors—were excellent, none below the 85th percentile, and some of them higher than mine had been at her age. But still her grades fell. When she came home in early February with three Cs on her report card, Dad lost patience and spanked her for the crime of having a potential greater than her performance.

One evening, as I searched for a comb I had loaned to Liz a few days before, I dumped her purse out onto the couch. Dad looked up from his easy chair at the pile. "That was all in there?" he asked, amazed, and came over to look just as Liz walked in. As Dad picked up one of Mark's school photos and peered at it, Liz shrieked.

"To Liz," he read aloud, "who is a very nice person to listen to." Liz stood horror-struck, but Dad only chuckled and dropped the photo back onto the pile, probably relieved that it contained nothing even remotely suggestive. Liz fell upon the mess and glared at me as she stuffed her treasures back into the purse.

Late in February, as I sat on a hall bench eating lunch with Cheryl, who edited the school newspaper, *The War Whoop*, Mark sat down beside us and handed her some drawings. "These are so good!" Cheryl gushed, and we spread them out on the bench and chirped over them. Mark lifted one thin shoulder in acknowledgement. He cracked his knuckles and peered down the hall. Liz came around the corner and sat down beside him. As Cheryl studied the drawings, I slid looks at Mark and my sister. His face was changed, his drawn pallor gone. He focused all his attention on Liz, and when she spoke, he listened, really listened, as no boy had ever listened to me.

That afternoon, Wendell delayed the bus for ten minutes so the upriver kids could see the end of a wrestling match between Etna and Happy Camp. When Liz finally flung herself down in the bus seat beside me, I turned to her. "I take it back," I said. "He really does like you. I thought it was just that you had a crush on him. But he really does like you."

Liz nodded. "I know. But he's never even tried to hold my hand. And I doubt he'd try to kiss me, even if it was dark in the bus or something."

"Maybe he thinks you look too young with all those metal bands on your teeth," I teased.

"No, even when I get these off, he won't think of me that way." She sounded sure of that. "It's like he just needs someone to talk to."

As the days lengthened and the endless rains let up in the afternoons, Liz sometimes played her flute in the back of the bus, and as Mark watched her fingers pressing the valves, his tense face relaxed. Liz had begun learning the flute only a year and a half ago, in Beginning Band. Had we remained in Happy Camp, she would have been playing in Intermediate Band this year. But the intermediates met at 7:30 in the morning, so Mr. Tristan had allowed her to jump ahead and join Advanced (high school) Band. Now, in addition to her regular schoolwork, she struggled each day to catch up to a year's worth of musical education in a few weeks. "You're not practicing enough!" Mr. Tristan shouted at her once, and flung his baton across the room as she lost her place yet again in the maze of notes. But somehow she stayed in the advanced class.

By the middle of March, with her grades up at last, Dad told Liz that she could get her hair cut. She visited Mr. Lee one day and came back with her thick golden hair chopped off just below her ears and a look of proud sophistication on her face. That night, she practiced the flute with new determination.

Two weeks later, without warning, Mark disappeared from the school bus, and from school. The official story was that his parents had sent him to a sanatorium far to the south. He had had rheumatic fever as a child, and his thinness and nervousness were lingering symptoms, now getting worse. Mark, the story continued, had asked his parents to send him away so that he could recover. That was the story. But the truth got out eventually. Mark was in a mental hospital.

At the spring concert in May, in between band numbers, Liz sat high up in the gym risers with Vern and held his hand in the dark. But when the yearbook came out later that month, Liz turned the pages of the *White & Gold* and found all of Mark's photos. "I wish he was here to sign them," she mourned. "And why aren't there any pictures of the wrestling team?"

145

In that 1966 yearbook, the posed photos of the senior class showed Mark as I remembered him from all those bus rides—the tilted head and slanted smile, the careless hair. What struck me afresh was his beauty. His brother Danny, beside him on the page, was handsome with his sleek brown hair and thick football neck, but in Mark the photographer had caught something more.

A few pages further on, the football team stood, in shoulder pads and numbered jerseys, all fierce and competitive. All except Mark. Mark's jersey looked too large for him, and he seemed to have been placed in it against his will. His neck was thin between the shoulder pads, his head cocked at an angle like that of a hanged man. His cheeks were sunken, and his eyes—his eyes were those of a prisoner, a hostage, begging for help.

ON THE LAST DAY OF SCHOOL, on a hot June afternoon the day after graduation, the bus drove past Mark and Danny's driveway without stopping. Danny had graduated the night before, and Liz, laboring gamely through "Pomp and Circumstance" beneath the gym stage with the rest of the band, had looked for Mark, but never saw him. "Someone said he was home, that they saw him at the store, but I hope they didn't make him come to see Danny graduate," she said.

Danny had driven his own car into school the next morning to clean out his locker. Now we saw Danny's current girlfriend coming toward us, walking on the river side of the road, a stunned look on her face. "What's she doing down here?" Liz wondered, and turned to look back at her.

The next day, we left for a trip to the Oregon coast, so it was two weeks before we learned that Mark was dead. He had died alone in his parents' house. He had shot himself with a rifle. Danny and his girlfriend had found him not long before we rode past in the bus.

After a year or two, Liz and I sometimes talked about Mark's death. "To their parents," Liz said, "Danny was the perfect one and Mark was the screw-up—at least, that's how Mark thought they saw him. Mark was the kid who flunked out, who couldn't be the football hero that Danny was, who never made the honor society. So I'm not surprised that he got depressed enough to kill himself. But why in the world did they let him come home for Danny's graduation? Couldn't they see that that was just rubbing it in, how much of a failure he was? Who let him come home? Why didn't they have sense enough to keep him away?"

Forty years on, another possibility inserted itself into our reminiscences. Even at fourteen, Liz knew there was something different about Mark and about his response to her. What do you do, then, if you're a beautiful, artistic, gay young man living isolated in a forest canyon, in hiding? What if you don't know that the world contains—even in 1966—faraway pockets of tolerance like San Francisco? Do your differences—which your family believes are your failures—so prey upon your mind that you finally seek an escape through the widest gate of all?

146

The Girls of Springtime

MR. BACKSTROM WAS A SLIGHT DARK-HAIRED MAN with a bored expression who resembled Patty Duke's television father. Before he came to Happy Camp in the fall of 1965 to teach high school mathematics, he had been a mechanical engineer for Lockheed. One rainy winter day in algebra class, he told us that he spent so much time driving around in a golf cart, looking for people and not finding them, that he thought he would stop wasting his time and become a teacher instead. The story was more interesting than quadratic equations, but I thought it likely that his wife's family's ownership of a large chunk of riverfront real estate near town had more to do with his sudden career change. Right now, he looked as though he thought that pounding algebra into our heads was a waste of his time, too.

By tradition, male math teachers also coached junior varsity basketball and tennis. The tennis year began in March, with a sign-up sheet posted on the sports bulletin board, in the hall between the girls' and boys' locker rooms.

I never learned why tennis was the only exception to the "no girls" rule for interscholastic sports in California, but with only five or six slots, the opportunities were limited. Years later, when girls played full schedules of basketball and volleyball and track, the biggest fans, the most rabid sports mothers, were women of my generation who had once yearned to play sports themselves.

DeAnna offered to loan me her sister's racquet, since I didn't have one of my own, but I felt uneasy about borrowing a racquet that I would have to replace if I lost or damaged it. Better to do what I did every year and use one of the school's. Just after third period gym class, I slipped into the musty equipment room and moved aside a trash can full of field hockey sticks to reach the racquet collection. I found four: two of wood, two of some kind of light metal. All good racquets were wood, in those days. One of the metal ones had a few broken strings; the unbroken strings on the other one were rusty. One of the wooden ones was so badly warped that it looked like a soup spoon. I picked the one with rusted strings as the best of a bad lot.

At noon I carried the racquet and a can of tennis balls, bought with the last of my Christmas money, onto the school's two tennis courts. The day was cool and sunny, and I sat down with my back to the green wooden backboard and ate my peanut butter sandwich and an apple. Then I started swatting balls against the backboard. I missed now and then, since I hadn't practiced all winter, but I soon recalled the rhythm of swing, connect, swing, connect. I slammed the ball harder, and the noise echoed off the wall of the science building across the lawn. Now and then my school shoes—sensible lace-up brown oxfords—slipped on the flaking concrete. I wouldn't know until years later that tennis was ever played on something besides concrete or asphalt.

Sometimes I sent the white ball over the top of the backboard. The courts were enclosed with chain link fencing, with a gate in the corner farthest away from the backboard. I ran out through the gate and trotted around behind the backboard into the wilderness of weeds and beer cans between the backboard and the hillside, found my ball, and trotted back, with a pause at the porcelain drinking fountain next to the gate. Flakes of ash drifted down on my sweater from the school's trash burner.

The boys' tennis team practiced during seventh period in mid-afternoon, and they were allowed to skip their regular gym classes for it. The girls had to practice at noon or after school, and show up at gym class besides. Marie and I had to catch the bus right after school ended, unless we could find another ride home. Mr. Oamek, the principal, wouldn't allow the girls to practice tennis during seventh period: we had already asked. There weren't enough courts, he said.

148

A week before our first tennis meet in Butte Valley, the ladder tournament schedule to determine the team's make-up still hadn't been posted for the girls. Mr. Backstrom had fobbed that chore off on Mrs. Pritchard, who had forgotten it. The six girls who had signed up gathered in a huddle and agreed that Jamie would be our top player, followed by Carla, Marie, and DeAnna. When Vicky dropped out, I had the fifth spot by default.

Tennis meets were always held on Wednesdays; on the Monday before, Mrs. Pritchard managed to find two more metal racquets, not new but in better condition than the one I had been using. She gave them to Liz and me, and at noon we volleyed across the newly erected tennis nets: two girls in leather shoes and wool plaid skirts, trying to keep the balls out of the puddles.

Just getting to the first meet was a challenge, as Mr. Backstrom hadn't bothered to arrange transportation for the girls' team. I was out chopping kindling on Tuesday evening when Marie's mother drove up and asked if I knew who was driving to the tennis meet. I shrugged and said I was just going to school as usual tomorrow, since I hadn't heard anything. She shook her head and said she guessed Marie would just have to do the same. After she left, I went inside and phoned Mrs. Pritchard, who also knew nothing. Mr. Backstrom didn't have a phone.

On Wednesday morning I climbed onto the bus and looked down the aisle at a grim-faced Marie. The bus creaked up Seiad Creek and stopped for several precious minutes to wait for someone who didn't show up. By the time Wendell had pulled over to bawl out Charlie for being, well, Charlie, Marie, and I were ready to scream. At school at last, we ran down the hall, flung our books into our lockers, snatched up our racquets, and raced for the front parking lot. Mr. Backstrom and the boys' team stood beside a station wagon borrowed from the grade school, ready to leave. Carla's mother was in the back parking lot with the girls' team, they said, but they were already leaving. We raced around the school building to the back parking lot, almost flattening Jimmy, the smallest member of the boys' team. "She's already gone," he said.

We walked back with him to the station wagon. Mr. Backstrom's mouth pulled down into a sour little line as the boys crowded into the backseats to let Marie and me ride up front. On the back side of Cade Mountain, at the roadblock, we saw Mrs. Smith's car up ahead, gathered our things, and ran to climb in with Carla, DeAnna, Jamie, and Mrs. Smith.

"What happened?" Marie asked.

"We drove down to Backstrom's last night to ask," Carla said, "and would you believe it, he said *he didn't know!* So Mom said she'd take us. We thought we'd pick you guys up along the way."

Marie and I looked at each other. "You could have called us," I said.

I turned to look back as Jamie, her olive skin pale, made a noise. "Stop the car!" she groaned, and Mrs. Smith pulled over. Jamie leapt across DeAnna's lap and vomited her breakfast onto the gravel.

149

Mrs. Smith sighed, set the brake, and turned off the engine. She walked around to the trunk and pulled out a jug full of water and a towel. "Carla used to do this all the time," she said as we all took the opportunity to stretch our legs.

"I did *not!*" Carla shrieked.

We stopped in Yreka so Carla could buy a pair of gym socks and Marie a pair of white underpants that wouldn't show through her white tennis shorts. The rest of us played in our regular gym clothes—blue shorts and a white blouse. We had never heard of tennis dresses. By the time we reached the hamburger stand at the south end of town, Jamie was feeling better, so we ordered hamburgers, fries, banana splits, and Cokes. We carried them to the city park up on West Miner Street, and as we ate them, I looked across the shaded pavement toward the house where Aunt Jo had taken singing lessons, back in the 1950s.

We drove on into the eastern half of the county, through a land of sagebrush. We crossed ridges crowned with ponderosa pines where snow on the ground reminded us that we headed toward a higher, colder land. The streets of Dorris were wide and bleak, but Butte Valley High School was much larger than ours, and they had four tennis courts. We took our time getting into our gym clothes in the girls' locker room, since the boys played first. As the courts emptied, girls filled them. DeAnna had scoped out the competition and declared that she'd rather play the fifth-place girl, so she and I switched places, and I found myself up against a braces-clad girl named April.

"You must be the one I heard about," she said.

"Which one?" I shouted across the court.

"The one who hits it where the other player isn't," she answered.

I beat her, 8-5. The girls played so-called Kramer sets, on the theory that girls had no stamina, but time was also a factor. Even the boys played only best-two-out-of-three sets, or the girls never would have reached the courts at all.

Jamie sat on the sidelines, rubbing her lean brown calves. "They're cramping up," she complained. "Can you go see if Mr. Backstrom has any salt tablets?"

Mr. Backstrom paced outside the chain-link fence, his arms crossed over his chest. "Who wants them?" he asked. I pointed at Jamie, and his lip curled, ever so slightly. He looked back at Jimmy, engaged in a fierce rally with a husky Butte Valley player. For a moment, I thought he wasn't going to answer me.

"Look in the back of the station wagon," he said at last. I stared across the wide dead lawn to the parking lot, and began to trot. I rummaged in a cardboard box stuffed with extra cans of balls, athletic tape, band-aids, and someone's old sneakers, and found the bottle. It rattled satisfactorily, so I shook several out into my palm and ran back with them. Jamie tossed them back at the drinking fountain with a flick of her short dark hair, then sat down to massage her calves again. "Will you play doubles with me?" she asked.

"Sure," I said, and she stood up, picked up her racquet, and began to jog around the outside of the courts to loosen up.

In singles, Jamie lost to Butte Valley's number one player. In doubles, thanks to her blazing serves, we won 8-6, even though her legs cramped up toward the end. As I played the net, my school racquet broke in two just as I smacked the ball. I snatched up the racquet face from the pavement and prepared to play out the point as Jamie whipped the ball past both our opponents. DeAnna ran out and handed me her racquet.

Jamie and I were the last players on the courts that day. Mr. Backstrom and the boys had not stayed to watch. We wore our gym clothes for the long ride home.

For our next meet in Etna, in Scott Valley, Mrs. Smith drove us again. On Tuesday, I had tried to claim third place from Marie, but she towered over me and her serves were fast and accurate. I had recently acquired a decent backhand, but it did me little good.

151

Etna High School had only two courts, and the boys took so long to play that we walked downtown to kill time. Etna was rich with the kind of steady wealth that came from land and crops and cattle. The high school was new, and the town was full of churches and Victorian houses with neatly fenced yards. We bought Popsicles from a freezer in the meat market, and strolled back to the tennis courts, where the boys still played. At four o'clock, a court finally opened up and Jamie began to play against an Etna girl.

Clouds appeared, sultry mare's-tails that held in the heat and irrigated humidity of the valley. We found some shade and the Etna girls came over to talk. When the Happy Camp boys lost their last doubles match,

Mr. Backstrom left for home with them. Jamie and I played doubles again and had our opponents beaten by five o'clock. By seven o'clock, Carla had won her singles, Carla and Marie had lost their doubles, and the girl who had been waiting to play against me had given up and gone home. The stars were coming out. We drove back to Yreka, ate more hamburgers, and drove down the river. I crawled into my pajamas in the dark house at eleven o'clock.

Mr. Backstrom caught up with me in the hall the next morning. "How did the girls' games turn out?" he asked.

"We won three of the four that we got to play," I said. *Why the hell weren't you there?* I added, but not aloud.

I went out that day at noon full of righteous wrath and beat Marie, who promptly challenged me again. For the rest of the school year, we switched places about once a week.

After the spring break, we played a match against Yreka in Happy Camp. With a baseball game scheduled for the same day, I knew that Wendell would hold the upriver bus at least until after that game, but if the tennis meet lasted longer, I had no idea how Marie and I would get home.

Jamie was sick the day of the meet, so we all played one up. As I watched Marie and Carla struggle in doubles, I ran over to get a drink from the water fountain. The Yreka coach, a woman, stood nearby chatting with Mr. Backstrom. "I understand you're not much on girls' tennis," I heard her say.

"No, I'm not," Mr. Backstrom said. "It's primarily a boys' sport, and anyway the girls don't come out during seventh period to practice."

"Mr. Oamek won't let us," I protested, wiping water from my chin with the back of one hand. They looked at me—Mr. Backstrom with impatience, the other coach with interest, and I slunk away, embarrassed.

"Like talking to a wall," I muttered, as I threw myself down on the sloping lawn east of the courts, beside Jamie and DeAnna. "How do you feel?" I asked Jamie.

"Better," she said, smoothing her sweatshirt down over her stomach. "My mom drove me down. Must have been something I ate."

The bus left without us, but Marie's mother showed up, and I rode home with them, hating Mr. Backstrom for despising the girls' team. It didn't help that I had lost, too.

In April, Mrs. Smith drove us to Dunsmuir, at the south end of the county in the Sacramento River canyon. For the first time, Jamie simply refused to go, without even bothering to plead sickness. "But why won't you go?" we asked.

Jamie swiped at her eyes. "Carla says I might as well not go," she said, as she glared at the Smith car in the parking lot, where the others were loading up the trunk. "So I won't."

"She's just sulking," Carla said, as we pulled out of town. But I had seen her exchange a look with her mother. With Jamie gone, we had room for Carla's little sister Cindy, who brought along her battery-powered record player and a stack of 45 rpm's that took up the middle of the backseat.

Dunsmuir High sat on a terrace gouged out of the mountainside above the new freeway, and once again we played on only two courts. Houses in Dunsmuir clung to the walls of a narrow canyon and looked down on railroad yards and tracks, for it had been a railroad town. I knew that my real father had gone to high school here, and as we climbed the streets to the high school, I wondered which of the houses had been his. I knew that his father had been a railroad engineer, but I did not know that his mother had loathed Dunsmuir and been depressed by its dark damp winters. I knew, in fact, very little about my father's family, but I did know better than to ask my mother about them. My father's older brother, our Uncle Dave—whom our mother had actually liked—had died just after the '64 flood, but we had only learned about it months later, from Aunt Jo, not Mother. About my paternal grandmother I knew only that she and my father had eaten Sunday dinners together in Boise, without inviting my mother, and that this was just one of many reasons for which I ought to hate both of them.

153

Now, I looked up at the mountainside above the school and saw that, as Yogi Berra once said, it did indeed get late early here. Our boys sat in a row, tapping their knees with their racquets while goose bumps rose on their bare legs. The Dunsmuir girls' team had only three players. I beat the third player while wearing my sweater against the chill; Carla and I played doubles and won while Marie and DeAnna lost theirs.

The following week, as we prepared to meet the Fort Jones team at Happy Camp, Marie said that her mother would pick us up after the game. Dad shook his head when I mentioned this at the supper table.

"Marie's mother is a good lady," Dad said to me as he passed me the mashed potatoes, "but don't ever get in a rig if her father's driving."

"Why?"

"Reuben drinks a lot," Dad said. "He's never really sober. It's just not safe to ride with him." I knew that Marie's father was a logging contractor, owner of his own company. Sometimes he phoned our house in the evenings to talk to Dad, and I didn't remember him sounding drunk when I answered the phone, but from the way Dad spoke to him, I knew they didn't get along. Just how bad the situation had become, however, I would not learn until later.

REUBEN'S FAMILY COULDN'T AFFORD to have him hit bottom, at least not until the oldest son was old enough to take over the business. Marie's mother and her three children lived as allies against the old man, and, sustained by religion and his horrid example, none of them ever drank. They lived in a house without electricity on an old homestead near Horse Creek. Marie and her two brothers were handsome, clean, quiet, and smart, and their knowledge of the cold realities of life was thirty years ahead of mine.

When Dad started work for the Seiad Ranger District, he worked both with old acquaintances—logging contractors he had known in Hilt and Happy Camp—and a few new ones, including Reuben. One of his jobs was to enforce the provisions—the "C clauses"—of timber sale contracts. He spent a lot of time walking the logging units and telling loggers what they had to do to keep the Forest Service happy. Sometimes loggers didn't like what he had to tell them.

One day as Dad walked back to his green pickup after checking out one of Reuben's sales, Reuben himself pulled up next to him. From a distance, the meeting might even have looked friendly, as the logger leaned out of his truck, his elbow cocked on the open window, the brimmed hard hats of both men tipped back from their white foreheads. But as Reuben talked to Dad, his attitude grew less and less friendly. The piss-fir was telling him things he didn't want to hear, things that would cost him money. The piss-fir was telling him that he could shut him down if he, Reuben, didn't follow the contract. Reuben had signed that contract last winter, sure, but this was now, this was the logging show,

154

and by God this guy oughta cut him some slack. He fixed Dad with a bloodshot eye.

"Well," Reuben said, "you better be careful, or something just might happen to your kids."

The noise of the loader on the landing behind him faded from John's ears. "Reuben," he said, "if that ever happened, you wouldn't be able to run far enough." He held Reuben's wavering gaze long enough to make his point, then climbed into his Forest Service pickup and drove away.

AT THE END OF APRIL, the Mount Shasta tennis team came to Happy Camp, and Mr. Backstrom left us alone in algebra class while he went out to watch the boys' matches. The girls didn't start playing until after lunch, but to our astonishment, Mr. Backstrom called us all together and announced that from then on, boys and girls would share the courts at meets. I looked around and saw Mrs. Smith and Jamie's mother standing at courtside, their arms folded, and Mr. Oamek trapped between them.

Marie's mother came to pick us up after the games, with Marie's freshman brother Dwight jammed into the pickup seat with us. As we reached the roadblock, we looked back and saw Reuben, his fedora tilted back on his head, behind the wheel of his work pickup—the one with the tank of oil and diesel in the back. Dwight slid out the door to ride with his dad, and as we waited for the roadblock to lift, I peeked in the side mirror at Reuben's hatchet face. He didn't look drunk, and Dwight obviously had no problem riding with him, but as his eyes met mine in the mirror, they didn't look friendly.

Tennis, like golf, seems to bring out the worst in some people. At one match in the first week of May, my opponent went after a ball, tripped, threw down her racquet, and actually began beating the concrete with her hands and feet. She was losing in the face of my hit-it-where-they-aren't technique. When one of the boys in the other court flung down *his* racquet in a passion, the coach rushed in and fairly leapt upon him, cussing him out so vehemently that I thought a fistfight might erupt. The other girl and I paused, awestruck, and watched. Mr. Backstrom looked up in vague annoyance from his copy of *Time*.

I hadn't expected to go to the county tennis meet in Yreka in mid-May, at which only the top singles and doubles players competed, but

155

one day at lunch Carla and Marie approached me and asked if I'd like to play doubles with Marie at the end-of-season event. Carla wanted to go to San Francisco for the Senior Sneak instead. Mrs. Smith had other commitments that day, but the boys were going out in Frankie's new car. Dad shook his head. "Maybe you'd better not go," he cautioned, probably thinking of me in a car with three boys and a student driver.

"No, it's okay," I said quickly. "Jamie's mom's taking a car out, too. And besides, if I don't go, Marie won't get to play."

So on Wednesday, I stood at the bus stop as a truck pulled up with Jamie at the wheel. I peered in the passenger side. Jamie's mother, her cousin Sheryl, and Jamie's friend Ruth were already inside. Ruth held a baby on her lap, on her way to the county jail to visit her husband. I stepped back and waved them on, and hoped that when Frankie's car came along, it would stop. It did, already loaded with Mr. Backstrom, Rod, and Jimmy. We picked Marie up in her driveway and were in Yreka by nine.

The girls' tournament was played on the courts in the Yreka city park, and once more I looked around that green expanse and imagined myself as a city girl, growing up here, going to school here. I imagined myself walking down to the courts on a Saturday morning from one of those shady houses on Miner Street. I thought about these things as Marie and I walked over to change in the park restroom. We played our doubles against two girls from Etna and—playing real sets for the first time—we proceeded to lose, 6-2, 6-0.

As Jamie began her first match, Marie and I took turns as her line judge. She demolished her first opponent and moved on. Over her gym outfit, she wore a long-sleeved purple sweatshirt that hung nearly to her knees. Her bangs stuck to her forehead. As Marie watched the lines, I sat in the shade of the maple trees beside the courts, next to Sheryl. "Why doesn't she take off that darned sweatshirt?" I asked aloud. "She must be roasting in that thing."

Jamie's mother stood up and walked toward the chain-link fence around the courts. She clapped her hands and shouted encouragement as Jamie aced another serve. Sheryl leaned toward me. "She's pregnant, silly," she whispered.

I stared at her and then out at Jamie as she raced to cut off her opponent's backhand. Of course. The vomiting. The sudden illnesses.

"How far along is she?" I asked with my best attempt at clinical detachment.

"Six months. Baby's due in August."

"Somebody in school?"

"No, no. Flagman on the road project. He took off when he heard."

Good grief. I was reminded once more of how little I knew about the lives of my classmates. I remembered how Jamie had looked as she sat behind the steering wheel of her dad's truck, her blouse outside the waistband of her shorts. For me, this would have meant a big breakfast or premenstrual bloating. Jamie didn't look pregnant, but her body must scream to her every day that she was.

Marie took a break to walk down to Klander's Deli and brought back soft drinks and sandwiches for us. We ate them as Jamie won her third match. After lunch we looked up to see Mr. Backstrom and the boys, back from the high school courts. Frankie and Jimmy had already lost in doubles, and Rod in singles. Jamie sat beside us on the grass and bumped her calves against the ground to keep them loose while she waited to play again. Still in her purple sweatshirt, she leaned back and sipped a Coke and crunched ice cubes between her teeth. Mr. Backstrom had not come to watch Jamie play. He had come to fetch Marie and me. He wanted to make the five o'clock roadblock.

Jamie won, with the fierce competitiveness that had once led her to rub her tailbone raw with two thousand sit-ups. The next day, we gathered around her to admire the trophy that she carried into all her classes, her walk a bit stiff but her smile one of true, vindicated delight.

In August, she delivered her son with ridiculous ease, and by fall she was back in school, the first girl ever at Happy Camp High to break the unwritten law that females who had (openly) reproduced were not eligible for an education. The following spring, she played tennis again, and her mother came to the home matches with her grandson on her hip.

"Oh, he went over the hill," Jamie said once when someone asked her where the baby's father was. Her expression dared the questioner to make anything of it, and the desertion, she implied, was his loss, and not hers. Unashamed, she trotted out onto the court and won yet again. Jamie was my first glimpse of a paradigm in which sex—and its consequences—was just another part of life, and not the end of it, nor of the world.

Seven years later, as Billie Jean King met Bobby Riggs in Yankee Stadium, and beat him soundly, I stood in front of the television and cheered, and cried for joy and for the memory of all the girls of springtime, who had played without hope and without respect, but managed to win more than we lost, in the teeth of those who despised us.

Choices and Secrets

BETWEEN MARK'S SUICIDE AND JAMIE'S PREGNANCY, Liz and I had a lot to digest in the summer of 1966. In early July, after two weeks of clamming, crabbing, and fishing on the Oregon coast, we fell back into our summer routines. I ran up Grider Creek Road in the mornings. We worked in the garden. On hot afternoons we piled into the station wagon and headed for a swimming hole. And as we floated side by side on our inner tubes above the green depths of Seiad Creek, or pulled weeds in the garden, we deconstructed the events of the past year.

With Danny graduated, the Sullivans almost vanished from sight. Occasionally we saw his mother at the store, behind a pair of dark glasses. One day, Liz and I took Tommy for a hike up the steep trail that led up to Lower Devils Lookout, a thousand feet above the valley. He strode ahead of us with his toy rifle, his belt cinched tight, ready to protect his sisters against bears. As we paused on the five-mile-long trail to rest, we looked down on Mark's house. "Do you think that Mark's still around here somewhere?" Liz asked, her hands cupping her chin. She had never cried for Mark in my presence, not once, but now I heard her sniff.

"I don't think so," I said. "He wasn't happy here. I think when you die, you go back to where you were happy."

"Like to Grandmother's house in Hilt," Liz whispered.

We had no news of Jamie over the summer, either. But in her story we heard echoes of our own family's most notorious scandal, in which Aunt Jo had had a baby and given it up for adoption, before she met Uncle Carl. Late in the spring, rumors flew at school that one of Liz's classmates had undergone an abortion; we felt only relief for her. Yet here was Jamie, pregnant and apparently unashamed, and supported by her family. Their only outward displeasure was aimed squarely at the young man who had promised marriage and then hit the road.

Happy Camp was not Hilt; views on sex and divorce were more easygoing on the river. Many of our classmates didn't share the last names of their parents or siblings, and no one seemed to care. Perhaps

Jamie's parents simply couldn't afford the expense of either a clandestine abortion or a home for unwed mothers. As for Jamie herself, she was, she had said, coming back to high school as a senior that fall. It turned out that the tradition that barred mothers from high school was just that and had no actual force in the face of a determined student.

One afternoon, as Liz and I pondered aloud the differences between 1956 and 1966, between our aunt's history and Jamie's, Aunt Jo telephoned Mother to tell her that she was divorcing Uncle Carl for the second time.

A week later, on an afternoon in mid-July, Mother opened a letter from Jo and groaned. "She's coming to visit, and she's bringing a gentleman friend," Mother paraphrased, scanning her sister's looped consonants. "His name's Jess, and she says he's her fiancé." Mother glanced at the calendar. "Oh, my God," she said, and sat down at the table to scribble a shopping list. Jo and her beau would arrive on the same day as Grandmother and Grandfather. "I don't know where I'm going to put everybody if they want to stay overnight," she said, and Liz and I looked at each other. This, we said to ourselves, was going to be good.

OUR GRANDPARENTS DROVE UP as I hoed the strawberries in the garden. Liz clattered through the garden gate and announced them, even as I heard the whale-bodied Oldsmobile's engine dieseling in the driveway. "Grandmother's crying," she announced.

By the time I had splashed water over my face and exchanged my grubby T-shirt for a blouse, Grandfather was peering beneath the hood, his sleeves rolled up to reveal his hairy, well-muscled forearms. Mother spoke to Grandmother through the rolled-down passenger-side window, and sure enough, I saw Grandmother wipe her eyes as Mother shepherded her out of the car and into the kitchen, planted her on the far side of the table, and stuck a cup of tea in front of her. One by one, we presented ourselves for hugs and approval, and the conversation was not allowed to turn to what had upset her. She wouldn't mention *that*, I knew, until she was alone with Mother again. Liz looked at me. "Whaddya bet they were at Jo's before they came here?"

Dad came home for lunch, peered into the Oldsmobile's viscera with Grandfather, and as they came up the steps together I heard him say, "Well now, Bill, if it ain't broke, don't fix it." Halfway through our sandwiches, a strange car pulled into the driveway, and Aunt Jo unfolded from it, her ringing voice carrying across the lawn. A man—thin, blond, and diffident—followed her into the house. Grandmother shot a furtive glance at Grandfather, who had looked up as though poleaxed, his lower lip falling slack.

"This is Jess Schoolfield, my fiancé," Jo announced.

After a strange and silent lunch, during which Grandfather barely acknowledged either Jo or Jess, Mother pounded cracker crumbs into an acre or so of round steak, while Grandmother chopped onions and parsley on the worn cutting board. The rest of us dispersed around the property. Grandfather took a nap in Mother and Dad's bedroom, and Jess dozed on the lawn, a newspaper over his face. At Mother's suggestion, Liz and Tommy and I took Jo and her children for a walk up Grider Creek Road.

As the toddler's stroller rolled over the chip seal, the conversation drifted, as it always did with Aunt Jo, to the old days in Hilt, and I sucked in my breath as I remembered something I had just read in the Yreka newspaper. "Ronnie Chase is dead," I announced.

Liz and Jo stared at me. "How?" they demanded at once.

"It didn't say," I answered. "But it wasn't a car wreck. Remember he got married last year?"

"Had to, you mean," Liz said.

Jo looked puzzled for a moment. "Ronnie?" she said.

"He was a year ahead of me in school," I explained. "He had an older brother named Lester, and a sister named Gloria."

"Lester," Aunt Jo murmured. "He was Lester Sr.'s son."

"Yeah," I said. We walked on for a few minutes. Jo sat down on a stump beside the road as Liz ran ahead with Sid and Tommy to look for wildflowers.

"I knew their father very well," she said, and her voice deepened. "When I was just thirteen years old, I used to go over to Candace's house, and we'd look at him over the back fence. He was so handsome, with that black hair and those blue eyes and those long black lashes. And those muscles ... We used to watch him chopping wood. And when I came back to Hilt, after I left Carl the first time, he was still there." She looked over at the little girl in the stroller, and something clicked at last.

161

"He was right next door," I said.

"Yes," Jo said.

LATER THAT AFTERNOON, with Jo and the kids down for a nap in their turn, Grandfather came outside and walked with Liz and me. He admired the garden and his strides lengthened as we led him up Walker Creek Road. "Where's Jess from?" Liz asked. The strange thick drawl with which he had thanked Mother for lunch marked him as a southerner. Grandfather's wide nostrils pinched inward. "He's from Arkansas," he said, "an Arkie, an ignorant, white trash … Arkie." Behind his trifocals, his brown eyes swam and his voice had grown thick with something like anger or grief. And we knew, right then, that in his eyes Jo couldn't have made a worse choice unless she had fallen in love with a Negro. Grandfather despised southerners of any color.

Dad came home early, having been telegraphed an earnest plea for help from Mother at lunch. He washed his hands and opened two cold cans of beer, and sat with Jess in the cool living room. And now I saw a new side of Dad, for he spoke kindly to this stranger, and Jess, sipping on his beer, relaxed visibly as Dad asked him about hunting and fishing in Arkansas. His pale eyes lit up as he talked about gators and catfish and white-tailed deer thick in the woods—species that Dad had never seen. Dad asked about buckshot loads for deer, and Jess told him about gigging for bullfrogs in the swamps, and about hounds that treed coons and possums at night. Dad asked Jess what he did for a living, and upon learning that he had always worked in the woods or in lumber mills, the conversation veered into a technical discussion of logging and sawmilling methods in Oregon and Arkansas, with each man learning something from the other. Dad rose and offered the visitor another beer, and they adjourned to the front porch to continue the conversation, while Grandfather hid behind the newspaper and ignored them.

162

THAT EVENING, I DRAGGED THE PHOTO ALBUM that Liz and I shared out from under her bed and flipped through the pages until I found the picture I sought, a school photo of Gloria Chase, taken when she and Liz were both in the second grade. The black-lashed eyes stared out at me; the curly dark hair framed her white face. "Jesus Christ," I said, and ran to fetch Liz.

After dark, Liz and I lay in our sleeping bags on the side lawn, and talked about Jo and her youngest child and Lester Chase. We both knew that when Jo lived in Hilt for those few months between her first divorce and remarriage to Carl, she had flirted with Lester, who lived next door with his wife and three children. Mrs. Chase, at least, suspected something, and Grandmother and Mother had, too. As long as Jo lived with her parents, their opportunities to meet alone were limited, but after Jo was back in Talent with Carl, Lester came to visit while Carl was at work. And so she enjoyed the company of a man with wavy black hair and blue eyes, a man who smelled like the Hilt sawmill, like the home she had lost. In years to come, Jo would tell us that she knew he would not come to her forever, and so she set out to conceive his child, a bit of the old lost world that would remain when he was gone.

"But isn't it wrong to sleep with one man while you're married to another?" I asked, looking up at the constellations. "That's adultery." I had read the Bible all the way through the winter before, and thought I had a good grasp of sin.

"But what if you really love the other guy, and you don't love your husband?" Liz replied.

"Then you should get divorced first," I said primly. "That's what Mother did."

"Well," said Liz, "the Catholics think *that's* still adultery, and even the Episcopalians wouldn't let Mother get remarried in the church."

As I pulled the canvas up over the sleeping bags to guard against the falling dew, I had no answer for her.

"Well, Jo says they're getting married in September," Mother announced at supper a couple of days later, her house blessedly clear of company.

"Grandfather doesn't like Jess, does he?" Liz piped up.

"Of course not," Dad said. "Why do you think she's marrying him?"

ALTHOUGH THE FINAL BREAK WOULD NOT COME for a few years, by marrying Jess, Jo set in motion a chain of events that eventually put a couple of thousand miles between herself and her father. Dad knew,

163

as he talked to Jess and heard the homesickness in his voice when he talked of long nights on slow rivers, that Jess would return to Arkansas someday, and to a way of life foreign to Jo and her children. For Jo's fiancé, whether consciously chosen or not, did indeed represent everything that Grandfather hated, the opposite of the life he had wanted for the daughter who had once been his baby, his favorite. Jo had discovered many ways to rebel against her father, but her second husband was the most effective of all. When she left us that summer, with smiles and waves, I watched her two children—their eyes brown and blue in tanned faces—staring back at us as they leaned from the car windows and waved good-bye. Sidney's brimmed with tears at leaving his grandfather, and as the car turned onto the highway, Grandfather removed his glasses and blew his nose.

I watched my cousins leave and for the first time felt a tug of attachment to them, a sudden yearning to yank them from the car and back to our house, back to a place that was safe, and clean, and orderly. I wished we could adopt them.

"Those poor little kids," said Grandmother, and Mother linked arms with her, and gently led her into the backyard to look at the zinnias.

EARLY IN AUGUST, RIGHT ON SCHEDULE, the sky grayed and the air cooled. We shoveled the long-cold ashes from the Ashley heater, and built a modest new fire. Liz appropriated one end of the kitchen table to make a dress, and ran up seams on Mother's portable Singer, filling the room with a pleasant rumble. The noise mingled with the tap of typewriter keys as, with the collegiate dictionary open before me, I worked on my summer project: a lexicon of English words derived from Old Norse. Mother, perhaps inspired by the coolness, stirred cake batter and cookie dough, and as I glanced out the kitchen window onto the yard and the gray ribbon of highway below, I felt a happy coziness.

With the cake in the oven, Mother reheated a cup of coffee in a saucepan. Liz, her mouth full of pins, narrowed her eyes and asked—as though Jo had left only yesterday instead of a month ago—"Why was Grandmother so upset about Aunt Jo? It's Jo's life, and she can't do much about it, so why was she so worried?"

Mother took a sip of coffee, sighed, and said, "Because she thinks it's her fault."

"Her fault? How could it be *her* fault?"

"It doesn't make any sense, I know, but she thinks that something she did, a long time ago, is somehow responsible for how Jo turned out. Your grandmother," Mother said, "believes that she's cursed. It's the Old Country coming out in her."

We stared at her. "It's because of the baby, the one that died," she said.

"What baby?"

"Your grandmother had a baby boy who died."

"But there wasn't time, was there?" I asked. Mother had given me her Bible, in the back of which she had written down family marriage and birth dates. I knew that in the year between Grandmother and Grandfather's wedding day and Mother's birth there was time for only one gestation period.

"Oh, not when she was married to your grandfather. I mean with her first husband."

"*What!?*" Liz and I yelped.

"She was married when she was very young, to someone her parents didn't like."

"What was wrong with him?" Liz asked.

Mother shrugged. "Apparently, he gambled, and her father—your Great-Grandfather Dithmart—didn't like that."

"So she had a baby …" I encouraged her. "Did she *have* to get married?"

"I never asked her," Mother said. "Although," she mused, staring over our heads at the river canyon, "that might explain why her father allowed the marriage even though he didn't like the man." She shook her head, took another sip of coffee, and continued. "But when the baby was born, something was wrong with it. He couldn't keep milk down. And then they both caught scarlet fever, and the baby died."

"What happened to her husband?"

"Her parents had the marriage annulled after that, and knowing Grandfather Dithmart, he probably told the man to go away and not come back."

I remembered the stories about Niels Dithmart's horrendous temper. He had once horsewhipped a barber who shaved off his prized handlebar mustache as he snoozed in the barber's chair; he wouldn't have hesitated to chase off his daughter's wayward husband.

"Does Grandfather know about this?" I asked.

"Oh, she had to tell him about the marriage and the child, but later on, when Jo turned out so wild, she thought that it was her mistake carrying through into the next generation and continuing to punish her. And in the end, because she married your grandfather, it separated her from her family. She still has a lot of guilt about not being able to be with her own mother when she died."

"But Grandfather thinks that Jo inherited her bad traits from *his* grandmother's family—those Kentucky moonshiners," I said. "He doesn't blame Grandmother."

"And women don't *have* to get married," Liz pointed out. "She didn't *have* to marry Grandfather."

"But back then, most women didn't have a chance for a real career," Mother said. "Her parents could only afford to send her as far as the eighth grade; after that she went to work at the bakery. She always wanted to be a nurse, but she couldn't afford the schooling. And after the annulment—well, all her friends would have known what had happened. She needed to get away."

"And then when Jo turned out so different from you, it must all have come back to her," I said.

"There was enough blame to go around," Mother said bitterly, "without your grandmother taking any of it upon herself. And Jo's a grown-up now, too."

Liz ran up another seam, then picked up the scissors to slash at threads. "We know about Lester Chase," she announced.

"Did Jo tell you?" Mother asked.

"She dropped some hints," I said, "and then the baby looks so much like Gloria."

Mother nodded. "Well, you were bound to find out someday. But don't mention it to your grandfather. I don't think he knows. Or if he does," she added, "he doesn't want to admit it to himself."

Fire on the Mountain

IN THE LATE 1950S, Dad became a bow hunter. Back then, reverting to such a primitive weapon was considered odd, and the compound bows now widely used were unknown. He used a straight bow with a fifty-five-pound pull that took a great deal of strength just to string. On summer evenings in Hilt, he walked down to the old baseball diamond and shot at box targets. When his quiver was empty, Liz and I ran ahead of him onto the knoll behind the target to search for stray arrows, for he missed a lot at first.

Mastering the bow gave Dad access to an early archery season for deer that began in late August. But after seven years, he had yet to kill a buck with his bow. He missed several, and once he tracked a wounded buck for miles before the blood trail gave out. But every season was a new one, so on Saturday of the Labor Day weekend of 1966, House Brannon loaded weapons and sleeping bags and the camp stove into the back of the pickup, and drove upriver. We turned off into the Horse Creek drainage and zigzagged on wash-boarded logging roads up into the high country below Dry Lake Ridge. White fir and hemlock displaced ponderosa pine and Douglas fir. Dad pulled over to string his bow and rest it on the seat between Tommy and Mother. Liz and I rode in the pickup bed, the 12-gauge shotgun rolled up in a blanket near our feet.

As we approached the ridgeline, we saw Dry Lake Lookout above us, and broke out of the forest onto a series of wide meadows pocked with gopher mounds. We rolled under the lookout and followed the ridge toward the east. We passed a camping spot called Deer Camp, but the last campers had left it in a mess, so we drove on and found a grove of trees on the south side of the ridge. Once, Dad said, this flat spot had been a logging camp. The buildings were all gone now, but a stream gurgled nearby, bordered by a thicket of stunted alders. A hundred yards away, the northern edge of the Haystack Burn began: an ocean of eleven-year-old brush.

Dad strung rope between two trees and threw a sheet of canvas over it for a tent. Mother clipped low-hanging fir boughs with the pruning shears, and Liz and Tommy and I dragged them into the tent to make a bed. After lunch, Dad took up his bow and slung his quiver of tanned deer hide over his shoulder. I loaded the shotgun and called the dog. Together we walked the road to the top of the ridge. To the east was Buckhorn Mountain, epicenter of the great fire of 1955. Above the road, atop the ridge, stood a jumble of donagers—jagged boulders a couple of stories high, like megalithic monuments.

"Go ahead and hunt down in below them on the north side," Dad told me. "Keep bearing toward the sun. There's alder thickets down there, should be some grouse."

Then he left me, and dropped over the horizon on the south side of the ridge, down into the burn. I climbed up to the base of the donagers and looked around. On the north side of the ridge, an alder patch spread before me, and I called Bob and walked down toward it. Bob charged ahead, and three bucks popped up from their beds in the brush and pronked away into a draw. They floated high in the still hot air, as if in slow motion, and then Bob's high breathless yips rose as he leapt after them. I whistled at him but knew he wouldn't hear me until he tired. I leaned against a boulder and waited. Five minutes later, muddy and panting, Bob flung himself at my feet. I unrolled some cookies wrapped in waxed paper and ate them. Over his panting, I heard the skittering of towhees in the snowbrush. Grouse should come to water soon, but the dog had doubtless disturbed the whole neighborhood. Something wriggled in my peripheral vision, and I turned to see the ears of a doe in the foliage just uphill from me. Bob had fallen asleep.

Branches moved in the breeze, birds called and rustled, chipmunks flirted their tails and squeaked at us. High in the trees on the ridgeline, Douglas squirrels scolded. We hunted their larger cousins, the western gray squirrels, but these reddish mites weren't worth a shell. And just for now, in all the world, I heard no human voice, no truck engine, no chainsaw or airplane. I was alone in the universe, and in the absence of civilized noises I had time to think. This was, after all, Dad's hunt, not mine. If I managed to get a grouse, well and good, but that wasn't the purpose of the trip. I wouldn't be held accountable, at the end of the day, for where I had been or how hard I had hunted. No demands were made, no results expected. Dad would hunt for miles into the burn, and at dark we would find our separate ways back to camp. For the rest of this day, until the sun fell—I had to keep reminding myself—absolutely nothing was expected of me. I had no obligations at all. If I liked, I could simply sit here, with the boulder warm at my back and the spicy tang of bruised snowbrush leaves in my nose, and wait.

Across the swale with its slow clear stream and alder thicket, the forest began again, a gathering of pointed firs that marched up to yet another ridge. No roads cut across the hillside; the Haystack Burn ended here, and with it—so far—the logging. Across the creek an ancient world began. I cradled the shotgun in the crook of my arm and worked my way down the slope and across the creek, then went up into the timber. Mountain quail spoke to each other in the alders, and I heard the whirr of their wings as they panicked at the approach of the dog. I wondered when quail season started; I had forgotten to check.

I hiked toward the far ridge, up into the fir forest, and the closer I came to it, the larger and farther apart grew the trees. Undergrowth thinned and then vanished, except for such plants as did not love the sun: trillium and twinflower, pipsissewa and the dried brown stalks of snow plants and pinedrops. The trunks of the old trees, four feet in diameter, were scarred by fire, but around the occasional giant sugar pine lay piles of shed bark, like pieces of a jigsaw puzzle poured out upon the ground. Duff covered the forest floor in a thick carpet.

I reached the ridge, where the signs of a deserted trail were visible: the compacted surface once trodden by mules and horses; the bark of a trailside tree scarred by an axe blaze now almost healed over; a silvery log cut away not by a chainsaw but by a crosscut. More recent deadfalls had not been cleared away, for this trail had been abandoned by the Forest Service. But like the beckoning nave of a cathedral, the forest pillars flanked the pathway, and I saw that it must connect to Dry Lake Ridge. I followed it south, and as the sun touched the western horizon, I glimpsed the donagers again through the tree canopy, and worked my way toward them. By the greenish light of dusk, I found the road again and walked into camp, where Tommy shot his toy bow and arrows, Mother worked on a watercolor, and Liz prepared to build a fire in the

169

circle of stones near the tent. I heard Mother wonder aloud whether she should start the Coleman stove and heat some water. I broke the shotgun and removed the shells, and just then Dad strode into camp.

He had gone out wearing a red wool shirt and a red wool cap—fluorescent orange was a decade away—but now his head was bare and his light brown hair, sticky with sweat, stood out from his ears. He wore a very bloody T-shirt, and a dark bundle dangled from his left hand.

"I got one!" he announced, and leaned his bow against a tree. "After all these years!"

He set down the bundle—a heart and liver wrapped in his red shirt. He took a long drink of water from the canteen that hung from a tree branch. "The buck's way over on the other side," he said in answer to our questions, and in a few moments we had piled into the pickup and were bouncing down the road. I soon lost track of where we were, but after several miles Dad parked on an old road that ended on yet another ridge. Around us, the low brush of the burn rustled in the almost dark. We walked downhill behind Dad, until he knelt beside a blackened stump. He stood up grasping the antlers of a forked horn, and I slid down to help him drag the carcass uphill. Behind us, Liz and Mother lifted a hind leg apiece, and together we pulled the stiffening body toward the truck, while Bob clamped onto a cloven hoof and seemed to try to help.

Back at camp, Dad skinned the buck by the light of the campfire, and tossed scraps to Bob, planted five feet away. Mother heated beans and made coffee and boiled corn-on-the-cob atop the Coleman stove. Liz and I spread another piece of canvas over the fir boughs beneath the tent, and rolled out the sleeping bags over that. Late that night, as we tried to sleep, a waning moon rose, and Bob barked from his post under the kill.

We broke camp in the cool of the morning and were on our way home while Liz and I still shivered under our sweatshirts. We stopped only once, when Dad saw a rabbit by the side of the road. "Want some rabbit stew?" he called back through the open window. "Shoot the rabbit." I slid two shells into the shotgun barrels and shot the creature with one of them. It bounced and fell dead. At the outflow of a culvert beneath the road, Dad stripped the loose pelt off with one smooth motion, pulled the innards out, and tossed them away. I tucked the rinsed carcass into a pillowcase while Dad washed his hands and then fished the hunting regulations out of the glove box and consulted them. "Season's been open since July," he said, and we put the rabbit into the cooler and drove to the mouth of Horse Creek, and then down the river to Seiad.

We stopped at the Ranger Station in Seiad, to have the buck tag validated. We saw Laurie, wife of one of the junior foresters, riding her bicycle around the compound. "Wait till I tell Ray!" she shouted, and pedaled off to their trailer behind the office. Ray trotted over and grinned as though the feat had been his own. "Look what ol' Brannon did!" he crowed.

The fire crew gathered around to look, as Tom Neenan, the district ranger, came out to sign Dad's tag. "What'd you shoot it with, a .30-caliber bow?" I heard someone say, and looked up to see Wilbur, the game warden's son. Wilbur, only in his twenties, was already a tub of lard, which I found odd since both of his parents were thin. The older Mr. Straight patrolled the Klamath River basin as far west as Seiad and as far north and east as Hilt. We had known him while we still lived in Hilt, and I remembered that he had once suspected Dad of poaching. To this day, his eyes narrowed above his dark mustache whenever he ran into us in the store.

"No, I did this legit, now," said Dad pleasantly enough, but I recognized the flash of anger in his blue eyes. Some questions from the other members of the fire crew brought out his terse account of the hunt. He had shot the buck in the brush, from a range of about seventy-five feet. His arrow had gone through the ribs and penetrated the lungs. He pointed out the place on the carcass, jabbing a finger into the hole now shrouded by a cotton deer bag.

When the deer at last hung in the cool garage, Dad took a nap, Mother baked a pie, and Liz and I took Tommy fishing down at the mouth of Walker Creek. We dined that night on fried buck liver with onions. The next morning was Labor Day, and Dad slipped out of the house before sunup to swathe the carcass in heavy blankets against the coming heat.

Around five in the afternoon, just as Dad prepared to take Tommy fishing, the telephone rang. "I have to go," he announced as he hung up. "There's a fire down by Happy Camp."

171

As he climbed into the pickup, he called to Mother. "If I'm not back by Thursday, take the buck in to Yreka and have the butcher cut it up." When deer were butchered at our house, Dad was always in charge of cutting and Mother of wrapping.

We had seen Dad leave for fires many times before. Fire calls usually coincided with a thunderstorm, so when we heard the first rumbles, we set the table early while Mother hurried supper. We let Bob in the house so he could hide beneath Tommy's bed, and the air filled with ozone, static electricity, and a taut expectancy. Dad came home, ate, and left wearing one of the new orange fire shirts that were supposed to be flame-retardant.

Of this fire, we knew only that it hadn't been started by a lightning strike. But just as the sun went down, something rose above the trees west of the house—a white, boiling cloud like a cauliflower that expanded into a fading sky.

"Oh, dear," Mother muttered as her eyes followed our pointing fingers, and ran inside to make some phone calls. As she returned, we heard the first low grumble of a B-17 retardant bomber, headed downriver.

"Well," Mother announced, as she stood on the front lawn with her arms crossed above her floury apron, "they say that it started right above Happy Camp, across the road from Zink's place, and burned up into that old burn above the road just as you start up Indian Creek. The convicts from the honor camp are on it, and it's about three hundred acres. Maybe," she added caustically, "if everybody hadn't been downtown, somebody would have seen it before it blew up."

172   This Labor Day had marked the inauguration of Bigfoot Days, one of those perennial Chamber of Commerce-type events germane to small towns. This one honored Bigfoot, our region's contribution to cryptozoology. The festivities had included a parade that featured one of the town fathers in a gorilla suit, posturing in a cage on wheels towed by a truck.

After dark, Liz and I unwrapped the buck. We swiped a few hairs and blood clots from the chest cavity with a damp cloth before pulling the cotton bag shut again. Dad didn't come home that night. At three o'clock, the yard light at Alexanders' went off, and when I got up to look around, I saw the whole neighborhood dark except for a muddied sliver of moon behind the smoke.

The power was still off when we rose at six o'clock. We draped the buck in his blankets again and used a trickle of water—for the well pump was off, too—to wash our faces and teeth. We dressed and ran for the bus stop. As we approached Happy Camp, the smoke grew thick. In the mill parking lots lines of buses, Forest Service trucks, and fire engines waited. Tanker trucks stood backed up against the river to suck water. Men milled around the vehicles.

At school, our teachers seemed more than usually clueless, and all except Mr. Tristan had a hard time keeping our attention. In the afternoon, the wind picked up and blew hard from the southwest, taking the smoke out of town but driving great boiling columns of white into the sky, colored an angry reddish-brown at their base. This meant a running crown fire, with great heat at the base, and flames that seared the tops of trees. On the bus ride back upriver, we watched a bomber drop a load of retardant onto the fire.

We ran up from the bus stop to fill Mother in, but thanks to Mr. Alexander's CB radio, she had already heard that the fire was about twenty-three hundred acres. At school we had heard that the fire had raced across the mountainside above the houses on Indian Creek. "Last night, it lit up our whole yard," one girl told me. The fire had a name now—Indian Ridge—and it had spread eastward into the Thompson Creek drainage. With the daytime temperature stuck in the nineties, rain was out of the question.

The next morning at the bus stop, Eddie Alexander told us that all the people who lived at Thompson Creek had fled upriver with all their furniture. As we passed Thompson Creek, we looked up to see smoke rising only about four hundred yards behind the houses. We crept past fire engines parked along the road. In Happy Camp, smoke hung like winter fog.

A girl in my class nursed a baby rabbit in a shoebox, its legs burned by the fire. At noon, as I shopped for new gym clothes at Hooley's, I heard someone say that three firefighters were missing. Rumors abounded. Slater Butte Lookout had been evacuated. No, it hadn't. Slater Butte Lookout was burned. No, it wasn't, and the lookout was back on duty. The sun had vanished, cars ran with headlights, and streetlights came on against the gloom.

173

As we passed Thompson Creek that afternoon, we saw a thin line of fire, about twenty yards above the road, too regular to be part of the wildfire. Strings of flame looped around tree trunks. The firefighters were doing a burnout to hold the fire above the road. The night before, the fire had jumped the river and sent smoke jumpers after spot fires near China Creek. In Seiad, the smoke hung so thick that our eyes smarted. Visibility had shrunk to fifty yards.

On Thursday morning, I helped Mother load the buck into the back of the station wagon. On the school bus, as we drove slowly through the smoke, we saw a dozen Greyhound buses parked along the road east of Thompson Creek, near Fort Goff. "They're setting up another camp here," someone said. At Thompson Creek, files of strange dark men lined up beside the highway, tools in hand as they peered upward at the flames that crawled through the duff. "Indians from New Mexico," Wendell said.

I saw Tom Neenan stride along the road, but we had not seen Dad for four days. Someone at the ranger station claimed to have seen him on the fire lines, and told Mother that he was working the night shift. Reports of injuries came in—branches fell on heads, men panicked in a tight spot and spread fear down the line. With smoke so thick, no retardant bombers could fly. Mother phoned Trella Loquet up Indian Creek, and they comforted each other. Trella credited a timely burnout behind their house with saving their place from the main fire.

We came home that day to find Mother cutting up the buck at the kitchen table, all by herself. She had taken the precaution of phoning the locker plant in Yreka before she drove in. "Can't do it today," they told her, "we're swamped with all this 4-H beef from the county fair."

174

The buck weighed more than Mother and I didn't like to think about how she'd gotten it into the house, but Liz and I changed our clothes and pitched in to help. We sawed up the ribs and cut and wrapped steaks and tenderloin. We gave the dog several bones, which he guarded jealously from the cat. Mother had to saw the buck's head off further down the neck than usual to cut out the maggots. We piled scraps into the roaster pan and shoved them into the refrigerator to be ground up later for hamburger. We put a box of unusable bones and fat into a cardboard box, to be taken to the dump later (we had learned the hard way that too much of either wreaked havoc on Bob's digestive system). Hours later, we straightened up and looked at each other, proud of having cut up a whole deer all by ourselves, with no male help. Mother heated tomato soup and we put our feet up and chuckled at our competence and cleverness.

Friday was a school holiday, so we slept late before a morning of grinding hamburger. We wrapped the lumps of ground meat and put them into the freezer with the other packages. A man came to the door and told us that Dad would probably be home soon. "I was just with him on a fire up Tim's Creek," he told us.

"How is he?" Mother asked.

"Getting grouchier all the time," the soot-covered man laughed. "We only get around three hours' sleep out of twenty-four." Mother gave him a package of venison steak as he left.

That evening, a Forest Service truck pulled into our driveway and Dad climbed out, bearded and dirty and reeking of smoke and ash. He laughed as we gathered around him and told him how Mother had dealt with the buck.

We had already had supper, but we sat at the table and watched Dad eat. "Last night," he told us, "they sent us up to Tim's Creek—that's way up in Thompson Creek. We started walking at seven o'clock and got to the fire at three-thirty in the morning. We had a crew from Yreka, and one man got hysterical, said his brother's house was down there in the path of the fire. Of course there wasn't any house down there, but I finally had to have someone take him back down."

"What was wrong with him?" Tommy asked.

"Booze," Dad answered as he picked up a venison sparerib and bit into it.

175

"The paper said the fire was started by lightning," Liz said.

Dad shook his head. "No, it wasn't. They've arrested a man for starting it."

"How big is it now?" Mother asked.

"Probably twelve thousand acres," Dad said, and then we all shut up and let him eat. Then he took a bath and fell into bed.

We awoke to see truckloads of horses headed downriver to haul supplies up to fire lines where no roads ran. More Greyhound buses plied back and forth, strangers to the river highway. Dad drove down to the station after breakfast, but when he learned he wouldn't be needed until that evening, he came home and slept again. In the afternoon, he loaded the garbage cans into the pickup and made a dump run.

By evening, I picked zucchini and crookneck squash under a clear sky. The temperature fell to eighty, and when I tapped the barometer next to the front door, it had dropped a bit. The B-17s returned. After supper, another Forest Service truck climbed the driveway. Dad put on his hard hat, slung his packsack behind the cab, and climbed in.

On Sunday morning, as the four of us sat down to breakfast and looked out at a cool and cloudy day, Mr. Straight knocked on the door. I opened it and was about to ask him in for coffee when he cut me off.

"What did you do with your buck ribs?" he said. Mother and Liz stood behind me now.

"We ate them," we answered, almost in unison.

"Someone dumped some buck ribs at the Seiad dump a day or two ago," he continued. "I'm sure it was you." He looked very angry as he went on to say that although in Dad's case, he wouldn't press charges (*Why not?* I thought. *You already think he poaches*), wasting game could get him discharged from the Forest Service.

Mother, her voice remarkably steady considering that Mr. Straight had just threatened her husband's livelihood, explained how we had thrown out a couple of ribs because of the arrow hole and some maggots, and maybe all the meat wasn't off of them because she had never cut up a buck before. When he demanded to see the hide and antlers, Liz and I led him out to the woodshed roof, where we had laid them out of reach of the dog. A few sated yellow jackets gnawed on drying fragments of fat and muscle.

"Well," Straight rumbled, "I had a complaint, and I want John to go down and see Judge Toleman about this." He scribbled something on a pad of paper, turned his back on us, marched back to his truck, and drove away.

I tried to remember what had been in that box of bones that Dad took to the dump, but all I could picture were the neck and back vertebrae, one hind leg bone, and one front leg bone. I couldn't understand what Mr. Straight was so upset about. We had always thrown some deer bones away. Some people boiled them, but the results were scarcely edible.

I walked back to the house and found Mother sobbing at the kitchen table, while Liz patted her shoulder. "It's all my fault if he's fired," she wailed.

"Nobody's getting fired," I said stoutly, but I hadn't liked the look on Straight's face.

Mother had just calmed down enough to start clearing the table when Dad drove up. I ran outside to meet him. "Straight was just here," I said. "Don't be surprised if Mother's crying when you go in."

He dropped his hard hat and pack on the front porch and as he opened the door, Mother flung herself into his arms and bawled. Between the three of us, we repeated what Straight had said, as Tommy hugged Dad's legs. Dad patted Mother on the back and looked at Liz and me over the top of her head. "None of you did anything wrong," he assured us. "I seen his truck down at the station," he added, his usually impeccable grammar failing him in the face of Mother's distress. "I'll go back down and talk to him." He jumped into the truck again, and was back in twenty minutes.

"Everything's all right," he said as he sat down on a kitchen chair and began unlacing his ash-smeared boots. "Straight just wrote out a warning ticket. He got a complaint so he had to investigate."

Later, over supper, he once again assured Mother that she hadn't done anything wrong. "Somebody who was jealous," he said, "probably told Straight about it. Lots of people think bow hunters shoot the deer with a gun and then stick an arrow in it," he added. "And everybody in town knows we got that buck."

As I turned the matter over in my mind, I decided that Dad, usually so careful not to show off his kills, not to parade them around as so many other hunters did, had allowed the joy of his first successful bow hunt to go to his head. Rather than driving over to see Frank Waldo or Ernie Weinberg—two Forest Service officers who lived away from the compound—he had driven into the station and let everyone see his prize. He would never again, I guessed, expose one of his bucks to the public gaze.

"Who do you think told Straight?" I asked him.

"Probably Wilbur," Dad said, forking in mashed potatoes.

Days later, a woman who worked in the ranger station office filled Mother in on Dad's confrontation with Straight. "I thought John was going to punch that little weasel out," she laughed. "I've never seen him so angry. He told Straight he'd better never even look cross-eyed at you ever again, and that if he had any problems he should come to him, and

177

only to him. Straight practically threw that warning ticket at him, he was in such a lather to get out of the office. Hasn't been back, either."

And it was true that from then on, Straight seemed afraid of our mother and even of me and Liz. He ducked his head and gave us a wide berth when we met in the confines of store or post office.

The run-in with Straight created in my law-abiding brain second thoughts about peace officers. I remembered something I had heard Indian kids at school talking about the previous spring. A middle-aged Indian man had wrecked his car near Happy Camp, and rather than summon an ambulance, the sheriff's deputies who came upon him bundled him into the black-and-white, then took their time about driving him back to town and the jail. He bled to death from his ruptured spleen before a doctor ever saw him. Word spread that five hours after the accident, the driver's blood still contained enough alcohol "to hold up in court." Otherwise compassionate white people repeated this, as though that was a good excuse for not getting him to a hospital. On a visit to Bev Collord's house, I heard her father, Happy Camp's senior highway patrol officer, musing about the incident. He hadn't been on duty that night, and he seemed puzzled and upset that the man had died. "He wasn't a troublesome Indian," Mr. Collord said. "I never arrested him."

In the halls I heard bitter words from Indian schoolmates. "The county Mounties don't care if an Indian lives or dies," they said, and the suspicion that the deputies had themselves beaten the man and caused his death lingered. I had shaken my head in disbelief—then. Now, still trembling with anger from the memory of Straight's cruelty to Mother, I was not so sure.

178

BY MONDAY, THE FIRE HAD BEEN CONTAINED at about twelve thousand acres and the fire camps were breaking up. Dad went back to working regular hours. Frost covered the grass in the mornings and mist hung over the river until noon. A hint of smoke lingered, but by the middle of the month, rain had washed the air clean, and now the full extent of the damage could be seen from Happy Camp: black stems and ash in place of green timber.

Dad told us that the fire had been set by an arsonist who used a simple timing device—several wooden matches stuck headfirst into the butt end of a lit cigarette, then placed in the brush beside Indian Creek Road. "It burns down to the matches in about sixteen minutes," Dad said. "Perfect time bomb."

The fire burned no buildings, but several Forest Service trucks, parked in a brushy saddle, were incinerated when the fire blew over them. The metal on the bodies, Dad said, had melted like plastic. In the burn, deer wandered, confused and unafraid. We took a drive up into the burn and saw how in some places only ashes remained, while in others the fire had swept through so rapidly that the needles on the trees were merely singed. In a few places, thickets of trees stood untouched. We drove up Indian Creek Road once more. The fire had begun just above the road near a meadow called the Duck Pond, then blown up the canyon until it reached Loquet's place. From there it raced straight uphill toward Slater Butte and crossed Thompson Ridge onto the Seiad District, where it had killed timber equal to over three years' cut for the district. All the places behind the blue house on Indian Creek, where I used to hike, were burnt, and I knew the land would be logged next year, and it would not be the same for lifetimes to come.

By the end of September, Dad was already lining up timber sales and writing contracts for the salvage logging to come. "It'll take us two years to log our half of it," he said.

IN JULY OF 1968, Ranger Neenan sat down to write up Dad's annual performance review. Reading it so many years later, I get a sense of what life was like for a Forest Service timber staff officer in the halcyon days before all those troublesome environmental laws—the National Environmental Policy Act (NEPA), the Endangered Species Act (ESA), the National Forest Management Act (NFMA)—came to disturb the peace of the agency. The Forest Service never really accepted those laws, never really thought that it should obey them, and never quite accepted that what has been called "a conspiracy of optimism" was over. As I write this, forty-one years after the Indian Ridge Fire, the game is all but played out, but in 1966 the Forest Service still prided itself on its ability to handle any catastrophe that came its way. "We're a 'can do' organization," its employees said, without irony.

So I now read Dad's report card with a mixture of pride in his skill and chagrin that the Forest Service could operate with no checks on its power to manipulate the landscape. No one talked about "alternatives" for dealing with the aftermath of a major wildfire. The solution was obvious: log the burned areas as quickly as possible, before bugs and blue stain got into the logs, before they "went to waste." If a forester wanted to minimize erosion from roads, that was fine, but the important thing, the only real thing, was to "get out the cut." And at this, I learned, my stepfather was very good indeed.

The allowable cut for the District is 24.5 million board feet per year ... during the period from September 1966 to June 1967 he supervised the preparation of 95 million board feet of fire salvage timber, a modification of an existing sale involving 25 million board feet of fire-killed timber, and 2 million board feet of small salvage and settlement sales.

He developed a complete plan for the salvage of 120 million board feet of fire-killed timber before the fire was mopped up. He supervised the preparation of as many as four sales at once with constantly changing personnel. The first sale was sold three weeks after the fire was controlled. Six months after the fire 110 million board feet were sold or involved in contract modification.

Because of his extensive background in logging and road construction he was able to recognize needed changes in location of roads in the burned area. In spite of his greatly increased workload and the lack of time, he was able to demonstrate the need for these changes, which prevented unacceptable damage to both watershed and near-view values.

After completion of the salvage program, he began an intensive program of reconnaissance of the remaining timber on the District in order to make a logical plan for harvest of scattered and marginal areas as well as areas that will require other than normal logging methods. He suggested a timber sale requiring Skyline logging and on his own initiative demonstrated its feasibility so that it was included in the sale program.

The normal cut for the District is 25 to 35 million board feet per year. During the 1967 season the cut was more than 90 million board feet. Contract compliance was outstanding on all sales. The sale administration work was accomplished with three sale officers, only one of which was added for the increased workload. The three sale officers had a total of only one year of sale administration experience among them at the beginning of the logging season.

He coordinated the administration of twelve fire salvage sales in addition to the regular green timber sales and salvage sales. The fire salvage program involved as many as thirteen logging operations at once in the same area and as many as six operators hauling over one road. He maintained harmony among the loggers and obtained outstanding contract compliance in spite of constant conflicts among different logging operations.

NO ONE WAS EVER TRIED FOR STARTING the Indian Ridge Fire. The man arrested on suspicion proved to have an alibi. "It wasn't him," Dad told us, "but we have a pretty good idea who did it. But without witnesses, we can't place him at the scene."

He refused to tell us the name of the prime suspect. "We don't want him to know that we'll be watching him," he said. "Maybe he'll get careless next time."

But he never did. He reformed, or died, or moved, and the creation of major forest fires on the Klamath reverted to lightning and carelessness.

Seniors

THE SENIOR CLASS THAT ENTERED Happy Camp High School under the smoke of the Indian Ridge Fire was only a remnant of the largest freshman class ever. Back in September of 1963, sixty of us had filed into the gymnasium for the first time. We clattered up onto the wooden bleachers and sat clustered together like ducklings. The principal, Mr. Oamek—a penguin-shaped man with a gray comb-over—strode out onto the polished basketball court and regarded the student body with resignation. But what set us a-tingle was that he talked about us, the freshman class. We were, he told us, the biggest class ever to enter these halls. We looked at each other with anticipation and pride, and ignored the sneers from the upper classes.

Our presence seemed to vindicate the foresight of the administrators who had built a modern campus on the flat beside Indian Creek, complete with football field, track oval, tennis courts, and outlying buildings for science and music. Our school dated only from 1957: across a side street from the music building was the old log structure where many of my classmates' parents had gone to high school. Built in the 1930s with volunteer labor and donated materials, it was said to have been the only log high school in the United States.

The building was still used as a polling place, and for community pinochle parties. I had been inside once while I waited for Mother to vote. I wandered down its single hall and marveled at the ingrained smell of chalk and books that still haunted the place. The blackboards—real slate blackboards, not the green chalkboards in front of our classrooms—were still on the walls, shammied clean as if the last class had left only the day before. Two ranks of lockers stood at attention in the hallway. The proud little school had served its purpose, and two of its teachers—Mrs. Toleman and Mrs. Applegate—still taught at what they referred to as "the new school."

Our high school was a direct result of the lumber industry's invasion of Happy Camp. As the old school burst at the seams with the children of loggers and millworkers, the county couldn't ignore its obligation to educate them. Fortunately, the industrial boom had created a pile of money: the so-called 25 percent fund. Those counties with National Forest lands received a quarter of the receipts from timber sales, to be spent on schools and roads. Some of that money had been pried away from the population centers of Yreka and Scott Valley and used to build a new grade school and high school in Happy Camp. In the rush to modernize, the log high school might very well have been lost, but its oddity saved it, and it was moved across the street and preserved.

As we ran laps on the track and swatted balls on the tennis courts, as we walked to classes, flecks of ash filtered down on us from the tepee burners east of town. It never occurred to us to complain, but even if it had, someone would surely have pointed out that we should just shut up and be grateful, for the mills were, in effect, paying for our high school education.

Nevertheless, the attractions of Happy Camp High were not enough to keep some of those shining freshmen of '63 on the path to enlightenment. Our numbers dwindled over the years, as boys dropped out to work in the woods or the mills, and girls left to marry or seek their fortunes in larger towns. A few girls never even made it to high school. One of Liz's eighth-grade classmates, a bosomy girl who could pass for eighteen when she wore lipstick, was engaged at thirteen and married soon after her fourteenth birthday. What with one thing and another, then, by the fall of our senior year, the class of '67 numbered only forty-one.

Those of us still around as our senior year opened in the fall of 1966 had various reasons for sticking it out. Some wanted to play football or basketball. Many stayed under parental pressure. Some needed a diploma to go on to college. For others, sheer inertia probably played a part. But having come this far, all the seniors expected to graduate, expected to stand on the stage in the gym on an evening in June wearing a rented cap and gown to receive a piece of paper in a faux leather folder provided by the state of California.

Several of the senior girls were engaged and met with their fiancés between classes. The men appeared at least once a day, seemingly out of nowhere—Johnny and Gerald were especially faithful. Johnny worked for the Forest Service as a fire technician; Gerald worked at Siskiyou

Mills, learning the trade that would eventually make him a millwright: the man who knows how to fix everything in a sawmill. But just now they were intent on snatching five minutes with Donna and Carrie, behind half-open doors or in corners, hidden from the glaring eyes of teachers. Girls smiled slyly at the furtive caresses; even jocks regarded the older males with admiration. Along with their tang of sawdust and smoke, they carried with them the aroma of the real world, the important world beyond high school. We are doing things, their looks said, and you're not. Their arms around the shoulders of their future wives were possessive and jealous—not of the boys roaming the halls, but of the building itself, of the whole idea of formal education. We concede you this, girls, those arms said, but after graduation, you are ours. And the young women looked up at their mates with pride, serene in their choice of career. They had already left the rest of us far behind.

FOR ME, COLLEGE LOOMED, and then a career as a teacher. I had long since capitulated to my stepfather's demands on that subject, thus proving that even if my choices outmatched those of my grandmother, they were, in this year of 1967, still relative. Teaching, I told myself lately, was a good enough career: three months off in the summer, and a chance to live in the country I loved and pursue my own interests in natural history. That a fondness for young people and a certain amount of patience with them might come in handy for a high school biology teacher never crossed my mind. Instead, I wished for a flamethrower to incinerate the boys who tossed spit wads over my head at the teachers.

184

I was a bookworm still; history and thick Victorian novels, science fiction and anthropology, politics and poetry flowed through my fingers. I wrote stories and essays that my English teachers praised; they told me that I should take Mrs. Applegate's journalism class, where students saw their work in print every month in *The War Whoop*. And each semester, I thought about it but pulled back when I remembered that my real father, whom my mother hated, was a journalist. If I took the class, it would only remind her, and she might think I was growing up to be like him.

Sometimes I abandoned my sweet daydreams of murder and tried not to despise the boys in the hall who shoved each other up against lockers, tried to imagine the lives of the girls who stood before the mirrors in the restroom ratting their hair up into mounds of frizz. Mark's death had coaxed a bare curiosity about them from the depths of my uptight soul. But on no other faces, in no other photographs, did I ever catch the withdrawn sadness that I had seen on Mark's. Whatever happened to the rest of us wouldn't, I thought, involve suicide. And I was right.

Meanwhile, I had only one goal: to make valedictorian. The way to do this was to make as many As as possible. But I soon slammed headfirst into a reality called trigonometry.

"Your problem," said Mr. Salter, the new math teacher, one day in late September, "Is that you expect this stuff to make sense." A first-year teacher from Arizona, he had a habit of gazing out the window at the timbered peaks across Indian Creek and muttering about feeling closed-in. "But geometry made sense," I retorted, as I recalled the math class that had been the easiest for me. "I thought trig was just more geometry."

"Not exactly," said Mr. Salter, as he paced back and forth and jiggled a piece of chalk in one fist. Among a dozen students, I was the only girl, an isolation I felt acutely when I remembered that Lee, my chief competitor for honors at graduation, was taking no math or science this year, but was taking both choir and band, where her positions as first clarinetist and lead soprano assured her of two easy As. Physics, where I memorized formulas and rolled ball bearings down slopes, was easy after two years of algebra, but with trigonometric equations, I hit a wall.

It wasn't that I couldn't solve the equations; it was just that the way I solved them was, according to Mr. Salter, wrong. My face burned and I grew damp under my heavy school sweater as I contemplated the red C on my latest test paper. I couldn't see over Robert's shoulders as he sat in the desk in front of me, but I knew his bore an A. Robert always got As in math. And although I was by no means the slowest in the class—the chorus of groans as Salter returned our papers that morning assured me of that—the fact that my C was one of the higher grades wasn't comforting.

Liz, caught in the same situation, would have attached herself to Robert like a limpet and charmed him into tutoring her. I would rather have died than ask anyone for help, especially Robert. The simple expedient of asking the teacher did not, weird though it seems to me

185

today, even occur to me, but neither did Mr. Salter offer me any extra help. I knew I had to do something, but what?

Mr. Salter turned back to the chalkboard and worked his way through the solutions to the test problems. Up on the board, white on green, the answers seemed so clear, so simple. But why couldn't I have seen them during the test? I copied down the solutions. Later, in study hall after lunch, I would stare at them and work backward through all my mistakes, and they would seem obvious.

I looked over at the built-in bookcases that ran the length of the classroom beneath the windows. Here were extra textbooks, editions never used, and my eyes wandered over their spines. When the bell rang, I crouched down beside them and pulled out a trigonometry text.

"Can I borrow this?" I said to Mr. Salter's broad back, as he erased the morning's futilities from the board. He turned and looked down at me. "Sure," he said, and turned away again.

The days were still warm and dry, so at noon I sat beneath the goal posts, ate a peanut butter sandwich, and leafed through the book. I had chosen the teacher's edition, for the answers in the back. Perhaps if I started over, fresh from the beginning with a different book, and worked through it page by page, the subject would grow clear in my mind. I moved my finger down the first page of the first chapter as Liz and Cheryl came running up.

"Ray just got shot!" Liz panted, as she sank down beside me and slurped the last of the milkshake she had bought at the Frosty.

Cheryl nodded agreement. "The ambulance just went up to Donald's," she said.

"What happened?" I asked. Ray had never looked like the type to shoot himself, but perhaps you never knew, after all. Liz and Cheryl shrugged in unison. "He was up there, with Donald and a bunch of other boys, and they got to fooling around with a revolver," Cheryl said.

Ray was a tall thin boy with a flattop haircut and black plastic glasses. He was in a couple of my classes, where he sat in back and never raised his hand. He had a mentally handicapped younger brother who had been allowed to drift through the public schools because no one could think of anything better to do with him. Good-natured and gullible, Barry was an easy mark for smarter and meaner kids, who in grade school goaded him into such hilarious activities as eating dirt.

186

After lunch, the halls buzzed with the news, but I heard no details until I climbed onto the upriver bus. Kathy Robinson, fairly bouncing with excitement, filled me in. "The bullet went in under his chin," she elaborated, jabbing her index finger under her jawbone, "and it came out"—moving the finger up onto her headband—"through the top of his skull."

"Russian roulette?" someone asked.

Wendell heard us. "It was an accident!" he shouted, his blue eyes snapping in the rearview mirror. Ray was buried the following Tuesday, and his death was a source of horrified wonder for a couple of weeks. Had Ray been showing off with a gun he thought was empty? Had he been drunk? For obvious reasons, the boys who had been with him weren't talking. Some of us made an effort to be kinder to Barry, but whenever I smiled at him, I felt vaguely guilty, for Ray had been one of the amorphous herd of spitballers that I mentally expunged, every day. I had never exchanged a word with him.

"Why do we feel so differently about Mark and Ray?" I asked Liz one night, as we sat cross-legged on our beds brushing our hair. "Why don't we care that Ray's dead?"

"Because we never knew him, not really," Liz said, "and we never rode the bus with him."

"But he was in my class. I should feel bad, but I don't. It's sad, but it's like it didn't even really happen, you know?"

Liz nodded. "One of the kids in my class wasn't even sure who he was," she said.

We turned out the overhead light and crawled under the blankets, and I opened a book about Galileo and read by flashlight until the book fell onto my chest.

187

November

IN THE 1960S, EVERY NATIONAL FOREST had creatures called junior foresters. Just out of college, these apprentices followed journeymen foresters around like puppies to learn everything they weren't taught in forestry school: the Way of the Forest Service. In Dad's new job at Seiad as timber management assistant, he supervised several of them. Sometimes he brought one of them home for supper, and Liz and I discovered that college men were not nearly as good-looking as in the movies. Liz managed to get in some surreptitious flirting, but they were usually too frightened of Dad to return more than brief eye contact. Once I caught one of them throwing glances at my breasts. I hunched my shoulders forward and took advantage of the plate-clearing break before dessert to race back to our bedroom and throw a loose blouse over my T-shirt.

"Why did you do that?" Liz hissed at me after supper as we stood on the porch. "He was just getting interested."

"I don't want him interested," I said. We waved to our guest as he drove off, full of my pot roast and apple pie. In the summer, Liz and I each had to cook supper once a week. "They're all dorks." I remembered one in particular, whose sleepy good looks ascended to a level that Liz termed "cute," but who turned out to have narcolepsy. He fell asleep in his Forest Service pickup in the middle of the day, sometimes while actually driving. No, the only junior forester who didn't make me want to hurl was Ray, the safely married one. He arrived in Seiad in the spring of 1966 and immediately bent upon our stepfather the eyes of worship.

Slender, with already-thinning brown hair, Ray was a graduate of the University of California at Berkeley and was raised in the Bay Area. His wife Lori didn't join him until June. She had to graduate from high school first. As he sat at our table for the first time and mentioned that Lori had given birth to their first child several months before, I rested my fork on the rim of my plate and stared at him. Why, that would make her only a year older than me! How in the world had they met, courted, and married with her in high school and him in college? But those questions would have to wait until Lori herself arrived, for at our supper table she seldom drew a mention. Ray's non-job interests centered—passionately and almost exclusively—on deer hunting. One evening when we had venison tenderloin for supper, I thought he would slide under the table with appreciation.

Ray's hunting had been limited to a couple of unsuccessful outings into the Sierra Nevadas. Here on the Klamath, he hoped to improve his luck with the help of a mentor—Dad—who was also teaching him to cruise timber, scale logs, map clear-cuts, and survey roads. With this in mind, Ray bought a new .270 Remington rifle. Dad took him out to help him sight it in and soon realized that Ray was a terrible shot. But as they practiced together, the younger man improved. Liz and I were discouraged from tagging along on their outings. "You're both better shots than he is," Dad told us.

At about the same time Ray arrived, Larry was hired on as a scaler on the Seiad District. About thirty years old, with a high school education, Larry could not hope to ascend to the heights of a forester, but in the paramilitary command structure of the Forest Service, technicians were the noncoms. Unlike their professional bosses, they often stayed on one district for their entire working life. They fought fires, planted trees, maintained equipment, graded roads, helped to lay out timber sales, inspected logging operations, scaled logs, and trained many a wet-behind-the-ears forester in the practical realities of the woods. Ernie Spinks, for example, the frighteningly intelligent son of a Karuk mother and a Welsh father, had worked in Happy Camp for twenty years, and had devised the calculation tables used by Forest Service scalers all over Region 5 (California).

Scalers measured logs on the truck or at the mill and determined the amount that timber purchasers paid to the Forest Service for logs removed from the woods. Volume was measured in board feet (a board foot is a piece of lumber one foot long, one foot wide, and an inch thick), with deductions for flaws like fire scars and rot. Stories about Ernie's ability to hold the defects and net volume of several truckloads of logs in his head were legion, but he was most famous on the Klamath for the house in Happy Camp that he built on government time. On

189

slow days, Ernie walked across the street from the scaling ramp and hammered a few boards into place. If a truck pulled up to the ramp when Ernie wasn't there, the driver went to fetch him. No one ever remonstrated with Ernie for this. He had taught scores of foresters and technicians to scale and was simply too valuable to offend.

Like most men on the river, Larry could have made more money working for a logging company or in one of the mills, but a permanent job with the Forest Service provided both stability and health insurance for his wife Sonja and their two young sons. And as he worked with Dad, first as a scaler and later in the woods, something between them clicked. They began hunting together.

Mother and Sonja had nothing in common beyond their husbands' partnership and the fact that their sons enjoyed playing together. Sonja wasn't a reader and had little interest in current events; Mother shuddered at Sonja's obese body. "But she's a hard worker, I'll give her that," Mother admitted. Sonja kept her house and her children clean and neat, and took in ironing to earn extra money. When Liz started babysitting her boys, she saw Sonja's framed graduation photo: she had been a stunning brunette with only a hint of plumpness. It showed, I thought, what could happen to women who Let Themselves Go. I wondered if the absent Lori, having given birth, was blimping out, too.

THE DEER-HUNTING SEASON USUALLY RAN from about September 21 to November 1. But in 1966, the Department of Fish and Game extended the inland blacktail season until November 12. Dad and Ray and Larry licked their chops at this, for by the end of the first week in November, they knew, the first serious storms would batter the coast and move inland, driving deer out of the high country. In the hot weather of summer and early fall, deer bedded down all day, and only rose at dusk. But when the rains began, deer roamed in the daytime, slipping through soaked brush and fog, their senses dulled by the downpour. With every hunter able to purchase two deer tags, this season promised to be a productive one.

September and most of October were dry. Dad and Larry took their bows into the Marble Mountains early in September, and Dad shot a

190

bear in an alder patch. Mother rendered out the fat and fried up the best donuts we had ever tasted.

I kept track of the hunting season of my senior year in excruciating detail. It would, I knew, be the last for a long time. Chico State's schedule made coming home during hunting season impossible. I had a new rifle that year: a Remington Model 600 in .243 caliber, with an eighteen-inch barrel and a scope, replaced the old .250-3000, which Dad had traded for a .44 revolver. Other hunters who saw the 600 marveled that a deer rifle could be so small and light, but Dad assured them that it packed a wallop. He loaded the cartridges himself, as he did all the ammunition we used.

One morning early in the season Dad and I rose at 4:30 and drove to the high bridge over the Shasta River on the old highway into Yreka. We hiked up a bare ridge in the darkness, between the shadows of sagebrush and scrub oaks. Two miles up the ridge, we paused in a saddle, and I looked back and saw the sun rise as Mount Shasta glowed beside the dark silhouette of Black Butte. To the northeast, Pilot Rock, a bump on the Oregon horizon, was backlit by the lightened sky. Below us on either side, the Shasta and Klamath rivers ran like threads of mercury.

That morning, we circled the summit of a bare peak called Riverview, one of us waiting while the other walked a saddle or a draw. I sat beneath lonely ponderosa pines, rifle balanced on my knees as I waited for Dad to beat through an oak thicket. Later, we side-hilled through oak woods, a hundred yards apart, and met in on a ridge. We fought our way through brush patches, knelt beside rare springs and sipped, then scooped out a pool for Bob to drink and cool his belly. By the end of the day, we had seen only a few does and the flocks of quail that skittered through the brush. Far below us, the tinkle of goat bells came up from the Klamath side. As the sun set, we retraced our steps down the knife-edged ridge to the truck parked beside the high bridge. I rode home with a bruise on my hip and scrapes and scratches on my legs, under my worn corduroys.

We hunted in the Haystack Burn at our old place near the West Fork of Beaver Creek, and now the routine of drive-and-wait came easily to me. One day Bob drove out a deer exactly as if he knew what he was doing.

Dad shot at it, and as he watched, I followed the deer down into a draw. I found the dog standing over the fat three-point, grinning up at me.

Acorns ripened, and black bears descended on the oak groves. Dad and Larry and Ray hunted together, and shot two bears in three days. Several days later, as the families gathered to cut up the meat, we met Lori, who turned out to be a beautiful young woman with clear white skin and glowing red hair. She'd met Ray, it turned out, simply because they'd been neighbors for years. Besotted with her infant son, she seemed perplexed as to why her husband wanted to get up at four o'clock in the morning to hunt.

By October, Dad often hunted with Larry and Ray and left me behind. On those days, I drove up Seiad Creek in the station wagon—there were some advantages to having a driver's license, after all—to a series of overgrown clear-cuts where, I was convinced, I would find a buck if I just hunted long enough. Tracks were plentiful, deep tracks made by deer heavy with antlers and summer fat, but I never found my quarry. Still, as I sat motionless with my back against the rough bark of a Douglas fir older than George Washington, the actual importance of another deer for the freezer faded. When a nuthatch looked me in the eye from a foot away and was not alarmed, when the blue jays stopped treating me as an intruder, when a chipmunk raced in to inspect my boot toes, I knew I wasn't wasting my time.

At October's end, Dad and I hunted across the river from Walker Creek in a red-soiled basin where a chrome mine had operated during World War II. The Ladd Mine was long since closed, but the old ore road still looped back and forth across the open slopes. We hiked up through damp stands of madrone and live oaks, across sidehills and along ridges. We met and parted, climbed and rested. We struggled through thickets of manzanita on south-facing slopes, and Dad pulled his binoculars from his shirt and glassed several does in a clearing, their coats already dark gray and ready for winter. As the sun fell and left us in cold shade, I shivered under my hooded sweatshirt. The air smelled of the end of summer, of Halloween. On our way down, Dad gave up on deer and shot two of the many gray squirrels in the oak groves.

We entered the house at dusk, and Mother laughed as she told us how Lori had called her, in a tizzy because Ray—who had gone hunting with Larry—wasn't home yet. "She doesn't understand that when we hunt, we hunt as long as we can," Dad said.

As I cleaned and skinned the squirrels in the kitchen sink, Ray and Larry pulled into the driveway with a buck in the back of Larry's pickup, and as Dad validated Ray's tag, his grin told me that he had shot the deer himself. "That should make him feel better," Dad said. "Lori, too," Mother added.

I awoke that night to the sound of rain on the metal roof, and the next morning Dad and I drove up Walker Creek toward Lake Mountain. We met Art Price, the Lake Mountain lookout, coming down in his pickup. "Too much snow up there for me, John," he said. "Fire season's over." By the time we reached the saddle below Slinkard Peak, I saw the Devils, newly coated with snow, across the river. We hunted in a drizzle that day, water pouring off Dad's hard hat, and I envied him his "tin" coat and pants. My sweatshirt and overcoat were thoroughly soaked. The rainy season was on.

On November 9, Dad took a day off work, went back to the Ladd Mine area alone, and shot a three-point buck on the same day that Larry shot a buck while hunting with his brother. Liz and I came home from school to find Dad skinning out the three-point in the garage. "Shot him as he was looking up at me from the bottom of a rockslide," Dad said.

I stayed home from school the next day. Dad and I drove upriver and crossed the Klamath to Horse Creek. The logging roads around Dry Lake ridge were the consistency of gray jam. Even with chains, Dad's pickup couldn't climb some of the jeep trails. We retreated, then pulled over to replace a spark plug. All the way down to the junction with the main Doggett Creek road that dropped to the Klamath River Highway, we met logging trucks whose empty bunkers slithered toward us and crowded the pickup into the ditch. Dad shook his head. "They'd better shut these guys down for the winter or they'll ruin the road surface," he chided.

The next morning, Dad and I arrived at Larry and Sonja's trailer near the mouth of Grider Creek at six o'clock. We found Ray and Larry drinking coffee in the cramped kitchen while Sonja packed Larry's lunch. In the gray wetness outside, Dad and Larry climbed into the

193

cab of Dad's pickup while Ray and I hoisted ourselves into the back. We drove up West Grider Creek, passed an intersection called Four Corners on Grider Ridge, and followed the main Grider Ridge road south through open timber, as a fine mist struck our faces. When the pickup lurched to a stop, Ray and I followed the turn of the heads of the men in the cab. "Can you see anything?" Ray whispered. I shook my head. Dad's rifle barrel poked from the window, and I held my breath. The rifle boomed, the bolt flashed out and then in again, and Dad flung open the door and leapt from the driver's seat. He ran up the hill, Larry close behind, and Ray and I followed, leaping logs as we went. Larry stopped and fired a shot, off-hand, with his .30-.30 Winchester. Dad and Larry fanned out into the timber, and I heard Larry shout, "You got him!"

Dad walked toward Larry, and in a moment we all stood in a knot and looked down at the buck as he threw out his last gasps. Dad and Larry looked at me. "Your buck," Dad said. "Better fire a shot." I worked the bolt, put a shell into the chamber, and fired into a log. Without ear plugs, the noise hurt my ears.

Dad and Larry dragged the three-point down to the road and knelt to gut him out. Just as they rolled the paunch over the edge of the road, two men drove up in a truck. Dad stood and talked to them. I tried to look proud but humble as Dad's chin jerked at me, but the longer I looked at the carcass the less I wanted to claim it. Dad had shot while the animal was partially obscured by a tree—all he could really see were the antlers—and had blown away part of the abdomen and one ham. Larry's shot had taken him in the lungs and ribs. But he wore one of my tags, which Ray had validated, and with the carcass wedged against the tailgate, we drove onward into a fog bank.

Ray pulled a ski cap down over his mouth and nose, but I could only snug my sweatshirt hood tighter and zip my coat higher. My knitted gloves were damp. We parked on a side road and hiked through a series of draws on the west side of Grider Ridge until late in the afternoon. The trick was to match your pace to those of your companions, so that no one got too far ahead or too far behind. Ray tended to walk too fast, as I had when I first started hunting, while Larry and Dad moved at a measured pace. I walked between Dad and Larry, and kept track of the occasional glimpse of Dad's orange hard hat as he stepped between the big-leaf maples, and Larry's red-brimmed cap, beneath which a wisp of cigarette smoke mixed with the fog. When the evening banished all color, we met on a ridge and hiked back up to the pickup.

As I sat beside the fire that evening and read to Tommy from *The Jungle Book*, I thought about the selective hunting ethics of my three companions. Good girl that I was, I had read the hunting regulations pamphlet cover to cover, and along with the bag limits on squirrels, I learned that it was illegal to shoot a deer from inside a vehicle, illegal to put someone else's tag on an animal one had shot oneself, and illegal to validate such a tag. Yet that was how Dad and his friends operated. They took care to cover their tracks—hence the shot I had fired into the log—and they would never have shot a spike or a doe, hunted out of season, or used a rifle in bow season. None of that was worth the risk to their jobs. But in the end, the hunt was about meat, not glory, and all over these woods, men both in and out of the Forest Service believed that a tag was a tag was a tag.

"If you see more than one buck," Dad often reminded me, "keep shooting. We'll find the tags." To do otherwise was foolish and even wasteful—as was missing a shot over some scruple about not shooting from the door of a pickup. No, the law of our pack differed from state law, and acceptance by the pack was more important to me than any written set of rules. Let the weight of the rules fall on rich trophy hunters from Down Below, not on those of us who needed venison for the freezer.

195

WET SNOW FELL IN THE NIGHT. The next day, Mother had to take Liz to Medford for an orthodontic checkup, so Tommy climbed into the pickup with Dad and me. We left Bob chained up to the garage. "Still too many hunters today," Dad said.

This time our hunting party drove away from Larry's trailer in two trucks, and Ray and Larry headed for Four Corners by another road. Dad put on his truck chains in Larry's driveway. We clanked uphill, through a tunnel of bent shrubs, until Dad stopped the truck and announced, "There's some deer," just as I saw them myself—half a dozen figures in the mist, heading into the woods. "Get out and put a round in the chamber," Dad said, but I had already worked the bolt. I stepped out of the truck and ran ahead a few yards to bring them back into sight. I saw the buck in the rear of the procession, and now the deer saw me and trotted faster, their slender legs reaching over logs and scattered branches. I raised the rifle, found the buck in the scope's crosshairs, held on him, and squeezed the trigger. He disappeared behind some young trees and brush, and when he reappeared, I shot at him again, and he fell. I ran up the hill and almost tripped over him. His dark eyes had gone unfocused, and his legs thrashed in a litter of pine needles. Dad ran up behind me and patted the top of my head. "You finally did it, gal!" he said, and grinned.

As we dragged the buck down to the road, Dad told me that he had seen the deer flinch at my first shot and knew that I'd hit him. He confessed that he had shot at the buck, too, although I hadn't even heard the report of his rifle.

Tommy skipped beside us. "Someone finally shot a buck while I was along!" he crowed. I looked down at my buck's antlers for the first time and saw that I had shot a fat four-point. I pulled out my pocketknife, rolled him on his back, and began to gut him. I found a bullet hole in one of his lungs. We rolled the paunch and intestines into the brush, hoisted the carcass into the back of the pickup, and drove up the road to Four Corners to meet the others.

After the congratulations, Ray and Larry climbed into the back of Dad's pickup, and we let them out at the foot of a clear-cut while Dad drove farther up the road. He parked the pickup and we got out and hiked up toward the top of Grider Ridge to follow some shadowy deer that moved past us through the brush. As we hiked, we heard five shots in quick succession from the other side. "Maybe they got one of those," Dad said, and after a while we made our way back to the truck and drove on to the spot where Dad had arranged to meet the other two men.

Larry appeared out of the trees first. He looked at Dad and shook his head. "We saw a great big buck in that clear-cut," he said as he leaned on the hood of the truck and lit a cigarette. "And he was lying down—with his back to us—and I had Ray lean his gun against a stump so he'd have a better aim. And he missed! Then I shot at him and missed, too."

"Where's Ray now—out drowning himself?" I asked, success making me bold. Larry gave a short laugh. "Probably," he said.

Ray came around the corner of the road, head down. The men marched away together, in search of Ray's buck. Perhaps one of them had wounded it. I waited in the pickup with Tommy, full of smug happiness, and watched the sleet hit the windshield. I had hit a moving target off-hand, the hardest shot to make with a rifle. I hadn't jerked the trigger, and I had hit exactly what I aimed at.

After a vain search for blood spots, the men came back and decided to call it a morning. The sleet was turning to wet snow. Back in our garage, I skinned out my buck, and Dad saw where a second shot had gone through the buck's shoulder and broken his back. That had felled him, but with one bullet through his lungs, he couldn't have gone much farther. On the following Wednesday night, as we cut that buck up, Dad dug his bullet from the shoulder wound. "But by all rights he was your buck," he said.

We slept in on Sunday, and that afternoon Ray and Lori and Larry and Sonja came over, and we all cut, wrapped, and divided the meat from Dad and Larry's two bucks. Lori sat in the living room and talked to Liz and me as we tried to do our homework. "I'm a city girl," she kept saying, and I looked up from a physics problem and wondered why she was telling us this.

Later, as we loaded their share of the venison into their car, Lori seemed mollified about Ray's desertion of her during hunting season. "She doesn't know how good she has it!" Mother said after all the company had gone. "She's living down at the base, with lots of company, and she's two minutes from the store and the post office. But she doesn't seem happy."

"She's pretty young yet," Dad said. "If she can make it for another six months, she'll be all right."

The next week, the temperature dropped and the logging trucks that crept down Walker Creek—the last of the season—were covered in snow. On the school bus, Bink Sherman was full of the tale of the two bucks Robert had killed—one on Friday, one on the Saturday on which I'd killed my buck—both four points, the largest one weighing 165 pounds dressed out and skinned: a mighty buck for a blacktail, and Bink made sure we all knew it. Robert wore the same aw-shucks-folks expression that had been on my face all week, too.

THANKSGIVING FELL ON NOVEMBER 24 THAT YEAR, a long and restful weekend of eating and chopping wood and playing checkers with Liz and Tommy, broken by Dad taking his meat saw and carving knives up to Thomases' to help Larry butcher a steer. By mid-morning on Sunday, with Dad at Thomases' again to butcher a second steer, I went out to the garden to cut the runners off the strawberry plants. About noon I drove downtown with Mother and Liz. As we stood in the store, the siren of a highway patrol car dopplered past us and we ran to the windows to see the black-and-white vanish beyond the school.

"Some boys had an accident," said Mrs. Hossick, behind the counter. "Mrs. Merriman up Walker Creek phoned Mrs. Sherman—she was working here earlier—and told her to come up there right away."

After lunch, with Dad home from butchering, I worked on the strawberry bed again, while Dad took Mother and Tommy for a drive up Walker Creek to look at a bee tree. Mother left Bob in the garden with me, so he wouldn't follow the truck, and I saw him wag his tail through the fence wire at a strange dog, a brown and white border collie bitch perhaps six or eight months old. She rolled on her back and thumped her long tail on the ground. I led her down the driveway and across the county road and wondered which of our neighbors she belonged to. Every year a new pack of pups followed the kids who lived in the cluster of houses on the river side of the highway. When the dog tried to follow me back, I hurled pebbles at her until she fled.

By the time I finished the strawberries and came inside, the pup was on the porch.

I chased her away again, hurled more gravel after her, and cursed whoever had left a dog alone without tying her up. She could get run over that way.

Back out in the garden, I scraped at the last of the frostbitten weeds with a hoe as Dad and Mother and Tommy came back. Dad came out in the garden, and I straightened up at the grim expression on his face. Oh, God, had I left the iron on?

"We stopped at Merrimans', to ask about the accident," he said. "It was Bink Sherman and Bob Cooley. Bob's dead." He nodded at me, his lips compressed over his teeth, then turned and left. I stood with my palms on top of the hoe handle for a moment, then struck at the weeds again. When they were all gone, I walked to the woodshed and

198

hauled in the chunks of fir that Liz had chopped earlier and stacked them by the back door. I made trip after trip, until my knees trembled. And I thought about Robert. Robert, not Bob. I had never called him Bob. I saw his red hair, his blue eyes, his straight nose. I remembered his straight teeth and the movements of his long legs. I thought of his bucks, frozen in packages in Blanche Priddy's freezer, and Robert not there to eat them, not there to scrape the hide and flesh from the skulls and mount the antlers on plaques and hang them on a wall. Not there on the bus, not there in trigonometry and physics. Not there, next year, at Chico State.

When the stacked wood on the back porch reached the top railing, I walked back to the garden. I looked up at the saddle beside Slinkard Peak, beyond which ran the treacherous snow-covered road under Lake Mountain, where he had died. But I didn't cry, not then.

At dusk the border collie pup came back, planted herself on the porch, and refused to leave. Dad ignored her, and Bob, chained to the garage, yipped and wagged his stubby tail at her. She ignored him. Then I saw something in the oak tree just below the rock wall that marked the boundary of the front lawn: a black ball of fur and a pair of round yellow eyes. I approached the tree and looked up, and a kitten, no more than ten weeks old, stared back at me.

After dark, I opened the front door and saw the brown and white shape still curled up on the cushions of the porch chair, but now the black kitten perched on the pup's back, paws buried in her warm fur. Boots the cat slipped up the porch steps, spared a hiss for the strangers, then slipped past my legs and into the house. Dad looked out the kitchen window at them, the newspaper between his fingers. "Doggone it!" he said. He sat back down in his easy chair and snapped the paper open with an angry jerk.

We all know, I wrote that night, *that if we can't find their owners, he'll have to shoot them.*

ON MONDAY MORNING, THE BUS WAS SILENT, all the way to school. The two grade-school boys who lived near Thompson Creek attempted some levity, but Mike Nowdesha thumped them on the head and they shushed. By afternoon, details of the accident filtered through the halls.

199

Coming down from Lake Mountain, Bink's jeep had struck a rock in
the snowy road and flipped over the bank. Robert, riding in the back,
on the lookout for bear with his rifle—bear season ran until January—
had gone headfirst into a rock pile. Bink, clinging to the steering wheel,
managed to stay in the jeep until it smashed into the wall of trees at
the foot of the toe slope. He crawled back up, found Robert's broken
body among the rocks, and somehow stood up and walked back down
the road. He reached Merrimans' house on Walker Creek by noon and
collapsed with a fractured spine. As trucks raced up the road to retrieve
Robert, an ambulance drove Bink to the hospital in Yreka.

The pup and kitten were still on the porch on Monday afternoon,
as Liz and I dragged ourselves up the front porch steps. The pup rose
to welcome us and rolled over at our feet, her tail slapping the porch
floor. The kitten, perched on the porch railing, blinked, and I noticed
how its hipbones protruded. Later, as they waited on the porch chair,
two pairs of eyes, round and quiet, looked at me. I picked up the kitten
and parted the short hair beneath her tail. Female. Damn. I might have
been able to beg for the life of a male kitten, which Dad could neuter
with a pocketknife, but I knew the futility of trying to convince him
that we needed a female cat. Spaying cost money; to spay both of these
orphans would cost over a hundred dollars, not to mention vaccinations.
I scraped out the remnants of a bowl of tuna fish and mayonnaise onto
the porch and watched them leap down and lick it up.

That evening, as I surreptitiously mixed more food to take out to
them, Dad went to the window once more. "Well," he said, "if we're
going to get rid of them we may as well be decent to them." Liz and
Mother leapt up then, to help me rummage through the refrigerator.
I mixed up a bowl of milk, cooked deer liver, leftover stew, cereal, and
other odds and ends, and set it out in an old square cake pan on the
porch. The two friends leapt down from the chair and shoved their
noses into the steaming gruel. As they lapped and snorted and ate, their
whiskers brushed, and I knew that they had always been together.

"Raised in the same place," Liz said.

"And dumped at the same time," I added.

Liz and I worked the phone that evening, but no one who lived in
our neighborhood claimed them. Desperate, I phoned Ernie Weinberg.
His three girls were magnets for strays. "We already have three cats,"

Ernie said, "and they don't like dogs. Why don't you keep them? Then you can have two of each."

"Because Dad will shoot them if we can't find homes for them," I confessed. There was a pause at the other end, and then a sigh. "Your father," said Ernie in the only Yiddish accent on the Klamath National Forest, "is a very practical man."

And Ernie knew from practical. His whole family had been killed by the Nazis in Europe. Only Ernie had escaped, because his parents had sent him to school in England to save his life.

On Tuesday morning Liz and I warmed milk for the pup and kitten, broke bread and leftover toast into it, then tried to find some dark clothes for Robert's funeral.

I HAD NEVER WALKED IN the Fort Goff cemetery before, only looked up at it from the highway. I knew no one buried there. When the school bus pulled over at Fort Goff and found a space among the cars and trucks, a crowd from Seiad was already there. We shuffled up the pine-needled path and stood in the drizzle as pallbearers carried the casket into the graveyard and put it down under a canopy. I cast a glance around at the tombstones and grave markers, some of the names almost obscured by moss and lichens. Then a clergyman began to talk, quoting scripture and speaking about the water of life. He smiled too much. I bit my lower lip and stared at the Klamath as it rushed along below the highway, with a roar that reached between the bare branches of oaks and the shiny madrone leaves, so that the Reverend had to raise his voice. I felt no tears behind my eyes, and no one else from the bus cried, either, but sobs came from a woman I didn't know, a woman who stood at the front of the clutch of mourners on the far side of the coffin, and clung to Blanche Priddy. Their black dresses merged into one, and a white wedge of Blanche's slip swayed as she rocked her daughter in her arms.

201

"That's his Mom," Liz whispered through stiff lips.

Men in dark suits stood behind the other women who surrounded Blanche and Robert's mother. The homily ended, and as the mourners filed by the coffin for the last time, I saw the pallbearers headed for the outhouse in the campground outside the fence. They carried boots and work clothes, and now I recognized one of them: Walt Robinson, Kathy and Donna's father. Of course, I thought. After we're all gone, they have to lower the casket into the grave, and fill in the hole.

I wondered what would happen to the pile of flowers on top of the polished brown casket. All of us on the bus had chipped in to send a wreath. As we filed back down the path and climbed on the bus, the silence was suddenly unbearable, and I felt the need to say something, anything. "Gee, I didn't know there were so many old graves up there," I said, and from her place across the aisle from me, Marie shot me a poisonous look, her lips tight, her nostrils flaring. She had gone absolutely white; her freckles stood out like pepper on rice. Shamed at my gaucherie, I turned around and ducked my head into my library book, seeing not a word of it. Not until we were almost home did it hit me that all those times I had watched Robert walk away from the bus, someone else might have been watching him, too. Someone else may have had plans for Robert.

LIZ AND I WALKED UP THE DRIVEWAY and onto the porch, heads down in the rain, and Bob ran off the porch to greet us, alone. Dad had come home at noon, lifted the pup and kitten into the truck cab, and driven them up Walker Creek, his revolver on the seat beside him.

I changed my clothes and went out to the woodshed to chop kindling, and then I sat on the chopping block under the low roof, and cried for a boy I had never really known and now would never know, and for two strays I had been powerless to help. Except for Boots, no wanderer that crossed our yard or huddled against our door had ever been allowed to stay. Only in that one case had rules been bent in favor of life and not death. Liz and I had packed puppies and kittens around the neighborhood before. Sometimes we found homes for them, sometimes we didn't. And when we didn't, they died with a bullet to the head.

Other families had more than one dog, more than one cat. But not in Dad's house. We produced enough table scraps for one dog and one cat, but not enough for more, Dad said. Besides the veterinary expenses, more animals would mean buying pet food. Now we only had to buy pet food when we went on a trip, for the convenience of whoever had to feed Bob and Boots. And if we had taken in these strays, what of all those to come? The county had no animal shelter, only a sheriff's pound, where prisoners were slain after three days. Unwanted animals were tossed onto roadsides, to depend on the kindness of strangers. But they wouldn't get it from Dad, I told myself, as I raged against my helplessness, and saw again the golden eyes of the black kitten. The pup had used ten thousand years of instinctive body language in an attempt to join our pack. The kitten, wiser than she, had known from the start that hope was futile.

Half an hour later, dehydrated, I picked up the axe; as I carried an armload of kindling to the back porch, past the row of deer antlers on the woodshed roof, I looked at them and remembered the sleek body of the buck I had killed, saw his antlers laid back along his neck as he fled, saw his clean legs tucked beneath him as he jumped. He was beautiful, and I had shot him without hesitation. He was mine, despite that other bullet in his body. But he had never had any illusions about me, while the pup had come to us in hope, and we had killed her and her friend, without even the excuse of wanting to eat them.

The death of a buck—of any of the bucks that had fed us through winters past—could be seen as a ceremony. We told stories about their deaths as we ate them, and for decades in the future, the sight of the antlers on the wall would remind us. Ancient cultures believed that an animal, properly honored and propitiated, would live again, that in fact the beasts would allow themselves to be killed by those who respected and honored them. But of the deaths of a lost pup and kitten we would not brag, we would not speak, and in their deaths no one would ever pretend to find meaning.

203

LATE IN JANUARY, WENDELL FORGOT, for a moment, that Robert was dead. He stopped the bus once more in front of Blanche Priddy's house, and opened the doors. We looked up, horror-stricken, silent. Three seconds passed, and then Wendell shut the doors, put the bus into gear, and headed up the hill toward the Robinson place.

That evening, as I sat at the desk in the living room trying to finish my physics homework, Dad astonished me by telling me to just let it go for this evening. "Just relax for once," he said. "You've been too nervous about your grades and college." Liz, struggling with geometry on the fireplace hearth, let her mouth fall open.

I put on a stack of records, then curled up in the corner of the couch next to the stove and dove into *The Cruel Sea*. Now and then I looked up at Dad in his chair, at his long-fingered hands holding a newspaper, their summer sunburn faded. He looked gentle and peaceful and as I looked at him it flashed through my mind that the deaths of Robert and our refugees might have eaten at his heart, too. In the fireplace, a madrone log fell apart into clinkers. Rain hammered on the roof. Mother knitted in her rocking chair, and Tommy lost himself once more in *Lord of the Rings*, with Boots curled up beside him. I wanted to hold this moment to my chest and never let it go.

By the end of January, I developed a rash on the insides of my elbows, a skin condition that had appeared years before in Hilt. The rash jumped to my neck, a virulent red flush that itched and burned and on which I splashed copious amounts of rubbing alcohol for the pleasant sting of it. Consumed by my final attempt to get perfect grades and make valedictorian, I didn't connect the rash with anything else. In the spring Mother took me to a dermatologist in Medford, who told me it was probably just nerves about graduation and handed me a tube of cream.

ON A MORNING IN LATE APRIL, I carried my transistor radio into the bathroom and brushed my teeth to the plaintive voice of Jonathan King singing "Everyone's Gone to the Moon." I looked out the bathroom window at Slinkard Peak, at the spiky trees on the skyline just turning from black to green as the earth rolled back toward the sun. The day before, I had learned that I would be valedictorian of the class of '67, but I hadn't felt nearly as happy about it as I once thought I would be. Lee Attebery had sat beside me as Mr. Oamek told us the order of finish. She hugged me and looked far more delighted than I felt. As we walked back down the hall, she confessed her relief. "I didn't want to have to give the biggest speech," she said.

I climbed on the school bus the next morning with a sense of letdown. What had all the work meant, really? Why didn't I feel happier about an achievement that had seemed so important only a few months ago? But as the bus rolled down into Seiad that morning, as I watched sunlight envelop the snow-capped Devils, as the reborn green pastures slid by, the clarity and hope of spring caught at my throat, and from some reservoir of archetypal myth, my mind coughed up the words, "the world has come full circle." I looked up at the head of Seiad Creek, at the line of mountains that bracketed Cook and Green Pass, at the washed blue of the sky, and in that moment all the darkness of the long winter slid away, and I knew in some deep recess of my soul that Robert was still out there, still striding the ridges on some quest of his own. He just didn't ride the school bus, anymore.

And before graduation, the rash on my neck had disappeared.

Departures

GRADUATION CAME AND WENT, and I wondered why I had been so worried. I gave a valedictory speech that praised learning and managed to say, in effect, that many of my classmates had merely put in their time and didn't deserve a diploma. I delivered it full of confidence, and even Dad praised the typed copy. "Good," he said. "You're right." But as I stood with the other graduates in the receiving line, one of the mothers focused her sad dark eyes on mine. "Academics aren't everything," Mrs. Davis said as she shook my hand. "Someday you'll know that."

Someday came soon: by August, I recalled my arrogant words with shame and was so embarrassed at the thought of running into any of my classmates that I often stayed home when Mother went to pick up the mail. When I did see them, I was relieved that they didn't seem to hate me. Then I remembered the boy who had swayed gently beside me, his eyes glassy, as we waited to receive our diplomas, deserved or

Mother, Dad, Tommy, Louise, and Liz on Graduation Day, June 1967, in front of the house on Walker Creek.

not. I remembered the furtive giggling at school that morning, and the noise of bottles being opened in the shelter of half-open lockers. Who was I kidding? Most of the class wouldn't have noticed if I'd recited Washington's Farewell Address.

One day I rode into Happy Camp with Mother to get groceries and saw Carrie, a married woman now, in Ealy's Market. I tensed, but she smiled at me as she piled items into her cart. We talked, and she told me about their new trailer house. She asked me when I was going off to college, but on her face was the same look of superior pity that I had seen in the school hallway when Gerald visited: pity for the unattached, the unengaged, the uninitiated. College, it seemed, was a consolation prize, awarded to those who couldn't go directly from graduation to a wedding ceremony. "How can you stand the thought of more studying?" she asked, laughing.

It wasn't as though I was the only senior girl on her way to college: Lee had a music scholarship to University of the Pacific. But somehow that was different, for Lee had been a cheerleader with a football player for a boyfriend. Lee was smart and musical, but I, God help me, had actually made learning into a contest with myself. The academic awards had never been important to anyone else, and now they tasted sour, even to me.

"Well, I hope it works out for them," Mother said, when I told her about Carrie and Gerald. "But girls like Carrie don't have much to fall back on, if their husbands ever lose their jobs, or get hurt." Or die, or divorce you, I added silently.

So I was happy, that evening, to go down to the river to fish, and to tell myself that there were bound to be good things about Chico. Any town with three libraries couldn't be all bad. I stayed until dark, trying to fix the river and the mountains in my mind, so I would not forget.

ALL THAT SUMMER, I allowed the quiet routine of ditch-tending to wipe away the embarrassments and neuroses of high school. And after three years of practice, I prided myself in my ability to keep the ditch flowing.

I loved irrigating, loved simply messing about in the ditch. I had recently read *The Wind in the Willows,* and I wanted to be the Water

Rat. On summer afternoons at Seiad, when the temperature rose to over one hundred degrees, the canyon walls swam in a golden haze of pollen and turpenes. Trees survived on soil moisture from winter rains and snowmelt from the high mountains, but all the bounty of our yard depended on the water that flowed through the irrigation ditch from Walker Creek.

During our first summer at Seiad, Dad led me up to the head of the ditch, both of us carrying a shovel. Vines and branches bowed over the waterway, and I knew I would have to check myself for ticks when we got home. At the head of the ditch, the cold rush of Walker Creek poured in, innocent of head gate or fish screen, providing irrigation water for us and several other families. Tiny trout, entrained in the ditch, ended up in our sprinklers and blocked the spray of water until I fetched a bucket, unscrewed the sprinkler head, and watched a couple of smolts shoot into the bucket. I carried the live ones across the road through a wasteland of flood-dumped gravel and poured them back into Walker Creek. The dead ones, crushed and broken by water pressure, I dumped in the garden.

The ditch had been built thirty years ago by Mr. Baird and his fishing buddy, Mr. Schultz—he of the green clapboard cabin on the point. The irony that salmon and steelhead smolts were entrained and slaughtered by their artifact went unmentioned.

On that first day on the ditch, Dad and I shoveled accumulated sand and silt from the entrance to let more water in. As we walked back in the dusk, Dad pointed out places where silt collected and needed to be shoveled out, where weak ditch banks needed shoring up. Every year, all the neighbors who used the ditch talked about renting a backhoe to rebuild it, but somehow that work never got done: it would have cost money, and besides, none of us except Mr. Schultz actually had a water right on the ditch—a little detail of law that no one liked to talk about, either. But for now, my instructions were clear: keep the mud out of the ditch and make sure that the orchard around Schultz's cabin got plenty of water.

The next morning, after Dad left for work, I drafted Liz to help me carry shovels and pruning shears and walk the ditch again. More silt had drifted into the ditch entrance, and we dug it out, then lined the first ten feet or so of the connection with rocks and big chunks of wood.

We piled rocks across the creek below the ditch, too, to raise the water level and send more water down the ditch. Then we worked our way back down the ditch, clearing out debris, shoveling mud over the side, cutting back branches and vines, while Bob crashed through the brush around us and sank belly-deep into the ditch to cool off. Home again, we found the ditch full of murky water and collapsed on the lawn with glasses of iced tea, feeling virtuous. Loaded logging trucks—up to twenty-five a day—groaned down the road beside us and sometimes honked at the two shorts-clad nymphets relaxing on the grass: we made no connection between their work and the sediment in the ditch.

The next morning found the ditch dry again, and Liz realized that this assignment was likely to prove both onerous and repetitive. She begged off in favor of cutting out a blouse on the kitchen table. I rolled up the legs of my jeans and walked the ditch bank in my sneakers, only to find that yesterday's clever engineering had blown out one of the weaker ditch banks. Water poured downhill from the ditch, through a madrone copse and across the Alexanders' driveway. All our work of yesterday had gone for nothing. Maybe Liz had the right idea. I hiked as fast as I could up the creek and into the frigid water to dismantle our rock dam, then back to the ditch breach to deepen the channel on the uphill side as the flow subsided. I shored up the bank with rocks, chunks of wood, clumps of soil and grass. An hour later, my shoulders ached and my ankles were bruised and scratched, but the bank looked stable. Sometimes, I decided, more water really equaled less water. I rolled a few rocks back into line in the creek channel and sat down to watch the water level rise in the ditch.

209

After that, I checked the ditch each morning, as soon as I finished my morning run. If too little water came through, I grabbed a shovel and walked up the ditch. One morning I killed a pair of mating rattlesnakes, chopping them down into the mud as they buzzed and attempted to slide away from me. I bashed them to death and cut off their rattles, then sat down on the bank and shook them like a character in a jungle movie where anacondas lurk in treetops. From then on, I wore an old pair of fisherman's waders.

I started to explore the creek above the intake and found a swimming hole several hundred yards upstream. It wasn't much compared to the ten-foot deep cleft in Seiad Creek, but it had a luxurious sandy bottom that soothed my feet. The pool had been deeper once, and the sand had ruined this particular spot as a nursery for steelhead eggs, but I didn't know that. I floated under the spray of the falls amid the white noise of water and felt only peace.

The Forest Service knew, in a general sort of way, that sediment in streams was bad for fish, but the Klamath National Forest would not have a fisheries biologist for another ten years. Foresters didn't seem to know—or care—that even a stream like Walker Creek that ran clear in the summer still moved loads of sediment kicked loose by roads and clear-cuts as the loggers moved farther and farther up the drainage. Culverts, in those days, were not friendly to fish passage, and road crossings often washed out due to poorly compacted fill or a too-small culvert. Before my eyes, the finely tuned hydrological system of Walker Creek was being dismantled by industrial forestry. As I sweated over my shovel, as I floated in the creek, I never connected the silt that made work for me with the logging trucks a few yards away, or the dust that covered the roadside blackberry vines. The problem was that older and more educated people didn't make the connection either.

Dad did know something was wrong, but what he saw was not so much the ecological harm as the economic waste of the Forest Service's five-year timber plans. "Sustained yield" was an attractive idea when timber prices were high, but when the industry went into one of its periodic downturns, it would have made more sense to postpone sales, to let the targets slide.

Busy as he was with the salvage sales on the Seiad District, he paid attention to the huge new timber sales that were planned downriver from Happy Camp—sales like Bunker Hill, with its nine miles of highly engineered main haul road, designed by an entire staff of Forest Service engineers in Yreka. They seemed to see their life's mission as the slicing of big road cuts through the decomposed granite of the Independence Creek drainage. A year and a half later, when he was promoted to timber management officer in Happy Camp, Dad would protest those very road specifications and try to make them less grandiose. But he laid out the sixty-acre clear-cuts to which they led, just the same. He would be a reluctant witness to the dedication of the Thornton Memorial Bridge that crossed the Klamath River to access Bunker Hill and a dozen other sales on the south side of the river. "Another big investment that won't pay for itself," he said.

For Dad knew, with an eerie precision, exactly how much old-growth timber lay beyond the expensive bridges and in the path of the over-engineered roads, and he knew what it was worth, and he knew that it wasn't enough. He doubted that the science of silviculture had advanced far enough to allow such large clear-cuts to be reforested within five years, as the standards demanded. And the timber targets themselves were based upon forecasts of reforestation and regrowth that time would prove to be over-optimistic.

Bets had been made that would never be collected. Timber was being cut in amounts that could not be replenished. Promises of timber forever were predicated upon calculations that would prove to be wrong. And I think he saw this, from afar, and he wanted his children to be far away, and engaged in some other line of work, when the chickens found their roost again. He wanted us to leave the river, get an education, and never return. What he didn't count on was that one of us just wouldn't get it, that one of us would wake every day with the river in her mind, and find her way back, to live out a love affair born in a green pickup truck in the rain.

Twenty years later, the fact that I had once scrambled myself into a college education would give me the resources I needed to leave, one more time. The tragedy for others, for Gerald and many of my classmates, was that they had believed the promises and had not recognized, until it was too late, that they needed something more. When the end came, they lacked the resources to start over. That a way of life could fall so far, and so fast, was beyond belief. The proximate cause indeed lay beneath the feathers of the spotted owl, but the seeds had been sown long before, in the minds and greed of men.

211

EARLY IN SEPTEMBER, I LEFT for Chico State College, two hundred miles to the south in the orchard-dotted Central Valley. As my parents helped me unload my things into a bare dormitory room on the first floor of Lassen Hall, as I hugged Mother and Liz and Tommy good-bye and shook hands with Dad, my mind caromed around my skull and screamed in panic. I had thought myself prepared for this exile, but now that it had come, now that the river would roll on and Dad would go hunting without me, I knew I was not prepared at all. Four years of college and another year of education classes and practice teaching, before I could go home for good, seemed to me, at eighteen, an immense stretch of time.

SEPTEMBER 28, 1967

Dear Louise,

"Boy! A passel of stuff shore took off taday, boy!" as Larry would say. Last night when Dad and Larry came home, Dad said, "Hey! Let's take the girl back with us when we go in tomorrow." Naturally I said "Can I? Huh? Can I?"

Larry gave that snortin' li'l laugh of his and said "Anxious, ain't she?"

The reason we had to go back in was that Dad killed a bear and a 4 point (3 on one side four on the other) on Saturday and Sunday respectively and they had to go in and pack the deer out that they had boned out and left up there.

Five o'clock this morning the alarm goes off and at five-thirty Dad and Mother groaned a little bit and Dad told Mother to jump out of bed and call Larry to be sure <u>he</u> got up on time.

Well, he wasn't up and he said he'd been "lyin' in bed cussin' John, and bear, and deer, and ever' blessed thing in general" after his alarm rang, when the phone rings an' Mother tells him to "Get up and get to work."

We left the house at 6:30 and took off on up Grider Creek. I wore your boots and they work real good. Dad and Larry made me because "We want our work mules well shod goin' up there!"

Anyway ... waaaay up Grider Creek I caught sight of Venus and was looking at it when Larry says "Hey! What're you doin' girl?!" Dad says "Oh she's lookin' at stars again." Larry says "I'll club 'er over th' head then she kin look at stars but we're lookin' for deer on the ground kid! My Gawd!"

I made some mumble and looked straight at the ground trying not to grin too much, when Dad turned the corner and we were comin' round a cut block. All of a sudden Larry yells "Hold it, John!" Dad slows up and Larry almost swallows his cigarette and starts to get out when Dad

212

*says, "Hold it! I'll back up!" Dad backs up and there is three little tiny
deer standing just below the road on this c.b. right out in plain sight!
Just looking at us! Larry asked for the glasses looks through them and
says "One's a fork, John!" Hands me his cigarette and suddenly all else
is forgotten but that tiny little buck. I put out his cigarette Dad says
"Yeh he's a fork!" Larry pokes the gun and Dad says "Hold still now
Lizabeth!" I hadn't been breathing for the past 30 seconds and didn't
need to and Larry pulled the trigger. Bang! And that buck just dropped.
The other two just stood there and looked stupid as only a spike can
and they were confirmed as too small. We piled out and Larry and Dad
changed into their corks and Dad had his on first and took off down the
hill, meantime the other two bucks finally moved on down the CB and
Dad got down to where the buck was and Larry yells "Need a gun,
John?" and Dad yells back "Only a frying pan!"*

*Larry and I took off down to him and he was a young buck that was
a spike on the right side and a forked horn on the left side. Gee! He was
pretty! The haul to the road took about a minute and we skinned and
dressed him right there on a tarp. His muscles still quivered when he was
skinned and when I remarked on it Larry said, "That's why we cut his
legs off so he wouldn't jump up and run away!" I told them, "I may be
stupid but not that stupid," and Larry just laughed.*

*Then we took on up the road and we saw a bear. He was moving and
Larry got only one shot and missed. Oh! I forgot. Larry shot the buck
with one shot in the neck. Clean as anything you'll ever see …*

*We shouldered our packs and began a two-mile hike into Stones Valley
that took two hours. We broke Dad's and Larry's old camp and headed for
home. My pack weighed about thirty pounds but it didn't seem too heavy.*

213

I LOOKED UP FROM THE LETTER. It had come in a box along with a
dried starfish, two Peanuts cartoons clipped from a newspaper, a postcard
of the River and the Devils, an Instamatic camera, a ballerina figurine,
and a loaf of banana bread. I sat on smooth grass with my treasures
spread around me, beneath the sycamores on the banks of Big Chico
Creek. Above me in the dappled shade, acorn woodpeckers racketed.
Far away in Seiad, my place had been filled by Liz, valued for her young
muscles now that I was gone, and happy to work hard for the privilege
of sitting next to Larry and his yellow curls and his cigarettes and his

dropped consonants. I had laughed and cried as I read her letter, and I sat there with tears on my cheeks and loved them all—Liz and Dad and Larry and Mother and Tommy and all the loggers and millworkers and the Forest Service, and the river, blue on the postcard beneath a clear sky and the snow-splashed summits of the Devils.

ROBERT WAS GONE, BUT IN CHICO, I talked to him. I told him about this place that he would never see, told him about Dr. Willis, my chemistry professor, and how funny he was and how he would look at me from under his gray bushy eyebrows when I came into the lab, and call out, "Birds in the trees seem to whisper Louise!" I told Robert that he would have liked it here, even though you couldn't really see the mountains, just the foothills if you climbed to the third floor of the dorm. Mount Shasta was gone beneath the curve of the Earth; the last glimpse of the white volcano had vanished as Red Bluff fell behind us.

But even as I talked to Robert's shade, I knew that had he come here, had he lived and studied in a room at Shasta Hall—the boys' dorm across the lawn from Lassen Hall—I would never have talked to him so much. A hello as he passed me with his books and binder cradled between arm and hip. Maybe a chemistry class together, and perhaps even (though the thought still made my palms sweat when I thought of it) an evening in the library to study together. Beyond that I would not have gone, would not have dared to hope. For if I had, he might have thought I was chasing him, and I could not have borne that.

214 But to his ghost I could speak as I sat alone between classes, beneath the ancient valley oaks near the science building. To his ghost I could tell the ugly secret I barely admitted to myself: that I didn't want to be a teacher, but that I saw no other way to go home. And I understood at last the great attraction that the Christian girls felt for Jesus. To confide in the dead is always safe.

So I spoke to a boy who fell off a mountain, and knew that without him, and without me, the seasons of the Klamath went on. Snows melted, water flowed, gardens grew again. Hunting seasons rolled around, and Dad found another apprentice. Deer died, and tags and freezers were filled. I read Liz's letter one more time, and stared down at the postcard, and longed for my own country, where the boys worked in the sawmills or the woods, and cut up trees from Dad's timber sales, and believed that they would do this for the rest of their working lives, if the draft didn't get them first. (Within a year, one of my classmates would die in Vietnam.) But for now, Liz's letter held that world in place, as it was. I blew my nose, gathered the box into my arms, and crossed the bridge over Big Chico Creek, on my way to class.

Bibliography

Arnold, Mary Ellicott, and Mabel Reed. *In the Land of the Grasshopper Song: Two Women in the Klamath Indian Country in 1908-09* (Lincoln: University of Nebraska Press, 1980)

Bower, Russell W., and Al Groncki. Dr. William Doron, ed. Chronological History of the Klamath National Forest: Volume VI, The 1950's. Yreka: Klamath National Forest, 1996.

Davies, Gilbert W., and Florice M. Frank, eds. *Memories from the Land of Siskiyou: Past Lives and Times in Siskiyou County* (Hat Creek: HiStory ink Books, 1997)

Harington, John P. *Bulletin 107: Karuk Indian Myths.* (Washington: Smithsonian Institution Bureau of American Ethnology, 1932)

Hirt, Paul W. *A Conspiracy of Optimism: Management of the National Forests Since World War Two* (Lincoln: University of Nebraska Press, 1996)

Kroeber, A. L. *Yurok Myths.* (Berkeley: University of California Press, 1978)

Siskiyou Pioneer, Vol. V, No. 6: *Stories of Jim McNeill.* (Yreka: Siskiyou County Historical Society, 1983)

Stuart, Granville. *The Montana Frontier, 1852-1864.* (Lincoln: University of Nebraska Press, 1977)

Tolkien, J. R. R. *The Fellowship of the Ring.* (New York: Harper Collins, 1974)